WHEN ONCE I LIVED

When Once I Lived

A MEDITATION ON A PERIOD OF TIME LESS THAN ETERNITY

by John S. Oney

Copyright © 2011 by John S. Oney

All rights reserved No part of this book may be reproduced in any form or by any electronic or mechanical means, including information storage and retrieval systems, without permission in writing from the copyright owner, except by a reviewer, who may quote brief passages in a review. Scanning, uploading and electronic distribution of this book or the facilitation of such without prmission of the copyright owner is prohibited. Please purchase only authorized electronic editions, and do not participate in or encourage electronic piracy of copyrighted materials. Your support of the rights of the author, and other creative artists, is appreiated. Any member of educational institutions wishing to photocopy part of this work for classroom use, or anthology, should send inquiries to the publisher at the address set forth below.

ISBN: 978-0-9818090-1-4

Library of Congress Control Number: 2011904392

Published by Angry Rabbit Enterprises LLC located at 16781 Chagrin Boulevard, Suite 318, Cleveland, Ohio 44120

Gratefully Acknowledged: Keith Witmer, Illustrator, of Portland, OR for illustrations and cover art; Stephen Tiano, Book Designer, of Calverton, NY for interior page design and layout; and Sheila Hart, Graphic Designer, of Strongsville, OH for cover design.

Printed in the United States of America

To My Mother
Who Read to Me

This book is intended to be read out loud.

Contents

Full and Complete

Introduction   xi
1 This Lofty Place   1
2 The Coffee Shop   10
3 I Dream   19
4 Starting Out   30
5 I Seek a Path   37
6 My Journey Begins   39
7 We Keep Count   45
8 I Become Lost   48
9 The Universal Pageant   51
10 The Natural World   57
11 The World of Intangibles   60
12 The World of the Senses   63
13 I Accept His Guidance   66
14 A Subtle Lesson   74
15 His First Prophet   77
16 Hidden Treasure   80
17 A Brief Diversion   89
18 Duck Duck Goose   91
19 I Come to a Crossroads   107
20 I Resume My Journey   111
21 What Fools   114
22 Shall We Gather?   123
23 We Count Up the Numbers   138

When Once I Lived

24 An Antique Land   140
25 My Assignment   146
26 I Add More to Our Total   159
27 That Place of Quietude   160
28 One True Thing   163
29 All of Them Kings   167
30 I Question My Guide   186
31 I Calculate Anew   194
32 The Wisdom of Stan   196
33 That Great Sovereign   214
34 I Travel Far   230
35 The Queen's Bower   236
36 My Journey Ends   253

Notes   267

Contents

Arranged by Topic

Introduction   xi

My Heart's Regret
Listed below are those chapters in which I set out an account of my life's greatest regret, and how, in my afterlife, I came to see and understand the lesson which it holds for me.

  1 This Lofty Place   1
  2 The Coffee Shop   10
  3 I Dream   19
  21 What Fools   114
  35 The Queen's Bower   236
  36 My Journey Ends   253

The Glory of His Creation
Listed below are those chapters in which I share instructive lessons (peculiar, unexpected and uplifting) which I was shown concerning the Glory and Wisdom of our Lord.

  16 Hidden Treasure   80
  22 Shall We Gather?   123
  25 My Assignment   146
  27 That Place of Quietude   160
  28 One True Thing   163
  32 The Wisdom of Stan   196

When Once I Lived

These Earthly Kings
Listed below are those chapters where I was permitted to see—from among all those earthly kings our world has ever known—some few who served His perfect Will.

    15 His First Prophet   77
    24 An Antique Land   140
    29 All of Them Kings   167
    33 That Great Sovereign   214

My Meditation
Listed below are those chapters which record the results of my meditation upon the course and direction of my journey in the afterlife.

    4 Starting Out   30
    5 I Seek a Path   37
    6 My Journey Begins   39
    7 We Keep Count   45
    8 I Become Lost   48
    9 The Universal Pageant   51
    10 The Natural World   57
    11 The World of Intangibles   60
    12 The World of the Senses   63
    13 I Accept His Guidance   66
    14 A Subtle Lesson   74
    17 A Brief Diversion   89
    18 Duck Duck Goose   91
    19 I Come to a Crossroads   107
    20 I Resume My Journey   111
    23 We Count Up the Numbers   138
    26 I Add More to Our Total   159
    30 I Question My Guide   186
    31 I Calculate Anew   194
    34 I Travel Far   230
    35 My Journey Ends   353

❧ ❧ ❧

Notes   353

Introduction

Please do not read this book.

Or rather, I should say, "Please do not only read this book." We all know what we mean by the word "reading." We picture some man or woman, perhaps in an airport waiting patiently at the gate for a flight which is destined never to depart, or hidden in the shade of a beach umbrella by the shore of some body of water in which the reader is destined never to be immersed. That reader—motionless, his focus fixed upon the page, and unresponsive to any claim which fate might make upon his time or attentiveness—is in no way present to the world.

Where has he gone? Well … if we should start our search by hunting for his "fancy," we know, at once, that it will not be caught in any other place (no other nook or cranny) than his (inflamed) imagination. Of the rest and residue of his consciousness, we find that it has descended upon only one beneficiary, which is that universe of characters, conflicts and emotions imagined by the author of the book he reads.

His eyes and attention fixed unshakably upon the page before him, his imagination racing ahead with the story, we know he is—for some brief time—entirely and authentically resident in that other world. This, we think, is as natural as these things might be. After all, as the philosopher Heraclites said (in Fragment 89):

> *"For those who are awake,*
> *there is only one creation;*
> *But for those who sleep,*
> *each turns aside into his own world."*

However, recently, we see that our familiar, gentle reader no longer so condescends as to bestow his full attention upon a simple "printed page" (which, we know—once being printed—will ever after have but one story to tell). Instead, it seems (our reader's fancy being not yet being kindled to any self-sustaining flame), he does no more than free his absent-minded gaze to briefly linger over shadows to be seen upon some digital device (as if some breezy, windy file of code did play across the surface of some field of gently waving pixels).

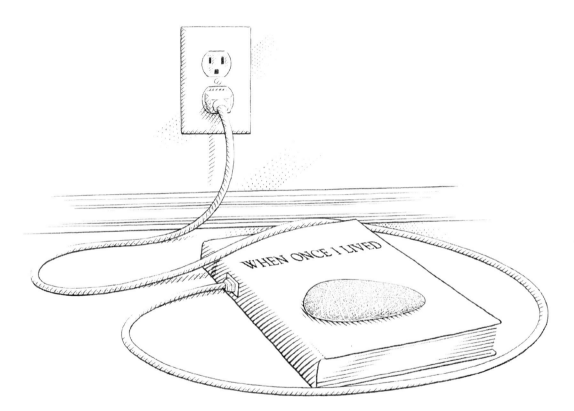

Watching that reader, we are soon reminded that even if we were to carefully take note of his demeanor and reactions, we would not be able to follow along with him on that path which the story lays out. In particular, we see that his lips are altogether silent and unmoving, his breath shallow, regular and unvarying with respect to his place in the story. Observing these things, we know without doubt that he was taught from childhood to read in this manner. After all, isn't "moving your lips when you read" some irrefut-

Introduction

able criticism of a person's powers of concentration? Some sure sign of shallowness of intellect, or lack of education?

Nevertheless ... what we are warned of at the age of seven, we eagerly seek out when we are twenty-seven. You, being urged to keep your lips still when you were taught to read, who is it (now that you have come of age) who could shame you into silence if you resolved to speak your truth aloud?

No, I urge you, do not only read this book. Instead, I challenge you, perform this book. Indeed, perform this book, aloud!

You will find in those pages following certain sections (My Heart's Regret, The Glory of His Creation, These Earthly Kings, and others) where, if you will venture to give voice to what is written there, you will by your own unhesitating voice recite (as if your own praiseworthy pledge) those pure, unblemished oaths of humble gratitude.

Thus, I suggest to you: find a place of quiet and solitude. Perform (out loud) for your own hearing, alone, those words of love and humility which follow. Find, I hope, that deepest pleasure of hearing words of grateful praise spoken aloud in your own voice. Resolve, if you will, that finishing this book, you will not leave off polishing your lines (of which you do, we know, extemporize) performing your own, supportive part in this great drama of life, and speaking, always, words of kindness, tolerance and tact. If you do so, you will learn, as I did, that each of us might rewrite that ancient Greek philosopher in this way:

> *For those who walk in the light,*
> > *there is only one Creator;*
> *But for those who are yet in darkness,*
> > *there are many false gods.*

CHAPTER 1
This Lofty Place

Our God is a great God; and a great King above all gods. Let me tell you how I know.

Yesterday was my retirement party, and what a wonderful send-off it was. How delightful to have seen my children, their spouses, and several grandchildren, plus friends from work, church and the neighborhood. Even a few of my classmates from college and law school were there, needing but little encouragement to tell those old, funny stories about how I almost didn't make it this far. The one note of sadness was the fact that Molly, my wife of so many years, could not be there to share that day with me, but I did feel (as I have heard others in this position say) that in some way her spirit was with me.

What door have I to some familiar world closed off, and to what unknown land must I this other door unseal?

Except for this party given by my friends, I have left off my former profession without ceremony; in all respects as if a farmer, pausing in mid-furrow, unhitching my team and turning them out into some nearby pasture to serenely graze. Then having no longer any care about my tools, I leave my plow out in the rain (which never would have done before, to such a treasured key that once I saw unlock my storehouse of productive gain). Then careless even of myself, I wander off to find my own contented meadow, where like some weary, withered steed, I put myself to stud (no races more to run).

And of my personal life, I am grateful to observe that, though now alone, I was for many years happily mated, and have cheerful and self-supporting children to show for it. I am likewise proud to say (as I do hope) that both in my work and in other ways, I have been of service to others. For example, I was, at varying times during my life: The sole support of enormous herds of gerbils, hamsters and rabbits (who depended for the names by which we knew them on my children); a volunteer coach for an offspring's team in more than one high school sport I never played; and an always faithful and diligent understudy to those all-important roles of "homeowner" and "consumer" and (not least of all) "taxpayer."

All of these endeavors being at an end, I ask myself, "What now begins?" The answer, I immediately perceive, is "my eternity." To which you say, with much surprise, "Your eternity begins! What eternity can you claim, having but some few years of retirement before you?"

Do not mistake me. I am not speaking any metaphorical language. I do not mean to say—despite what you suppose—(seeing before me only idleness, slow decline and endless reminiscences) that those few years which yet I might expect (bereft of any vital purpose) have nothing to impart but some "eternity of boredom" (compressed within that shorter span).

No, what I mean is that seeing the years of my retirement now upon me, my vision (heretofore absorbed in the daily minutia of this world) cannot help but look up and out upon that greater horizon which lies beyond. Here is how it appears to me: Were I of younger age (just starting out), and were I embarking upon some substantial journey (let us say, endeavoring to climb some lofty mountain), then standing at the foot of my chosen path, it would be vain of anyone to inquire of me, "What dangers might this path conceal? What of the weather? How rocky or how smooth, and at what distance does its ending lie? And if we need to stop and rest, what shelter will we find along the way?"

No one seeing me but standing on the threshold of such a path, or even coming on me as I climbed, would think my testimony true that claimed I knew this path or understood the climb, or yet could say if it might take me to the top (or only to some lesser spot along the way). But now imagine: you are transported to some remote and elevated location far above the clouds. You find me there (resting, no doubt) at that place which, for me, will be that highest peak that I will ever know among these mountain tops.

It is, I say, the place of my retirement. No longer will I climb. Indeed, looking about me you see that I have previously (along that winding, upward-tending trail) abandoned all those helps and aids on which my climb depended; no longer any ropes or harness, no climbing ax or pole to test the drifts of snow. I have my tent, my stove and fuel, and so this place will be my final, most secure encampment (you know, of course, that from this place there will be no descent).

Having found me here, at the extremity of my climb, you soon understand that my opinions and observations on the climb are of unique value. You ask

This Lofty Place

about the dangers which I saw along the way, and I have much to share with you. You ask about blind alleys and impassable slopes, and I list them out for you. You ask about rock slides, glaciers and rushing torrents, and I tell you where to safely cross. As they say, "Ask some one who has been there."

Now, trusting to my mountainous metaphor to bear yet more of my explanation, let us press on. You, coming upon me at my encampment, are satisfied with all that I have to tell you about this mountain and the climb. Then, going on to make conversation, you are soon astonished to learn that the value of my opinions is not limited solely to matters concerning the mountain … and the path. You soon perceive that there is much I have to tell you touching on those lofty topics which we only grasp when reaching highest.

Soon, you, with enthusiasm, are pressing me to tell you of those questions which, despite our greatest efforts, remain unanswered. You ask about mortality, about ethical choices, fault and error, and the place of forgiveness in our lives. Then, marveling at the wisdom and maturity of my answers, it dawns on you what is the source of these truths which I share with you.

It is this: That having climbed to this lofty place (at the price of a lifetime of effort) we find our vision shows horizons far from us but true. Our sight unobstructed, we see the motions of the stars (which by celestial divination, His plan for us thereby revealed). And being, now, above the clouds, we find our eyes no longer obscured by dust or rain or other intervening veils of dark but having, now, illumination which we need to trace horizon's boundaries.

You may be led to think that all that I might share with you about mortality, and truth and error, and His compassion (overseeing all) is but the product of this final destination. That anyone—having been brought to this place, and having the same senses as I—might see the same truth and know these things as well as I. But thinking so would be a grave error.

No. What I have gathered is not solely the fruit of this small orchard to which I have come at last. What I know, and what I might teach, is likewise the product of that journey which brought me here. Is this not clear? No one but I stood at that threshold, starting out that one unique path to which only I was admitted. No one else ascended those slopes (traversed by me alone) turning this way and that, first avoiding some obstruction blocking off my way, then going by some (briefly) downward-leading track, available only to my steps. Every journey up this mountain is like no other. Soon you will appreciate every truth which has its source in that one fact.

Being present, now, in my retirement, at this place of quietude and peace, where the burden of ever climbing upward no longer falls upon me, I ask what challenges or toils might occupy my time? Looking back upon the years it took to make this climb, I see I have only some few years remaining during which to make my home here. After that I will have a much longer journey to commence when, taking leave of this place, I embark upon my eternity.

My Encampment
Pressing on, as it seems I must, with my vivid and picturesque metaphor, you see me now seated not far from my tent, on an elevated, rocky crag, musing, pondering and (honestly) daydreaming in the sun. Have I not earned some few moments of renewal, when my spirit might more nearly attune itself to that inaudible sound of this mountain?

But it's no use. Such emptiness of purpose is foreign to me. Have I not lived a life of ceaseless struggle? Ever testing my strength and will against the steep, the footing and terrain? Who, knowing me, could expect that I would long occupy myself thinking about the past or going over ground long since abandoned? Is it not our nature that we look ahead, seeking out (at once) a better path, a more direct approach, a safer place to step? Does it seem likely to you that our Maker, seeing this about us, would (as our reward) lead us to some place in life where every future path is hidden from us?

No, that is not His purpose. Seeing those years of my retirement unrolled before me, I see, too, His wish for me, which (setting aside some time for recuperation from my life's exertions) I hasten to commence. I see it is His Wish that I prepare myself for my eternity. Seeing before me all the time I might require, yet still He tasks me to begin at once to plan, prepare and make ready. Offering to me, in my afterlife, a place free of any higher promontories to be climbed (and so, no labor, chores or struggles to attend) yet still He whispers in my ear, "Which way? How far? What is your goal?" He takes away my fears, obstructions and delays, and tells me once again "Press on!" into some unknown land.

Join me awhile here in my solitary tent. Look about you. You will not see much. I have my bedroll, toothbrush, a few articles of clothing (well adapted to a hike) and my lantern (there so I can read at night). You will notice, also, reposing in my reach a score of well-thumbed novels of the thicker sort: That need the first one hundred pages just to "set the scene" and then another hundred merely to prefigure doom. I love such books, that (fearless) rise up on their hindmost legs and stare eternity down.

Upon coming into my little tent, you quickly look around to find a place to put one foot so you might rest awhile before you start the search to find a spot to stow the other. I admit this tent is not over large; its advantage being that when the weather blows and rain comes down and hailstones fly, it makes a smaller target. We open up the flap at one end (though breathing but those rare perfumes of wisdom long-distilled, we still need air).

Looking around you, I see you are nearly in a panic. You want to say something complimentary about my tent, but you are not sure it can contain the entirely of your gesture. Likewise, you do not wish to deny me the opportunity of showing myself a thoughtful host, yet you have never heard of any such performance playing in so small a house. At last, in desperation, you say the worst possible thing (exactly what is on your mind): "Do you get many visitors?"

Now, recalling (as I hope you do) my story to this point, perhaps you will anticipate what next I said: That I well expected what you asked and, having given many years in painful toil to reach this place (this tent my burden taking every step), I am not likely to find any great offense in your inquiry.

"As a matter of fact," I reply, "I do … get … many visitors." Indeed, if you had come just an hour or two earlier, you would have shared this tent (I see your look of fell astonishment, that struggles three to fit within this tent we know too small for two) … with a visitor I just had. It was a Mr. Melville, a man well used to blows and mists who, stopping in from out the cold, he had some points he wished to make about a fish.

Then, last evening, before bed, I had another visitor (his name "Cantor") who shared with me a clever sort of answer to a puzzle which he knew: Forsaking any numbers (which any doing "math" are loathe to do), he showed me of those points upon a "plane," such "guests" might come to visit every "host" who has his tent upon a point upon a "line," and then we see (a goodly thing to know when entertaining) that every "guest" will have a "host," and never will a lonely "host" be found this night.

Now thinking to myself (this all unspoken) that finally waiting out your visit, I will, in all due time, get back my life. (The same as any other host who bides his time, who never lets his mind be host to that ungrateful thought, "Will he not leave?") Next guest, I know, will be Odysseus to this (my tent) which, though it be a humble stopping place, yet will he find its rough and rudely figured canvas prove as artful, welcoming and true as ever was his spouse's tapestry.

As night draws on the weather builds, with thunder, driving rain and lightning flash, and all at once the flap draws back, and now I have my guest. A shorter sort of man, he has that average height of men of such an ancient time. All clad in skins and pelts, I see his features rugged and his hair unkempt.

As small as you have heard my tent, I note he does not stint to look around (and check behind) that hidden danger he avoids.

"What story would you hear?" he asks, ignoring all those novels which I store throughout my tent. I see such things are meaningless to him. He knows of stories "in the air," of those performed, declaimed and acted out (which each one being shared aloud, such simple joy is by that joining multiplied). He never knew a story which by being written down in black and white would not but lose its luster, energy and spark.

"Now listen close," I hear him say. Then warming to his tale, he takes me to some place and time where ever since we know that every schoolboy goes (and thinks it all a royal bore). But I do not. Not sitting in my tent, alone, where weather howls and journey ends. I know these things of which he speaks are living still in mortal hearts. Thus now he tells of beauty, lust and treachery … of swords of bronze (all flashing color in the sun), of faultless honor shining bright, of hearts that burn with passion never giving up, until that end (we could not guess) in which a spirit noble, loyal and divine breaks down that ancient fortress gate, and thereby giving lie to those who claim that never could a horse deceive.

You have met (before) my most recent guest. He is, of course, Homer, that most ancient and revered storyteller whose name alone we now attach to oral, epic allegory or (some say) to any ancient, treasured record of unprovable truth. In fact, although we have his name, we cannot be certain that such name is that of some one man, or instead identifies some group or "school" of storytellers. (Not unlike our foremost playwright and poet, of whom we have only the "nom" of his poetic—and thereby all-too-transparent—"nom de plume." But more on this later.)

I will have many more such guests who visit in what way they can, sharing with me their stories: those they sketched, wrote out and passed along, others which bequeathed to one and all as their biography. In time, I know, even these guests (like my family members, who have climbing of their own to do) will visit me less and less often. After all, although I do not break or move my camp, yet still I find the air gets thin.

I Resolve to Prepare
Sit with me a moment. Let me tell you of myself. You see me here as if a lazy, carefree soul, as unaccustomed to those cares of life as any soul unburdened of the world could be. In this, you would not be mistaken. But this is not the whole of it.

This Lofty Place

No, you find me at that place and time where (weary of those hackneyed phrases which we all have heard) still must I answer this (which speaking as were His command): "Prepare to meet thy Maker." Is this not apt? That I, forsaking life and having but some briefest time remaining, must hurry (urgent to the task), unknowing of that moment when He comes for me (but certain it will not be long).

Who, being told that he will shortly come into the presence of One so Majestic and Grand, would not prepare himself? Who, feeling already that rush of dire anticipation (arising from awareness that his time grows short), would not (to his impending end) give over every moment's meditation? And who, knowing his Almighty Judge is temperate, just and fair, would not but labor tirelessly to quiet any anger, bitterness or blame which still beclouds his heart?

How then, I ask myself, might I be accommodated to His Wish? How might I prepare myself to hear, of Him, what judgment He commands?

I see He asks that I do not depart this life (if time I have in this way to prepare), nor yet arrive to claim eternal life, in careless disregard of His unblemished Righteousness.

Arriving at the end of my journey, and shortly to be admitted into the presence of one greater than myself, I shake the dust from my clothing, feeling it not altogether right that I should come before Him bearing on my person any evidence of wrongdoing. Thus all-attentive to those marks and scars and blemishes which I did suffer on my climb, I feel my greatest shame for imperfections in my soul. Now meditating on those errors which my heart admits, I ask, "Who have I wronged? What errors did I do? How might I find forgiveness?" This you will see is the unexpressed prayer of my Meditation: That ever pressing on, I seek that blessed forgiveness which (His gift in this world and the next) I hope to have delivered of His hand.

I invite you, now, to read and follow out this record of my Meditation; where I, guided only by His Word and Wish and Plan, seek out the path of my eternal journey yet to be.

When Once I Lived

❧ ❧ ❧

Now beginning my Meditation, I pick up the story at that place which commences in just a few pages ("The Coffee Shop"). Upon completion of my Meditation, I plan to return to my point of departure (to this same page, but immediately below), as if to the place of my encampment, where I will tell you of my lessons learned (and what emotions felt) during that period composing and writing my Meditation.

❧ ❧ ❧

I am grateful that you, sensitive to my need for solitude, were willing to go away for some period of years during which I had quiet and leisure enough to complete my life's final testament. Thus giving over those years of my retirement to meditation, reading, study and reflection, I made it my occupation to set out in written form an account of my (imagined) voyage in the afterlife. That account—of my (invented) journey after death—you have recorded in those pages beginning shortly.

You will not imagine that such an account (even granting that it takes as its subject some activity barely to be contained within an infinity of time) is a story taking an eternity to tell, as that would be both tedious for the reader and unprofitable (even) for the author. Nevertheless, feeling as I do a sympathetic fondness for any other soul who reads and thinks and meditates, I could not forgo that (anticipated) pleasure of sharing with you that brief but hopeful story which my eternal odyssey marks out.

Thus I am grateful to share with you all of those pages (following) which record the contents of my Meditation. All of that Meditation now having been written out, bound and sealed in tribute to posterity, I once again turn my eyes to the horizon, gazing forth in my final days from this lofty encampment (where taking in that universe of His portentous stars, I read that final pattern which to me spells out my end).

First coming here, I had the pleasure of receiving visitors from near and far who shared with me those rich and varied stories which they knew. But as the years went on, I found such treasures proved a burden to my mind. I made some time to hear the story of that noble, hollow horse (which dreaming of, I saw it run unfettered through celestial gates of bronze … into His boundless pasture where eternal stars shine forth), then found next day, when I to all my stories did return, I heard that epic yet again of that same horse (which then to me it seemed both wondrous fresh and new).

Wait here with me, and in time you will see: That I, having long before given up my work, career and family as but a burden, and having come to this peaceful place where I was soon satisfied with my tent, stove and books, in time our Maker, wishing to prepare me for some still greater ascent (to some more lofty place, which having other, more remote and grand horizons yet to show), now requires of me that I set aside (as but another burden) every earthly purpose which my life sustained.

Where before I trusted to my body, mind and wits to bear me up, here at the end He makes of all these things a burden which I now lay down. Leaving behind me this encampment, my flesh and bone and all perceptions, and giving up as well this record of my Meditation, I lay down all my earthly burdens; I am uplifted.

CHAPTER 2
The Coffee Shop

Everything is quiet. I stretch myself out in my tent, trying to find a position which will offer me comfort but not so much untroubled repose that my meditations are overtaken by sleep. Finally I am satisfied, and I turn my attention (unavoidably) to the sound of the wind and weather. Do I hear voices? Would I be giving myself over to madness or delusion to imagine that the wind (having, we know, no mortal source or inspiration) has any message which my heart must hear? Nevertheless feeling that if I only listen, I might find in those near-inaudible murmurs some words or theme or stories that will stave off slumber, I give myself over to such unorganized and untutored wisdom as they have to tell.

Soon caught up in the secrets which those fairy-voices whisper, or gone at once to sleep (I could not say which), I find myself now standing in a once-familiar place: A busy coffee shop where, in college, my friends and I did often find a place of refuge from examinations, papers and some dread professor's wrath. I step inside the door and see the line is short, indeed, though all the workers look attentive to what caffeine-based concoctions all their coffee chemistry will soon be challenged to distill.

Impelled as much by habit as by any need to stay awake, I step up to the counter and order what I always did. It being promptly presented to me, I look in the back of the shop to see if my favorite table is by some chance free—and see it is! I drop my backpack in the place I know is best then take my seat where then (in company of friends) I, more than once, did solve some crisis which our nation faced, or plotted out my own (or some dear friend's) next step in life, or found some theme which being written out to fill 10 pages (double spaced) did satisfy my teacher that such wisdom as those pages did contain (though many times rephrased, restated and repeated) deserved the highest praise.

I am on my third sip of coffee (and some greater number of reminisces of lively times had at this table) when I notice some person has come up to my table and is standing there, waiting for me to notice him. I look up and see a young man of similar age to my friends and I (when once we came to this place) and dressed the same as any of us might have been. I pause a moment to try to recall his face, but not placing him in any way, at last I find the presence of mind to speak. "Oh … did you want to sit down?" I ask, acknowledging the empty chair across from me.

"Yes," he says, "if it won't disturb you?" I motion my assent, and he sits down, shrugging off his coat to hang over the back of his chair. He takes a long swallow of his coffee (as if in preparation) then speaks, "You look like you've been here before. You know this place?"

"Of course!" I reply. "I have been here—this very table, this chair—more times than I can recall. And you know," I say smiling, "as long as I have lived, I have never had a better cup of coffee than you can get here." My guest finishes his sip (which he clearly enjoys) then observes, "I agree with you – about the coffee – but it doesn't seem to me you've lived long enough to become much of an expert on coffee."

Shocked at his comment, I look down at the back of my hand (grasping my coffee cup) and observe that, for some unaccountable reason, my skin is remarkably smooth and clear (for a man of my advanced age). Rapidly checking my other hand and seeing the same inexplicable but undeniable fact, I stand up next to my chair to check out my countenance in the big mirror behind where the coffee machine stands.

I am both surprised and gratified. I see that my face, the color of my hair, my features and my skin, are faithfully and honestly expressive of that younger, slimmer self of mine (who once existed when I was still in college and who visited this coffee shop so many times). I sit down, again, and the expression on my face no doubt reveals to my companion how deeply affected I am. He smiles a smile of generous understanding and continues.

"Yes," he says, "you have been brought here not merely so that you might find, again, some safe and tolerant venue which (in life) you knew and loved, but also this: To feel again that energy of youth; to look from out some lofty vantage point upon a land as yet unknown to you; to find within your heart some fresh and still-untrodden place from which your gaze might thrill to see this world in all its sympathetic wonder. Let me explain," he says.

"You are now at the commencement of your afterlife, and I am your guide. You see that you have been brought here—at the beginning—to a place familiar to you, promising only warmth and cheer. This is merely the first of what you will, in time, see to be many such arrangements which our Heavenly Father has made to reassure you and quiet your fears. Do you understand?"

He waits for my reply, and during that quiet I let the background noise and clatter of the coffee shop occupy by attention. Am I, indeed, in the afterlife? Or has my posture in meditation proved all too restful so that now, in fact, I dream? I cast about briefly to see if some aspect of my surroundings might give away the ruse (and so inform me what is true—and what illusion). But I find no failing in the set or scene.

It seems as if this place, which all too clear must be a sham, is yet constructed and upheld by hands as strong and deft as those that once sustained that coffee shop of old (which in that world of substance all agree did once exist). In truth, I see about me nothing that is but a "sham." To all my senses there is nothing I can see or touch or taste that does not seem as real as anything I knew in life. Thus I think, "This must be a dream." But still … we know that in our dreams we feel ourselves as much alive, at risk and in the moment as ever we might feel in life. How, then, can I determine which this is?

My guide, as experienced in these matters as I am ignorant, speaks up. "So … now you doubt yourself. You are asking, Is this real? Or is this a dream? Now, in any other case, I would make every effort to demonstrate to you the truth of the matter (whatever it is) and likewise use all my talents and powers to demonstrate to you the falsity of your conclusion (assuming you have misread your position, whatever it might be), but I ask you to think, now, what choices lie before you? On the one hand, this may be a dream, where, as if by magic, or spell of illusion, or some subtle power of our body acting upon our now unfettered imagination (as if, as has been suggested, all might be the product of some "underdone potato") we feel ourselves resident in some powerful and all-compelling drama (of which we see no imperfection which might break the spell) and thereby live this little life a fiction which we discover, now, as soon as we wake up. Or on the other hand, this may be the afterlife, where with His unbounded power, He does make of all our senses but the hues of which He paints the scene before us, racing on ahead of our dull wits to color out that set and scene and story which His purpose now requires.

"I ask you," my guide gently challenges me, "can you tell me which is true? Which the dream you cannot fathom? Which that drama of eternal tragedy where you play the central (mock-heroic) part? Have you so much wisdom, lived so long, and seen so much of His creation that you might draw that line? This no more than a dream (but even a dream real in its own way and ever faithful to its own laws), this other but the work of hands unseen, showing what His promise, here, has built for us: Where some moments we might find abode within those walls and rooms and gardens which express His love (as … has He not said that here, in our eternity, He prepares for us 'many mansions?').

"What say you?" my guide asks. Now, who, being given this choice, would not be humbled? Nothing could be more clear to me than that my poor powers of reasoning and observation are in no way adequate to say what is true. I look around the coffee shop, feeling in this instant lost, alone and enfeebled, a poor excuse for a man, unworthy, and unready to embark upon this, my eternity. Then, unthinkingly, I take another sip of coffee … and find my cup still full! The coffee still as hot as it has ever been! And then it dawns on me. That now I see these things made new again … my face and form, this place … my friends and all those dreams I had (that I might learn, discover and explore this world which He reveals to me).

In consequence thereof reminded of His unfailing grace, I give my guide's question my honest and fearless consideration. At last I have my answer.

"It seems to me," I say, "that if I am 'dreaming,' I can only be experiencing that one, most agreeable dream where, dreaming that I have passed away and come to the afterlife, I find myself thereby enveloped in His perfect and never-failing mercy (where, like any dream obedient to its own purpose, I find that all about me does uniformly and unceasingly declare His unrivaled loving-kindness).

"On the other hand," I continue, "if I am not dreaming, that can only mean that I, in the midst of my meditation, did sadly and untimely pass away, in which case all about me that I see is not a dream but no more than the commencement of that eternal life which was promised to me and which the evidence of my (now-eternal) senses does unmistakably show is but the work of our most loving Maker.

To my chagrin, my guide, upon hearing my answer, lets out a loud laugh, rocking back in his chair and slightly spilling his coffee. "Oh! I should have known!" he exclaims in a loud voice. "I forgot you were a lawyer! Oh, for heaven's sake, don't you know the old joke we have here about lawyers?" I shake my head.

"Well," he explains, "it goes like this: A lawyer comes to the afterlife, and he sees all his old lawyer friends are already there, so right away he concludes,

'I must be in Heaven.' Then, later on, he sees a fence, so he goes over to it and looks on the other side. There he sees a friend who he knew when he used to be alive, who is not a lawyer. So the lawyer calls out, 'Hey, Rick, what are you doing over there? You were a good person when you were alive, so how come you're not in Heaven?' So, Rick looks over at the lawyer and says, 'Well, all I know is, everybody here says *this* must be Heaven, 'cause over here … we've got no lawyers.'"

On that note, we each go back to our coffee, sitting quietly in silent contemplation.

The Coffee Shop

My Guide Explains

It is a few minutes before we resume our conversation, as I need a few minutes to acclimate myself to this dream-like state. As if a swimmer resolving to overcome the coldness of the water by the rapidity with which I throw myself into it, I ask my guide, "Alright, so you're my 'guide.' So … what is the program here? Is there some sort of 'tour'?" He smiles with humor "No. It's not like that. I'm more of a coach, a tutor, a … well, guide, and you're like an explorer who doesn't know the territory or the language, and you need someone to smooth the way for you. But still it's you who's doing the exploring, and it's you who's got to write the account of your discoveries."

He shifts in his seat, getting more comfortable. "Here is how I'd like to see you work," he says. "I am going to leave you here for a while, and what I want you to do is to meditate … just what you were about to do when you suddenly found yourself here. And I want you to plan your own journey. Decide what will be your first explorations; try to anticipate the 'rules' of this new land. And when you come up against some puzzling question or choice or imponderable, I want you to use your own imagination and decide what you think the answer should be, or what process you think best represents how the afterlife must operate.

"Now, periodically, I will rejoin you and check your work. And in those cases where you've got something … not as right as it might be, well, I will correct your work, and then you can go on to the next step. So you see, this process is not just about exploring and getting to the landmarks that are characteristic of this place; it is just as much about developing your skills as an explorer. Now I will be your guide, but in time, if you progress in your skills and understanding, you will be permitted to explore on your own, without any need for a guide. Does that make sense to you?"

"Yes," I say. "But one question: Can I … am I permitted to see friends and family members who I used to know and who passed away before me? Can I see them again, now, and talk about old times and things we did … when we were alive together?"

A shadow of thoughtful recognition passes over my guide's face. Then he replies, "No. Not now, at least not for some little while. You see, what is important at this moment is that you so refine and prepare your judgment that, being given some moral or ethical challenge, you will make that choice which is most expressive of your authentic, moral character. It is … as if He asks you to prepare yourself, in your own time, and revealing your own genuine voice, to answer honestly what justice you see in this world and where, with whatever wisdom, strength and skill you possess, you might add to that store of righteousness which is His eternal legacy.

"If you were to give over your time to re-connecting with old friends and family, you might forever lose this opportunity to refine and focus your better tendencies, to no important end. I can tell you, however, that in all due time, assuming you progress as I believe you can, there will come a point where you will be permitted to see again all your old friends and others whom you loved and cared and knew.

"Here, then, is your assignment in the afterlife. It is the purpose of each of those lessons which I will teach you and (of no lesser importance) the very goal and purpose of your meditation: It is to seek His truth in all of its many forms and languages, in this time and all others. For we cannot be made poorer by being placed in possession of a greater quantity of His truth, and there is no occupation which provides greater riches or returns than to cultivate those fields of His wherein we find His truth has taken root.

"Now, my job as guide requires not only that I be familiar with that unknown land into which you will soon journey but also that I take into account those talents and inclinations which you, my client, possess. Thus, I know, for example, that in addition to the law, you made a life's avocation of the study of mathematics. I wonder if you could, now, for my benefit, explain to me how it is that you, a lawyer, who makes it your profession to work with words (and ideas expressible in written form), should give so much of your valuable time over to the study of a subject which must be in its essence entirely alien to your linguistic skills?

I am taken aback by what my guide has asked. Here he is, mere moments into our first meeting, forthrightly telling me that he has already "made a study" of my life, and (by the nature of his question, subtlety insinuates) that by virtue of such inspection, he has "uncovered" some (heretofore undisclosed and, in some way, shameful) distinguishing inclination peculiar to my character. Then, far from apologizing for this intrusion, he now presses me to explain (and—if I understand correctly—to justify) some conflict or inconsistency which he imagines must exist between those two aspects of my personality (which I have already found to have established, over a lifetime of enforced partnership, a mutual accommodation allowing them to reside peaceably in the same heart).

"I take it this is my first lesson? A quiz on a subject I ought to know well?" He nods his assent. "Well," I begin, "it has been my experience that there exist certain natural affinities between the 'law' and the science of mathematics, and it is due to these shared qualities that I enjoy mathematics and find it meshes well with my profession as a lawyer. You see, I approach mathematics as … merely another language. We would likely all acknowledge, for example, that 'music' constitutes a language in itself and that the many forms and styles of music (representing that same number of self-sufficient musical 'dialects') offer that many more languages which a person (a musician) might employ. Thus we know that music speaks to us in moods and tones no other form of language can compare. And, likewise, the truths it tells are truths which we do not expect to exist or be expressible in any other language.

"Is it not the same with mathematics? That if we learn the language of numbers, soon we drink deeply of truths which could not be contained in any other vessel. Is mathematics difficult? Yes, but so is mastering a musical instrument. And (we know) not every person has that inborn talent allowing him or her to freely express himself in song or sounds or notes. But should we conclude that, because powers and formulae and transformations are similarly difficult to grasp, that we are thereby excused from hearing those truths which only numbers might express?

"Let me point out to you, in defense of this universally accessible language, that it was only recently in human history that a mathematician (a Mr. Godel) proved (by groups and signs and infinities) that there exist certain statements about mathematics and science and the fundamental nature of the world (which, no doubt, have their place also in this eternal afterlife) which are not merely 'seemingly' nor 'practically' nor even 'effectively' (but 'unconditionally,' 'categorically' and 'conclusively') unknowable and unprovable. We see of such statements (which are often of the utmost importance in mathematics) that if we should arbitrarily declare one answer 'true' and all the others 'false,' we soon find the truth of that one answer—and the falsity of all the others—forever indeterminate, and in all worlds irreducibly undecidable.

"Speaking, now, as a person well acquainted with this newly discovered theorem of mathematics (proven to be of universal application), and notwithstanding my lack of experience with the afterlife, I am nevertheless confident that if I were to greet some person newly come this coffee shop, I could greatly facilitate his lessons in the afterlife (and help him to avoid unexpected disappointment) by reciting to him these cautionary words: Not every answer shall be given; not every mystery shall be revealed.

"And continuing, I would admonish him with these final words: Even supposing that you, having lived out your life in ever-unwavering trust in His all-knowing, boundless wisdom, might come (as I have) to this afterlife having it your unshakable conviction that the answer to some insoluble riddle will at last be revealed to you, it may yet be that His appointed servant (knowledgeable in such things) tells you with a smile that even He is not able (by logic) to declare such proposition to be 'so' or 'not so.'

"This, I believe, is wisdom which no other human language could so well express or demonstrate. Thus, I do cheerfully say that I (indeed) love mathematics, which occupies no small or unimportant part of His storehouse of eternal truth."

My guide looks at me with what I surmise to be genuine admiration, evincing thereby his good-hearted anticipation of a friendship which we might find together. "I perceive," he says, "that if I am to challenge your curiosity and intelligence, I will have to introduce some aspect of 'numbers' into your lessons. Here is what I want you to do: While you are planning out the activities which you expect to experience in the afterlife, I want you to keep a running total of the amount of time you believe you will need to devote to those experiences.

"No doubt it was one of the first purposes of the science of 'mathematics' to express how much time would have to be allotted to some task or journey. For example, we can imagine the earliest human hunters saying something like, 'The river is five days' walk, and then our summer hunting ground beyond that is eight days' walk' (or some such thing). Accordingly, and for much the same purpose, it will be an essential part of your lessons here to keep an accurate, accessible and exhaustive 'cumulative total' of the amount of time which you estimate you will need in your afterlife to see and learn all of the truth which He has for you. Is that acceptable?

I readily agree.

CHAPTER 3
I Dream

I Dream
After the foregoing interchange, my guide and I sit silently for some little while, wordlessly enjoying each other's company; he giving thought to how his plan for me must now be modified, me letting my ever-active subconscious mind take in and process all that my guide has said. At some point, the idea occurs to me that I have at last found that Holy Grail of all the world's diners, coffee houses and luncheonettes (the "bottomless cup"). I likewise notice (my attention having been directed by this thought to the coffee cup in my hand, and so to my other hand, resting motionless at its side) that I am still wearing my wedding ring.

"Why would this be?" I ponder. Then giving it more consideration, I am boarded on some new and stimulating train of thought (freighted with possibilities). My guide has been at pains to explain to me that I am not yet permitted to contact or communicate in any way with friends or family who I knew in life. Now I can well see the logic of this limitation, and I feel no desire to test such boundaries as my guide (to all appearances kindly and seeming to wish me no ill will) might set for me. Still … I feel that, denied of all human contact, my spirit must soon wither and thirst (even in this lush and fertile landscape which He keeps for me).

Thus, I cast about in my mind to imagine what person or persons would not be denied to me (if I were to seek of them companionship, humor and … purpose). Now, in no little time it comes to me who might be my (permitted) companion.

Clearing my throat to rouse my guide from his reverie, I begin, "It occurs to me that when you said I would not now be permitted to visit with friends or family, you did not (perhaps) express any final judgment upon certain others—

person or persons—who I might have as traveling companions, hosts or guests along the way. I assume that, friends and family being ruled off limits (that even the value of their well-informed insights is over balanced by the distraction which they bring) there would be no possibility of my substituting those even more distracting 'perfect strangers' who we might find here in numbers.

"Nevertheless," I continue, "it seems to me that there is one 'special case' who, not only I, but also you (and our most-loving Maker) must soon agree is more than just a 'friend' or even 'family.' It is that one who, looking, now, upon this ring, I do recall was once to my eternal soul enjoined. That she and I did swear before the world that 'no more twain,' we thenceforth in that world and this did promise to each other (and to Him) that 'two is one,' eternally and more.

"Not meaning, in any way, to deprecate your sincere concern for my welfare," I say to my guide, "nevertheless I must tell you that I have my own plans for this afterlife. And among those plans is one, in particular, which I feel some urgency to commence. That is why I take this opportunity to press my case. My spouse, my wife, is no mere 'friend,' nor even blood relation. She is no little part of me; that me stumbling, it is she who bleeds, me doubting, it is she who despairs, and me passing away, it is she bereft of the world.

"I ask that you do not separate us, who knew in life but the one, same love. Who, having before us that one eternity which is promised to all, still we could not trust that we would find our (separate) selves again in that unbounded, endless infinite, but hastened, once, to seal our souls in ever-lasting partnership, having no more 'yours' nor 'mine' but only 'ours' to pledge against our souls' indebtedness to Him.

"So you see," I conclude, "I feel entitled to ask you … to implore you … to allow me to see and speak to my wife. There are things which I need to explain to her. Honestly, I don't see how I am going to get anything out of the lessons which you have for me here unless I can first talk to Molly and get some things straightened out. Really! She and were married for more than thirty years, and now you won't let me see her?!"

I am well-aware that, in voice and demeanor, I have worked myself into a state where what I said was all-emotion and very-little-logic. I see that my guide has weathered my outburst calmly, and even now I fancy I see the 'wheels turning' as he calculates how to deal with my heartfelt imprecation. He crosses his arms (no doubt the better to contain some angry, righteous reprimand which he intends), then suffering a scowl to 'ore-spread his face,

I Dream

he answers, "Yes, I understand your request—and your position—all too well. First, I do agree that pressing on at once into your lessons would be a fruitless exercise. You do have … some sort of thorn in your paw, and, unless we get it out, you will not be found pacing up or down the footpaths of our Maker's savanna of eternal truth."

"Nevertheless, I say to you, you are not ready to see your wife," he baldly pronounces. "Not ready. And not only that, if you will but give this matter some more patient consideration, it will, perhaps, occur to you that your wife (also), having come here some years before you, has had her own lessons, and (we might expect), her own thorns of which she needed to be healed.

"Having said all this (rejecting, I know, your request in its entirety), nevertheless I am not unmindful of what motivates your insistent and unyielding demand. There is, still, that thorn which now vexes me as much as you. So we will need to do something about it—something which the rules and regulations of this afterlife permit.

My guide pauses in silent thought and I, anticipating his as-yet-unrevealed solution, lean forward in my chair to hear what remedy he will prescribe.

"Who of us," he begins, "having some thorn in our flesh, would not wish to retrace our steps to find that time and place where we (unlucky or, perhaps, admittedly unobservant) did tread upon that thorn? Thus given our wish, any of us would (forthwith) go, once more, to that one fateful spot where we might step again with added care, or find some dry, unyielding rock to rest our foot, or choose some more protected road, and so avoid that hurt or sprain or life's regret which (all unnoticed) lay within our path.

"This, all too clearly, is what you desire (as might we all)," my guide acknowledges. "Lamentably, as will shortly be revealed to you, such an opportunity to altogether retrace your steps is not allowed to any mortal soul within this world. There is, however, one other 'world' within which all things (unalterably fixed in this mortal world you know) are as subject to our further amendment, erasure and revision as any written record (hurriedly jotted down in pencil) might be.

"That world you have already encountered: It is the world of dreams. Where you, seeing (regretfully) that your ill-omened thorn is unavoidable … still, you trust that in a dream you might revisit that time and place of your injury and, by some thoughtful, clever emendations to the text, cross out that 'thorn' and place, instead, some 'blossoms, buds or blooms' beneath your foot. In dreams, we know, though time and place and deeds may not be changed, the over-arching theme does but arise created by our mind's dramatic art; change but the tone or cadence, the accent or the emphasis, and all the drama (and so, the moral) is thus transformed.

"You asked to speak to your wife, and I have explained to you that this is not permitted. However, what I will permit is this: You will be allowed to communicate with that one, true and authentic 'self' (your own self) who, at the time that concerns you, was daily in communication with your wife. If you have some 'message' or emotions which you wish to communicate to her, you may do so by your own dumb show which you place before your own unseeing eyes.

"Here (in three parts) is what I will allow: You shall be transported into some dream which your then-living self did have. There, in that dream, you will be cast in the role of some iconic figure which we often meet in dreams (as if symbolic of your 'conscience,' your 'unacknowledged desire' or 'shame'), but being in the dream, you may not speak in words so plain or clear that give away the subterfuge. No, you must, as if in any dream, speak only in symbols, signs and auguries. Then, finally, having been given this stage where you may act out such wisdom as you would bestow upon your old and former self (and if your art be true, upon your wife), you must never speak to me of this again, but only trust that in due time all shall be revealed ... and every story (however sad) heard out to its prefigured end.

The Church
Quickly I give my assent, and my guide, motioning with his hand to some place not far off, instantly we are transported to a place which, after some few moments, I recognize. It is the area before the altar in the church where Molly and I were married. I see the altar lit from above, the pews on either side already decorated with sprigs and boughs of blossoms, and I notice some soft, preparatory music is to be heard if I but stop and listen.

My guide, standing next to me, leans closer to my ear and whispers, "You see. This is the place where you and your wife exchanged your vows. The church, you observe, is even now prepared for your marriage ceremony tomorrow. Shortly I will take my leave, as I prefer not to be seen in this dream of which you will soon be a part. In a few moments the dream will begin, and the dreamer is 'you'—that you who was the 'groom'—that young man who, in the dark of night before the dawn of his wedding day, did dream this place and persons, seeing about him all these things you also see, but being all unknowing of yourself, your message, or the truth you wish to tell. Before I leave, recall that all will be as if in any dream. You will see characters, creatures and events

I Dream

as strange as any imagination can invent. Therefore, do not be distracted from your purpose by anything you see much out of place.

My guide turns and walks away, in moments becoming invisible to me. Immediately I feel a most unusual sensation, and before my eyes I become aware of clouds and mists that take away my sight of walls and ceilings which did seal me in. I thrill to feel a sort of buoyant, incandescent lightness, sensing in the air some otherworldly scent of His intention (having in it but a hint of memory). I see, standing off to one side of the pews, a female figure, both tall and fair, dressed all in light (the color not apparent) and in posture revealing that she has some purpose here, of which she awaits only the proper moment when she will do her appointed duty, then fade away, all in obedience to some greater majesty.

Now, looking where the pews stand on the other side of the aisle, I am shocked to see crouching, watching and waiting, two lovely, tame and luminescent rabbits! Each all over white with attractive spots and splashes of black, these two creatures evince no fear of their surroundings. They appear to be a mated pair, which I—now evidently all too prosaically confined to mortal, human form—do only regard in silent admiration, in no way party to what secrets pass between them. I see their ears (erect) now quickly twitch to catch what sounds there are that now announce our (deep-dreaming) host, who I see is coming down the aisle in the direction of the altar.

It is, I see, my former self as I appeared (and wished and dreamed) that evening before my wedding day. I see that I (myself, the "Groom") am dressed in that dark and manly suit which I would proudly wear the next day, though it be but poor plumage in comparison to those others populating this dream. Notwithstanding, I see this Groom is as honestly and naturally suffused with joy as any bachelor (unshakably determined to commit matrimony) might be. His eyes sparkle; there is energy and lightness in his step, and (on his face) I see that look of childlike anticipation which promises a heart both guileless and direct.

Before I can react or in any way initiate any communication with my former self (this Groom), I become aware that there is another figure advancing down the aisle. Not only the Groom and I but also that shining female observer, and the rabbits, now fix our gaze upon this other figure who appears from out the dark. It is—to my surprise—my wife! (my Bride) Molly!

She advances slowly; her bearing graceful, modest, and having about her an air of wise beneficence. She is all over dressed in the most gorgeous raiment that any loving bride has ever worn; the colors of her gown all luxuriant in shades of white (of which, if we attempt to name them all, we soon overtax the vocabulary—if not the senses—of any Eskimo mother of the bride). Altogether, her appearance, the lights above the altar and the accompanying hymns create about her an aura of divine solemnity, in consequence of which I confess the beauty of this efflorescent female apparition to be nothing less than "angelic."

Her feet, I see, are shoeless (as, in dreams, we do not expect to suffer any toilsome hike). On her head, I see a wreath of flowers, freshly cut and seeming yet alive, their fragrance preceding her down the aisle, and there inspiring some grateful, approving nodding of the rabbits' heads. Under her feet, I see she walks on a seamless carpet of dogwood blossoms, both cushioning her step and likewise adding to that sweet odor which announces her coming.

What most attracts my admiration, however, is how she holds her arms. These she crosses closely before her, as if she cradles some now freshly newborn infant in her arms. But yet not any child of hers I see. Instead, clutched to her breast are lovely, fragrant bouquets of colorful blooms. There are Lilies and Marigolds, Blue Bells and Larkspur; great, upswelling bunches of blossoms, in numbers not easily counted, each species retaining that vitality which it so recently enjoyed (unceasingly verdant in His abundant garden). I am dumbstruck with wonder.

Seeing her resplendent in all this womanly beauty, it is at once apparent to me that in this dream authored by the Groom, she is not to be given any lines, but only appear (thusly) in silent show of her unequalled perfection, which to the dreamer promises as enchanting and gratifying a betrothal as any words she might be made to speak. The Groom, meanwhile, stands motionless, his every power of communication stilled in rapturous awe.

I see instantly that now is the moment when I must reach out to touch the heart of this attentive Groom. It must be now, or all is lost.

Those Oaths
I step forward, attracting the attention of the Groom and noting that my Bride suspends her step. Then next I pause—as dramatically as I know how—hoping by this device to keep the eyes of the Groom fixed upon me. In the interval, I find his eyes meet mine, though not with any excess of discernment or self-awareness. I begin to speak, in as deep and authoritarian a voice as I can manage, "Wait, Groom, I have much that I must show you! If you would be forever joined in inseparable devotion to this angelic maiden, then there are three lessons which you must learn, and so, three corresponding oaths which you must, now, forever, vow.

I Dream

The Groom looks not a little perplexed (as is this not *his* dream?), and what man is this, coming to him on the eve of his wedding, who nevertheless seems not to be proposing to him any activities which might profitably be part of any bachelor party? I name it, therefore, "Good Fortune" when I report that the Groom (a good sport to the end) compliantly gives over his attention to what I (this figure of All-Knowing Fate) will try to teach.

Being now in the dream but having, still, my wits about me, I venture an experiment to determine if this dream state might be as pliable to my will as it is to his (the Groom's). Looking up to where the altar stands, I motion with my hands, and immediately we see before us what I desire, which is: A lovely, snug and well-proportioned house having about it such "homey" features as any newly wedded couple could ever wish. There are large windows in the front to let in the light and large windows in the back, so that a mother might watch her children play (while she does the dishes). Then a chimney telling of a warm and hearty hearth, where toes and fingers (in the wintertime) might be restored to health. Not least, we see a fence and gate (of white), more decorative than real, which to all the world declare, "This is our home, and here we live and love."

Turning to the Groom, I ask, "Do you see this? This is but a symbol of that space (consecrated, alone, to the two of you) which it is your eternal purpose in life to create, preserve and devote to that union of your souls. This space, being ever and again dedicated by your (husbandly) labors to the safety and support of your mate, you reassure her by these efforts that she (and all that is promised by her fertility) will have some refuge in this world and will never fear to be alone, abandoned, or without shelter.

Having made use of these "visual aids," and having likewise made my speech, I hold my breath to see what reaction the Groom will have. His verdict is not long coming. At once he throws back his arms, tilts back his head and calls out to all the world, "I love this woman! She is beautiful! Caring! And loving! And soon she will be mine! And has the world ever seen so perfect a love, as my Bride and I do share?! No! No one has!

"Why … why, we have such love as has no need of doors or walls or windows! No need of roof or floors or picket fences! We two shall live unfettered, sharing out our love beneath the very sky, the stars, and all His colored pageants of the sun (that every day shall rise and set upon our heads, as naked to the wind and rain as live those rabbits over there). We need no such dwelling. No walls or roof that any vanity might think could keep such love as ours entombed. Our love needs no such shelter as you build for us.

For how could any mortal hands deform those perfect bonds of love which so surround our love (as like our wedding bands). Tell me no more!"

This is not the reaction I wanted or expected. Still, I must press on. Time is short; dreams do not long endure. Looking, once more, to that cozy dwelling which my dream-like magic has constructed, I motion, again, and now we see stretching out behind that cozy home, luxuriant fields and pastures. There are orchards of fruit trees, meadows where farm animals graze contentedly, and gardens growing vegetables and crops that might sustain a family (of size). All of this is as pleasant and natural as such things can be.

Once more addressing the Groom (and drawing myself up with all my counterfeit authority), I first declare to him, in manner most stentorian and grand, "Hear me now (!) and Heed my Words!" Then next, in voice (intended) calming, soft and confidential, I go on, "Although you may believe your love to be not merely essential—but also sufficient—to sustain your marriage, I ask you to consider this scene before you. Here you see fields and crops and pastures which will produce that bounty necessary to support your bodies (and necessary, as well, to nurture such children as you may be blessed to have). You see that, being resident here on some continuous basis (so as to timely plant and cultivate and harvest these crops) this cozy home represents no more than some convenient stopping place where you might cook and sleep and play when not out in the fields. Do you not see, at last, the value of these oaths I press on you to build this house, to keep these fields, and so live out your love (entire)?"

Once again, my Groom reacts as if performing his own (over-acted) part before some audience both hard of hearing and seated no where close. He leaps up from his seat in one of the pews and, as if shouting to be heard in some top-most row of cheapest seats, declaims, "Our love will be as fruitful and bountiful as the world has ever known! We shall not want for any common, mundane things that populate your fears. No! We shall live grandly, drinking only of His purest rain, eating only of His softest fruit, plucked freshly from His abundant orchards (planted by the wind, and cultivated only by the actions of His lesser creatures, like those two rabbits over there).

"I … who swear my love before this altar of His benevolence, can do no more than hope and trust and (so) believe that that same gracious Will which has given me my Bride will not fail to provide (in the same measure of generosity), whatever meat and drink and bread we two might need to sustain our perfect love. Do you hear me? I will not swear that oath you press on me!"

I Dream

I think to myself, "This is not going well. This Groom is not listening." Nevertheless, I have only one more lesson to teach, and this final lesson is that one commandment which I have many times promised to myself this Groom must surely learn.

Seeing that the time has come, at last, to teach this urgent and vital lesson, I make of that cozy home a "schoolhouse," now summoning its one (inattentive) student to take up his crayons and chalk and thereby copy out this last assignment (due—double-spaced with footnotes—at the cessation of his mortal life). Thus, by some power given to me in the dream, I hold up for the edification of my audience one characteristic and invariable feature of this home's design. I show a kitchen, dining room, gathering room (that holds the hearth) as well as baths and storage rooms, but that one, indispensable feature (which we dare not miss), is this: That this home provides but one bedroom for the couple living here (though as many nurseries as their love might populate). This point I stress.

"You see ... this house has no other bed which any resident of this home might occupy; no other bed where, some other woman coming in the door, she could expect of that one husband (living here) any touching, tenderness or bliss. There is only the one bed, only the one place where this husband's love and caresses might be shared, and only the one, same body (his wife's) of which he might gather those fruits of a woman's tender blush.

"Thus I say ... Behold! (Having reached that utmost climax of my persuasive drama, my voice takes on a tone and timbre altogether Biblical.) There are of your marriage Three Vows (!) which you must swear (!):

> *First ... To make of your love a dwelling place tranquil and tolerant, calm and restorative.*
>
> *Next ...To make of your love a fruitful and bountiful partnership, giving nourishment and support both to your own selves and to your offspring.*
>
> *Finally ... To make of your love (and union) a thing precious and undefiled, unsullied by falsehood or disregard, forever unpolluted by any thoughts uncaring or lacking in love.*

Having done my best, I fall silent.

It seems that the Groom does for some few moments hesitate, as if the force of my argument has not been wholly unappreciated by him. Still, in but a little while again he stands up, and now pacing over to that image of his

Bride (standing, still, before him) he steps 'round in front of her and, taking hold of her hands in his, he drops down to one knee and looks up into her face. But … we see that doing so, he takes away from her grasp those fragrant bunches of flowers which she holds in her arms, and we see them fall to the floor, lying desolate and disordered … in confusion at her feet.

The Groom, now kneeling before her, we see rashly tramples with his weight those same blossoms, unthinkingly scattering the Lilies and Marigolds this way and that, and treading upon those bunches of Blue Bell and Larkspur so that they lie broken and misshapen about the ground. He, despite this sad result, is all unseeing and unconscious of what he has done and how his actions (done with all good heart) now trouble her expression, giving rise to some inner anxiety with which her heart now struggles.

I see him now, as so do all, look up to catch her gaze. Then in some softer voice (than was before) he speaks his love. "My dearest, my sweetheart … I pledge to you these vows, which are not the same as that other voice (who knows but age and years and burdens weary to be told) would have me swear. No! Not those oaths! These vows I swear!

So long as burns my heart in all-consuming passion, replenished by vitality of youth, I shall be true!

So long as lives your beauty ever fresh and all unchanging, I shall be true!

So long as lives our love unbounded, free and self-sufficient in the world, I shall be true!

"A love like ours, that lives both innocent and new, I would not sacrifice to any bonds of oath, no matter what I vow!"

৶ ৶ ৶

Thus borne aloft by ardor, and so despite of Fate, my drama ends. Our somnambulistic playwright having performed these final lines of this, his final scene, a host of unseen stagehands rushes forward to strike the set. Of those orchards, fields and pastures which we saw, these are given over to their natural state where they soon revert to that wilderness and waste from which they came. Then that cozy house (which has its charms), now starved of any owner's upkeep or repair (by which it might defy all nature's wrath, and years, and children slamming every door), does quickly go to ruin where such shrines to our domestic bliss do molder, rust and waste away denied of our devoted care.

We hear those hymns (of promise) first grow faint then die away. Those lights above His altar (illuminating all) do flicker, spark and crackle in distress, then giving in to darkness, dissolve to black. Those fragrant odors in the air (which linger, gently touching heart's desires) are dispossessed of every subtle power of suggestion.

As if on cue (despite the final curtain being down) the image of my Bride fades all away, and before the altar there remain only those same characters you know, at our feet the ruin of her blooms which now mix wantonly with that carpet of dogwood blossoms I saw before. I see the Groom, yet kneeling where he last did speak, now grasping in his hands only emptiness, where before he held his Bride's sweet fingertips.

Knowing that my efforts have been unavailing, and that I have failed of my purpose, I find that there are tears in my eyes to see this scene of sadness (oaths unfulfilled, and others from the first declined). I look about for that shining female figure whose duty she all-patient did await. But I do not see her; she has gone.

I see, at last, those two fast-running rabbits, all attentive to the end, who turn their spotted backs to go. Then, in unison glancing over their shoulders, it seems to me they smile in undiluted pity, if one might witness such a thing of just a common rabbit.

CHAPTER 4
Starting Out

Here is my task as I understand my guide has given it to me: To plan now for how I will spend my time in eternity. My personality is such that I feel the need to make this plan. Doing so will give me confidence that I will be prepared for that challenge, but also it will give me pleasure and a sense of security to contemplate the activities and rewards that I believe I will enjoy during my life everlasting.

How do I know I will have this eternal life? It is a promise of our Savior, and I feel the strength and vitality of that promise more every day. I take comfort that not only does my church teach this doctrine, but so many other religions I know of also teach eternal life. It cannot be some empty wish that each of us should not be extinguished but should have life eternal. Here is my strongest proof of the certainty of this promise (and if you live long enough, you will come to see this also): That when you see a child born from nothing but the love of his parents (if he is lucky), and then that child develops quickly into a person with a character so rich and complex, so unchanging (in so many ways), from childhood into youth and then adulthood, that there is no other conclusion but that God – or some higher power or more elevated dimension of being – has brought this precious and unique personality into being in this tiny infant's body. And whatever has been brought into existence with such generous and loving forethought, it could not be intended that this child, at the elapse of eighty years or so, should be fully and finally extinguished, never to be any more.

So it is not from any religious doctrine alone that I believe that death is not the end. It is from ordinary, common experience with the world.

But what I do have from my church and from its doctrines and from so many sermons is that our afterlife will be eternal and unchanging. It is our promise that we shall be gathered to Him and that we shall worship Him and praise His name for all eternity. Not just our denomination teaches this.

I Pause at the Threshold
Here is the first question I must address as I commence my journey. By the answer to this question I will determine the direction that I will travel throughout my journey. My church teaches me that I will be saved and that I will have an eternity in Heaven praising His name. So … will I, upon my passing, proceed immediately to Heaven, or will some other events intervene? Is this not the moment when—with near universal certitude—so many of the religions of the world declare that I—my eternal soul—must first stand before the Heavenly Throne and submit to the judgment of God? Will my soul be found acceptable? Or will I be judged wanting, and so be sent to that eternal perdition which is the common fate of sinners, evildoers and non-believers? If I accept the teaching of so many religions, each with its own deep reservoir of wisdom, compassion and truth, I might, perhaps, end my meditation here.

Why, on this one point which you would think would be answered so differently by so many different religions of such divergent sources, is there so much agreement? Perhaps in some ancient time before we know, it was the common belief of all men (living then in a world of everyday brutality and violence) that their warrior god—who to his followers dispensed life and to any who opposed him, death—was possessed of such awesome and terrible jealousy that when called upon to deliver his judgment of any human soul who came before him, had only the one punishment (death) for any who fell short of his perfection in any way. But we do not live in such a world. We live in a world in which we know that the judgment of our God is perfect, just and true.

No, I would expect that, upon my passing, I would be judged, and an honest, just and compassionate determination I would expect it to be. Not an earthly trial wherein passion often rules the day, or vital facts and testimony—unknown to any but a heavenly witness—never gathered, never brought to court and which, if they were only brought forth, would plainly show my innocence. No, in this life we soon learn that if we come before an earthly tribunal, we will be subject to every occurrence and possibility of falsehood, and injustice may easily result. Thus we do not place our trust in any such court but only in His heavenly judgment.

And of this heavenly judgment, what might I expect? Here my mind and heart struggle with what I have been taught since childhood. What I was taught—on those few occasions when the subject was addressed—is that each of us must receive His judgment, which is of the utmost simplicity. On the one hand, we may be found "acceptable" (in which case we receive the reward of eternal life), or in the alternative, we may be found "wanting" (in which case we receive His judgment of eternal torment). It is, if I may characterize it so, a precociously "digital" process: We are judged, and we are—like a digital switch in a computer micro-processor—either "on" or "off." There is no middle ground, no other position where the switch might be moved. On or off. Holy or damned. An eternity of bliss or a like eternity of unbearable agony. This, we must honestly agree, seems to be the shared opinion of many of the world's great religions.

Now I would not lightly cast aside this offered wisdom of so many great religious teachers. What does this say but that, in a Heavenly judgment, our acts in life shall have their just reward? The guilty shall not escape their punishment. The righteous—who in this life may seem to suffer unjustly at the hands of the wicked—will have their true reward. Such a teaching—with this same measure of absolute justice—I could never disbelieve.

I Accept His Judgment
This is the point at which I, still feeling that I remain a "believer," must strike out in a different direction. I cannot accept that His heavenly judgment should be so lacking in subtlety. Let me explain what I mean.

Throughout my working years I was a lawyer, and during that career I had considerable exposure to a great number of criminal trials. Many of those trials were (in my estimation, then as now) of great importance. That is … they were trials in which the defendant was charged with a most heinous crime, or in which the punishment that might have been imposed included imprisonment for many years. As you might expect, in nearly every such case guilt or innocence was far from clear. Now, from having witnessed those trials, I see that there are lessons I have learned which will apply equally to His heavenly judgment, for these are lessons learned about people—about human nature—true in this world and in the next.

Having been present at so many such trials, I can describe for you what I witnessed and what I would naturally expect of such trials were they to be conducted today. First, the prosecutor will usually make a sincere effort to charge the defendant with the proper offense. That is, there will usually be an honest matching of the charge to the crime. Next, during the trial the judge will pay close attention to those aspects of the trial that provide the defendant an opportunity to refute the charges against him and cast doubt upon his accusers. So, even in the case of the most horrific crime with overwhelming evidence of guilt, every officer of the court will strive to uphold the honesty and integrity of the proceeding, feeling that the righteousness of their task—to vindicate the suffering of the victim—must not be tarnished in any way.

Then, determination of the guilt or innocence of the defendant is submitted to a small group of citizens randomly selected from the general population. These few, we trust, will have an equal commitment to the integrity of the process, and, upon completion of their deliberations, they give their honest verdict upon the question of guilt or innocence. In the final phase (in those cases where the defendant has been found guilty), the judge will take into account every fact and circumstance relating to the crime, the victim and the defendant, and will then impose a punishment which is most nearly just under all such circumstances.

This is but one trial in one court, and there are countless other courts throughout this country and the world. Every one of them having gone through a similar process, and with no little measure of common justice, will issue a like verdict: Innocent or guilty. Always the same.

But this final verdict, even if it rightly declares this one defendant "guilty," will often be seen by many observers to be deeply offensive to our sense of universal justice. Why is that? I have asked myself this question many times. What is there about this outcome that is so repellent to our sense of order and rightness with the world? I think I know now. Look at what we know: Every crime is a unique event, not easily reconstructed, and with much about it that is unknown or uncertain. Every defendant is a unique individual, with his own justifications, explanations, background and motivations. Every victim possesses his or her own story (some having a measure of culpability and others not). Nothing about any crime is ever clearly painted out in just black and white. Nothing is ever so simple that we might utter the one word "guilty" and feel that we have delivered a full accounting of the crime.

Thus we see that even if the trial is as fair as human effort can achieve, even if passions are excluded and all involved labor to do what is just, even if there is no mistake of fact or misapplication of law ... even so, there is always this one irreducible injustice. There is always only the one verdict, which is either "Innocent" or "Guilty."

Now let us consider the heavenly judgment which I am taught to expect. I come before this heavenly judge, and there is much to comfort me. There will not be any mistake of fact or circumstance. No witness shall give false or mistaken testimony. No misinterpretation or misapplication of law will occur. Nevertheless, there is in this heavenly court the same inadequacy we see in our earthly one. There will only be the one same verdict: Saved or damned. But here there is, in a sense, even less justice than what is common in our earthly courts. If the verdict is "damned" there is then only the one punishment (eternal damnation), while, in our earthly courts, the judge will often have a multitude of punishments or penalties from which he might select the one that is the most just.

There is more. The verdict of our earthly court, simple as it may be (and I think, too simple), has this virtue: It does not pretend to sum up the worth or character of the defendant, but only declares "Yes, you are guilty of such-and-so criminal act" (or if innocent, that he is not). So we see the verdict is strictly limited to the crime that was charged. It answers only the one question (innocent or guilty) and makes no pretense—even if the defendant has been labeled "guilty" of some terrible crime—that such designation constitutes some sort of universal and transcendent declaration of the defendant's absolute moral inadequacy, guilt and failure (but which, in the heavenly court, it is!).

Can you imagine! I am standing before this heavenly judge, and I have had a long life, with, I am sure, some actions to be proud of and others to answer for, but a whole life! Let us say 85 years, with all that that means, and I prepare myself to receive the Divine Judgment of a Just God. I want to know. Where was I acceptable? Where did my efforts fall short? A lifetime of uncertainty, of good intentions (but limited abilities), and fallibility, mistake, and so on, for 85 years! I am ready to hear the verdict of Him, our Heavenly Father, Creator of Heaven and Earth, the Source of all wisdom, justice and compassion. And I receive as His judgment—the *entirety* of His Judgment—a "Blue Sticker" ("Working at or above grade level.") or, I hope not, a "Red Sticker" ("Needs improvement."). And that's it. I'm done. Next case. So we Blue Stickers (I hope I get one!) go off on our way to Eternal Bliss (with a fruit drink and a snack) while the Red Stickers (dullards! lazybones!) trudge off to the Lunchroom Detention of the Eternally Damned (and let that be a lesson to you!).

Shall we briefly imagine the circumstances of some of the most notorious persons from history as they come before this heavenly judge? Let us say … a guard or soldier from one of the death camps of the Holocaust or the Gulag. Such a person comes before the heavenly judge, and many, many who suffered at his hands in life press forward to give testimony, that nothing should be forgotten. Their faces contorted with emotion, their voices clamor for the truth to be told—with nothing left out! Now is the moment which in life they guarded, nurtured and firmly affirmed even up until that last moment when there was nothing left but this promise of His heavenly justice—sure and true. But, a sticker ... and then ... it's over. No testimony needed. You can go now.

And the same for those others who labored, sacrificed and loved. You say you could not rest in your eternal peace unless you could give your grateful testimony—first hand, dramatic, heartfelt and complete—of this man's, this woman's, faithfulness, compassion and love? Sorry. We don't need to hear it. He got, she got, a sticker, so go home.

Does it seem likely to you that our Heavenly Father, having at His disposal an eternity of time (and, if it pleases Him, many more eternities, piling one upon another, in this and every other world which it was His plan to fashion) should arrange our heavenly judgment in such a way? We feel that if there is an omnipotent, omniscient God that there is nothing "hid from His sight thereof." That He knows the secret testimony of our hearts, our true intentions, and those acts which we hope and believe are known only to us. He knows all these things and is not deceived. Shall He not show them, now?

It does not seem possible to me that the judgment of such a God should be defective in any way. And if this is so, then this is what I know. That when I am brought before this heavenly judge, my soul on trial in that one court wherein no falsehood can be admitted, there must be set aside a time, at least equal to the duration of my life, where there might be entered into evidence a complete, uncensored and honest account of every thought, action and intention of my whole life (including my innermost emotions, wishes, fears and all besides). Every witness (and by this I mean every person who might speak truth about my life) must be sworn and give a full account. And every secret desire, hidden intention, and subtle scheme that I entertained at every moment of my life must be proved and entered into evidence.

And having brought together at this one place and time that final and complete assemblage of all that is true about my life (and let us say I have reached the age of 85 years), it must then be His intention, if His judgment be true and perfect in every way, that He then sets aside a like period of time to show me, by whatever method He might choose, but always in complete and exhaustive detail, His true and authentic verdict upon the case before Him— my life and all my words and deeds and choices (in this one court collected).

This, then, His verdict, which I and any others might freely read: All the events of my life, collected and written out, without omission, honest, fair and true, in the universal record of the human race ... and with it written out, His judgment, of equal duration, line by line, as true and complete as it might be, so that I and others who study this eternal record might always read these two together. The one ... lived by me, a drama written and performed with as much hope as I could manage, and the other ... His verdict, compassionate, just and fair ... a judgment perfect in every way.

CHAPTER 5
I Seek a Path

Do I have any reason to believe that the vision I have just described of heavenly judgment is in any way an accurate description of what occurs after death? How would I know? Well, perhaps I'll ask someone who has been there. Now, of course, I know of no one (an ordinary person) who has finally and permanently died and who has nevertheless come back to tell us of it, but still there are cases.

We've all heard that sometimes, when we are facing imminent death, some mental or perhaps supernatural process takes over and allows us to relive every moment of our lives up to that point. This is such a common story that there must be some truth to it. And we know that people who have experienced this reliving often come out of the experience completely changed. They develop different priorities, often focusing on the love they feel for those around them. Worldly ambitions for money and power are left behind. So is this reliving a gift that is only given to those in peril of imminent death? Or is it offered to all of us following our demise? It seems to be an exceptionally powerful experience, changing the soul in a way that nothing else in life seems capable of doing.

When we hear these near-death stories, they usually tell us that the person is permitted to watch the events of his or her life from the outside (as an omniscient observer), not feeling the passions of the moment but rather viewing the scene as a wise and understanding witness, seeing the frailties and weaknesses of the individual and thereby coming to feel pity and sympathy for such a fallible creature.

So for the purposes of this meditation, I am going to assume that, upon our passing, we are granted the opportunity to relive the events of our lives in minute detail and in vivid, authentic and uncensored completeness.

But if (like those who have had a near-death experience and live to tell of it) we can relive our lives—lengthy and complex as they are—in the blink of an eye, what does this say about our eternal life? If He can condense a whole lifetime into an instant, is there really any eternal life at all? Can He give us an eternity in an instant? How could I say that He could not? And yet, isn't that just playing with words? Words being used to evoke emotion (rather than to describe factual circumstances) need to be appreciated as such.

No, I'm not going to go down that dead-end street. When we are promised eternal life, I understand that this assurance refers to an authentic duration of time as we know it. Now, I don't expect there will be any sun to rise or set, so there will be no days or years as we know them. But still, there is the passage of time. What I remember of physics from college teaches us that, according to Einstein, time can speed up or slow down and even appear as a variable in some equation descriptive of natural forces, but it is no mere frayed garment to be cast off at our death as are our perishable bodies. No, it is His commitment to us that the sure passage of time will unfailingly follow us into our heavenly abode where we serve Him.

We will, I am convinced, experience in our afterlife that same intangibly real elapse of time which we know in our Earthly life. We will observe that there are intervals of time for this and that, and we will feel all the sensations that humans naturally come to expect from events happening over time—the boredom of inactivity, the excitement of stimulating sensations coming rapidly one after the other, the serenity of repose and reflection that requires the calm passage of time to allow our spirits to recover and learn from what has transpired.

We have been promised eternal life. That means to me that time will be part of our experience, that it will elapse just as it does for us in this, our Earthly life. I believe the promise of eternal life is not a trick or play on words. There is an eternity of time, and we will have our heavenly life everlasting, forever abiding in that eternity, as it pleases Him to prepare for us.

CHAPTER 6
My Journey Begins

I Prepare for My Journey
Giving my attention, now, to that aspect of my meditation most particularly prescribed to me by my guide, I wish to begin keeping that "running total" of all the time which I must allow in the afterlife to pursue His truth. Here is how I have decided to do this.

I assume, first, that in my afterlife I will wish to review and relive all the events of my life. How much time must I allow for this? Well, I assume I will live to the age of 85, which may be too short or too long, but even if my assumption is incorrect, will not be so terribly far from the fact. Already I am 67 so that's not far from 85, and if I make it to 100, for example, I can't imagine the years from 85 to 100 will be anywhere as eventful as a similar number of years earlier in my life.

Now a few words about our unit of measurement. What should it be? Years? Months? Days? No. Our memories seem to operate on a much shorter unit of time. If I think back on the important events of my life, I can most easily picture a mere moment: My son—walking across the stage at his graduation ceremony. My wife—coming toward me down the aisle of the church at our wedding. The moment I opened the letter of acceptance from my college. Try this yourself. There is no longer duration in your memory. Can you remember high school? Certainly, but not a memory of four years' duration. No, only as a series of isolated memories occurring here and there over that span of time.

What is the reason for this? No doubt because our memories are inseparable from the emotions that accompany them. Every memory has its associated feelings, and it seems that if I want to recall a particular memory, I have to be prepared to feel again that same emotion which (in life) accompanied the memory I wish to recall. Emotions come and go and have only the shortest duration. So if we wish to measure and account for our memories and the memories of others, we must choose the shortest unit of time—the minute—as our measure. No doubt even this is much too long for certain memories—I think of the first time I saw my wife, which was but an instant, but now seems as fresh as it was that day in March—but we must have something that any one of us can readily understand. So we will use minutes.

My Journey Begins
Here is my first excursion: A trip of 85 years—which is the reliving of my life. So taking out my calculator, this is 60 (minutes) times 24 (hours) times 365 (days) times 85 (years) which equals 44,676,000 minutes. When written out with so many zeros it seems daunting, but then it's only 85 years, which is something not unusual in our world. But let us put this aside for the moment and consider other possible excursions.

I might choose, for example, to see the lives of my mother and father. But is this permitted? Is it allowed for me to see all of the personal, and often private, life experiences of my parents? Perhaps there is nothing sensitive about the years of their childhoods, but what about after they reached puberty? Is it really allowed for me—a male—to see the private moments of a young woman, especially my own mother? And what about those intimate moments that she shared with my father? Are they to be fully revealed to all? Including, in this case, to a child, who should show respect for his parents? If they were still alive, I would naturally grant them a wide latitude of privacy, so why after death should they be exposed in all their nakedness?

This question has given me great difficulty. Here is what I have concluded. That if it is given to me to see the lives of others, I must see the entirety of those lives, without exception. Seeing only the public events of (for example) my parents' lives would be fundamentally incomplete. If I am to understand their choices and responses, I must see their private moments as well.

All this seems obvious. For example, I doubt that I could understand why my mother accepted my father's marriage proposal without seeing her reactions to other young men—and to my father—in their private moments. But once again, we ask, are those moments not ever to remain private, something precious to be shared alone by those two lovers? How can such moments retain (for them) their iridescent luster, if crudely and unthinkingly exposed to the world? Would we conclude that keeping all these private moments "private" will ensure these lovers never feel the glare of public shame?

My Journey Begins

No, even if my witnessing the events of their lives were limited to those moments which we think of as "public," nevertheless my observations (taking in, as they must, any moments of public shame and wrongdoing) cannot help but subject this couple to the glare of pitiless exposure, as much to be avoided as any similar exposure of shame or wrongdoing in their private lives.

So it seems there is no possibility of drawing a distinction between "public" and "private." Every private shame or fault must be exposed as surely as the public ones. But, I ask, which of us could willingly contemplate subjecting our loved ones to such spying? And which of us would wish our own lives to be similarly exposed?

Wait. Let us remember where we have come and what we have given up—willingly or not—to be here. Going only from memory, now, it seems to me repeatedly expressed in the Scriptures that, upon our passing, each of us lays aside our Earthly body and takes up a heavenly one. No longer are we subject to the appetites or indignities of the flesh. Whatever form and features we possessed in life, these things, no longer ours, we now show our spiritual face, long hidden. And if I do finally set aside my Earthly body, should I not also set aside, as all of one cloth, those fears, desires and appetites that accompany it? And among those modesty?

Not just that I no longer fear to have my own body exposed, naked and vulnerable, but also that my gaze (having in my eyes no longer any lust or disapproval, harsh judgment or scorn) no longer incites in those I might encounter, naked and exposed, any similar pain of modesty. It is part of our reward in our eternal life that all considerations of shame and modesty, pride (of Earthly beauty, shape and form) and physical perfection, are uniformly extinguished. If all of these merely transient attributes survived with us into eternal life, then they would be as imperishable as our souls, which is contrary to the teaching of every prophet and holy man of all history. No, He does not suffer that any such impurity should mark us in our heavenly home.

So I conclude that if we are permitted to witness the lives of others, then we are permitted to see all of the events of their lives—both public and private.

But are we permitted to witness any other lives at all? Or are we limited just to our own individual lives? Here it would be natural to conclude that, since in our eternal life we have left behind all human vanity, there should be nothing to prevent us from witnessing the lives of others in addition to our own. Others would have no reason to hide their lives from us, and we would have no reason to hide any events of our lives from them. For if it is true that upon our death we leave behind all shame, modesty and embarrassment and no longer feel the need to shield our past actions from the eyes of others, then what, exactly, motivates us—or others—to wish to relive those events? It is one thing to say that a near-death reliving will often profoundly change an individual in the most basic, moral foundations of his or her personality. But if I have died, and if, as I say, I have given up this measure of guilt, shame and embarrassment, then what motivates me to wish to relive my life and the lives of others? Is it just petty curiosity?

If He permits me and others to relive our lives, then there must be a purpose to this reliving which is not trivial. I need to meditate on this question.

I Pause to Rest
Two days have passed since I posed the question contained in the previous paragraph. I see now that I must have been tired to have been stopped at that point. Being now more rested, I have an answer to that question, an answer which should give us great promise.

Let me provide the answer by re-phrasing the question in this way: Assuming that, after my passing, I am able to put aside all considerations of modesty and shame, is there anything of a moral or ethical nature that I might learn from a loving, sympathetic witnessing of all of the events of my life and the lives of my parents, grandparents and others? To ask the question is to answer it. I can scarcely imagine what deep and profound lessons I will learn from seeing these lives. Taking away those sometimes overwhelming emotions which are inseparable from my body frees me to recognize the greater and more transcendent truths revealed to us in the mundane events of our lives. Yes, let me see it all. Show me truths which, but for the clamor and confusion of day-to-day life, I could have grasped in this life. Isn't this the true source of wisdom? Those truths which we might recognize only by looking out across the decades of our lives? What better way to teach His truth and wisdom.

Some Additional Stops Along the Way
Now that we have established that I will be allowed to witness my own life and the lives of my parents, and since I expect I will have the time to do so, there seems no reason why I could not expand the population of individuals whose lives I could relive. First, my two brothers. (Now I will finally find out which one of them broke my model P-51 Mustang!) Next, my friends from high school and college. Then there were some teachers who meant a lot to me and who influenced me to become the person I am today. Yes, a couple of bosses

and co-workers, too. And in the spirit of this exercise, there are a few former girlfriends and blind dates who I would wish to include in this number.

How many names might I list among those I have just identified? Perhaps 50, or if I have the time to really remember, this could be 75 or even 100 names. Then, what about the people whose lives changed mine but whose names or contributions or even existence are unknown to me? The people on the college admissions committee who granted me admission? The other youngsters in my first grade class who affected me but who I do not remember? The young man who dated my wife before I knew her (but who broke up with her, so that when we met she was not in a relationship)? All of these people are part of the story of my life, as much a part as those whom I know well. How many of them might there be? Who can even guess at a number? Another 50? Another 75 or 100?

Now, here is another group of names, no doubt larger than the first. These are persons who affected my life just as they affected many more lives. The presidents, congressmen and judges who shaped the laws of this country. The businessmen, inventors, scientists and leaders who made history. And don't forget the artists, musicians and performers who made the music, TV shows, movies and books that were so important to me during my life. No one doubts their influence, and though some might wish to list them here simply as celebrities whose lives we might now intrude upon, I would include their names here only in honest recognition of their talents and the products of their efforts and abilities. There should be many, many names on this list.

Mysteries Revealed
The next group of lives is one that I can truly say I am looking forward to witnessing, no matter that I am eagerly anticipating my own death to see these things. This is the group associated with the mysteries of the world. Show me the actual assassin of JFK. Or, if there was a conspiracy, show me who they were and why they did it. Show me the events at Roswell, New Mexico in July 1947. Was it a UFO that crashed? Show me the government officials who hushed it up. Or show me how the (false) legend grew. Show me who killed JonBenet and who killed Ron and Nicole. Show me the Loch Ness Monster. Or show me the non-monster the non-witnesses misperceived. Show me Bigfoot. Show me the real author of the works attributed to Shakespeare. Show me every person who was actually abducted by aliens or show me their delusions. There are many more such mysteries.

Is this petty curiosity on my part? I like to think not. Not petty. These are honest mysteries of our time (some more mysterious than others) and not trivial. Whatever truth they contain speaks volumes about our world. And even if there is no truth in some of these mysteries, I want to see the cause of the misperception. Was it honest error? Was it intentional hoax? Or some form of delusion to which we humans are subject? This list has to be part of the entire witnessing. Don't tell me I get to see why my high school biology teacher was afraid of snakes and then tell me I can't witness the truth about ghosts and psychics and spoon-benders.

More Names
Here is the next group of names, a group I trust more hopeful than painful to recall. These are the persons whom I influenced in some measurable way—for good or ill. Was there someone who, by my kind words, was guided or nurtured? Did my example or my efforts give encouragement to a child at some critical time? In my work, did my skills or judgment lead another person along a safer path? And what about the times my anger showed? Did a selfish action of mine cost another man his job or health or hope? This is nothing less than seeing the actual and authentic consequences of my actions as they affected other people.

I do not look forward to this exercise. Will my guide be there to point out to me all the consequence of my actions? Here a person damaged in spirit by my words? There a person supported by my optimistic encouragement? Then finally, some innocent person cruelly injured by a thoughtless action of mine? Truly, as he said, "I fear this most of all." Our God is a just God; He knows our secret faults, and as the Psalmist said: "Who can tell how oft he offendeth?" My faith teaches me that my sins will be forgiven me, but it now seems likely that I shall have to witness and acknowledge them if I am to be forgiven, and that I do fear.

CHAPTER 7
We Keep Count

Before continuing, I need to stop and count up the time I will be devoting in eternity to all the "reliving" I have been describing. We start with my life, which I have already estimated at 44,676,000 minutes. Then we add my parents and family, friends, classmates, and others close to me. For the sake of round numbers, I will say this is 100 individuals. To get the total, I multiply the number for my one life by 100, and so I get the product, which is 4,467,600,000 minutes.

Next we come to all those people who influenced my life, but whose names and identities I do not know. This group I am going to arbitrarily assume is another 200 names. Now here is a question: If I think about the elementary school principal who assigned me to a particular class—and thereby gave me many friends who were friends for life—do I need to witness his entire life to appreciate his influence? Or wouldn't I just want to witness that hour or perhaps that few minutes when he made that assignment? After all, although it had an enormous impact on my life, probably what he contributed to my destiny was a trivial bureaucratic action taken without any great thought.

My point is, perhaps I need not allow any great amount of time to witness the activities of this group. For most in this category, I need not allow the full 85 years of life. On the other hand, I don't really know how many names are in this group. So, again in the interest of keeping things easier to count, I will just say this is 200 individuals. As we have already seen, the number for 100 names is roughly 5,000,000,000 moments, so for 200 names the total is 10,000,000,000.

The next group is those politicians, scientists, celebrities and other important public figures who influenced me by the prominent parts they played in the wars, economies, governments, arts and sciences of the time. The difficulty here is to know where to draw the line. Take the cell phone. I have used a cell phone, and it has certainly impacted my life in a non-trivial way. I can imagine there must have been many people involved in developing the cell phone and bringing it to wide public use. Let me even assume that I could identify one single individual as the "inventor" of the cell phone. In this case, would I put that single "inventor" on this list?

I think the answer is "no." What I am looking for in my journey are the names of those whose contributions had an impact on my life, but only where that influence carried with it some sort of "moral" content. Important government officials exercise power, and in so doing they necessarily introduce some element of moral choice into their decisions. Decisions for or against war. Decisions that inflame or reduce hatred. Decisions that enhance the well-being of others or which reflect self-serving ambition. And this number includes not just government leaders but also leaders in the arts, religion and commerce. I acknowledge that this is another group where I am forced to draw a line more or less arbitrarily. So I might include Mahatma Gandhi because of his influence on Martin Luther King, Jr. who was influential in the United States during my lifetime. But I would not include, for example, Bill Gates because, although he was the richest man in the world, and his software was everywhere, there was no real moral dimension to his business, and computer software has a technological inevitability about it that obviates his moral influence.

No matter what I may believe now, I have to acknowledge that my judgment about who has had an impact on my world—from a moral viewpoint—will certainly be different after my death. Nevertheless, although names may be added or deleted, the number I will add—for our purposes here—is 1,000 names. In order to add these prominent names to my total, I must find that number which represents 1,000 times the number of moments of my one life (which is about 50,000,000). Thus, calculating the total for these "famous names," I multiply 1,000 (names) times 50,000,000 (moments) and I get the total, which is 50,000,000,000.

My Journey to This Point

My life	44,676,000
Family/friends	4,467,600,000
Others	10,000,000,000
Famous names	50,000,000,000

There are two more groups which I have identified but whose numbers I have not yet counted. The first is that associated with the mysteries of the world. Here the counting gets a little complicated. For the Lock Ness Monster, should I add another 85 years for the monster? What if his lifetime is only 30 years or so? And for a space alien captured alive when his UFO crashed, should I add another 500 years, if that is the alien's lifespan?

No, here I am just looking for the truth of those mysterious events and incidents. In fact, if there is no "monster," I might need to devote no more than a month or so to the various mistaken non-sightings. If there is some witness who sighted a UFO, I doubt I really need to experience his entire 85 years to learn the deeper truth of that brief incident. So I'm not going to go overboard allowing time for the entire lives of every participant in all these mysteries. I am just going to estimate this group at 100 names and accept that I've probably allowed more time than I will truly need. So for the names of the "mysteries" I now add another 5,000,000,000 (moments) to my prior total.

My Journey to This Point

My life	44,676,000
Family/friends	4,467,600,000
Others	10,000,000,000
Famous names	50,000,000,000
Mysteries	5,000,000,000

Now, the final group of names not yet included is those who have been helped or hurt by me without my being aware. This group includes those lives which have been nourished and protected by my Godly activities and those others beaten down or misled by my sinful, hurtful behaviors. I cannot even guess how to pick this number. Again, I am looking for the truth, the honest outcomes of my actions, not necessarily the whole "life story" of every person who might be included in this group. So, for my purposes here, I am going to take a guess and fix a number—300 names.

Calculating in this case, we multiply 300 times the number of moments given over to one single life, so this total is 15,000,000,000. Smaller than we might suppose, but then, like the mysteries, we only need to see the truth of these matters, not every day of every year of every person listed.

My Journey to This Point

My life	44,676,000
Family/friends	4,467,600,000
Others	10,000,000,000
Famous names	50,000,000,000
Mysteries	5,000,000,000
Helped/hurt	15,000,000,000

CHAPTER 8
I Become Lost

Up to this moment, the planning of my journey has been straightforward. I have identified people and events that I want to see or relive, and except for considerations of privacy, there seem to be few objections to my witnessing these past events. However, deeper meditation discloses some additional questions. Am I limited to seeing events that occurred prior to my death? Or, after I am gone, will I be permitted to continue to observe, for example, the events of this world occurring after my death? Can I be witness to the lives of my family, friends and others extending (after my death) indefinitely into the future?

This is a common theme in human history. In certain cultures, people believe that their deceased ancestors continue to re-visit this world and take an interest in the lives of their descendents. When I think about my wife, it is hard for me to imagine that she has not, in some way, continued to watch over me, her children and her grandchildren. Can the end of life really be such a "going through a door" that we cannot go back and see how the world progresses without us? At a funeral, we almost universally feel the presence of the deceased. If a man or woman has died by murder, do we believe that person to be forever absent, and taking no interest in the doing of justice?

Putting this observation in other words, we know that every culture has stories or legends of ghosts—who are nothing else but those who have died but who continue to exist in our world. It seems a universal recognition (independent of religious doctrine) that the dead sometimes refuse to cross over and are present in our world in a way we do not understand. If the soul were, without exception, extinguished at death, there could be no ghosts and no allowance for the dead continuing to witness the events of this world.

On the other hand, if I imagine myself present in the afterlife, where even there the years pass on to the "wearing out of the world," I see that there must be considerable doubt about how much interest I will continue to have in day-to-day events after my death. Today I care about my children and grandchildren, but I have to believe that, after many, many future generations have come and gone, I will no longer have any proprietary interest in my far descendents. No doubt that world (so far-removed from our chaotic time) will be a place completely altered in every way, and, again, I wonder if I will feel any deep connection or involvement with its then-current controversies. Aren't we creatures of our time? Our modes of thought, our prejudices, expectations, goals and styles of relating to others? All of these things will, after so many years, be mere antique historical curiosities, inspiring, then, no interest even in those of us who were so deeply immersed in them when they were fresh and alive.

So this question has put me in the mind of one who is lost. Where do I go? Can I (should I) continue to observe the people and events of this world after my death? I am no longer to be found there as an active participant and surely much of my interest in its newsworthy (perhaps even sensational) events and personalities is nothing more profound than ordinary human curiosity. We might well ask: Since I can't act in that world—for good or ill—what purpose is there in my being witness to every detail of its comings and goings? We recognize certain very personal ties I will have with a few of those left behind, but as their memory of me decays, it seems only reasonable to assume that my vital attachments to them will likewise fade.

I have meditated on this question: How to find my way out of this thicket of indecision? Here is what I have decided. That my authentic, moral interest in the affairs of the world—putting aside for the moment my loved ones—is this: That if I am to fully witness the consequences of my actions, I must be witness to every act and eventuality of which I am the author, notwithstanding that they occur after my death. My own death (quieting my every impulse) in no way stills that pendulum of cause and then effect which I (by what I said and did) put into motion during life.

To imagine a vivid example: If I am a murderer, and if I die shortly after committing my crime, it is divine justice and moral transparency that I should be made to witness the grief and loss resulting from my actions. If I could escape the consequences of my crime merely by my death, where would justice lie? The natural consequences of my actions in life may require years or more to fully bear fruit. Certainly He would want me to see that flowering, no matter when it occurs. I come back to where I was before. Our God is a just God. He is patient. He is not deceived. His justice is sure. And, as they say, His mill grinds exceedingly slow, but it grinds fine.

When Once I Lived

We have seen that I should make some reasonable allowance for the time (after I have passed away) during which I will continue to take an interest in the world and people I have left behind. So, in keeping with my practice of allowing a generous estimate for each group of events which I expect to witness in my afterlife, I will allocate a full 300 names to this further list. As we saw before, 300 names represents 15,000,000,000 (moments).

My Journey to This Point

My life	44,676,000
Family/friends	4,467,600,000
Others	10,000,000,000
Famous names	50,000,000,000
Mysteries	5,000,000,000
Helped/hurt	15,000,000,000
Afterlife	15,000,000,000

CHAPTER 9
The Universal Pageant

I Retrace My Steps
At this point in my meditation I take leave of people, places and events which I have witnessed or, in some few cases, been a participant, however minor or remote. I will have seen my life and the lives of my contemporaries, as well as the lives of my ancestors and near descendents. The people and events of my early-21st century world will have been known and seen by me.

But as in the case of my hunger to know the mysteries of our world—UFOs, the Loch Ness Monster, etc.—I have another hunger which is not yet sated. It is my strong desire to see the defining events of human history. Here I hardly know where to begin. I want to see how and when the pyramids were built. I want to see how beautiful and seductive Cleopatra was. (And while we're on the subject, I want to see Helen of Troy. History tells us her beauty "launched a thousand ships." Now I can see if her beauty likewise "floats my boat!") You can see that I'm feeling a little giddy, imagining the whole course of human history laid open for my inspection.

The assassination of Julius Caesar. The French Revolution and the execution of Marie Antoinette. King Henry VIII and his wives. The first Queen Elizabeth (I see her sign the Death Warrant of Mary, Queen of Scots). The destruction of the Spanish Armada. Washington crosses the Delaware. The fiery speeches of Thomas Paine.

I want to be in the audience at Lincoln's Gettysburg address and to be in the theater when he is assassinated. I want to see the Battle of Thermopylae—to witness the bravery of that little band of Greeks who saved Western civilization. It makes my head spin trying to decide what to see first, even trying to remember it all.

When Once I Lived

I want to see the life of Christ, a story I have known from the Bible and from so many Sunday school classes. To see his face, hear his voice, listen to his sermons! And to see the crucifixion and His resurrection. As a Christian, it is deeply satisfying to me to contemplate being able to see His life and share—however remotely—the joy and promise His life foretold. And to see those around Him—Mary, John and the other disciples. To see how vulnerable they all were and how great was their faith. It would all be so very moving.

If I do witness His life, I also want to see the lives of other great religious teachers. Buddha, Moses, Abraham, the Prophet Mohammad, Saul, Martin Luther. To see the Exodus—the truth of it—and the sacrifices and faith of the Jewish people. And what about the founders of other ancient, important religions? The Egyptians worshipped their own gods, and their hearts were lifted in faithful devotion to names that mean nothing to us now: Isis, Osiris, Set, Anubis. This religion was alive and vital for 3000 years! Now it has died out, but how did it arise? Was there another great teacher, another man of God whose name and contributions have been lost to history? I want to see that man, equally touched by God's spirit as all the rest.

Oh, and I want to be present for the most famous disasters of the world! The sinking of the Titanic, the Lusitania and the Yamato. The Great Fire of London. The years of the Dust Bowl. The San Francisco earthquake of 1906. The great Tokyo earthquake. Krakatoa exploding. And the Black Death—when the greater part of the population of Europe perished, victims of a merciless plague.

And what of the great battles of history? The siege of Troy—to see those epic battles portrayed by Homer and to see that great wooden horse led to some place of honor (its own anointed stall) within the city walls! Now I will see Alexander conquering the world. Napoleon invading Russia (Napoleon fleeing Russia) Napoleon at Waterloo.

I see Pearl Harbor, the Battle of Midway, Iwo Jima and Guadalcanal. Then not forgetting D-Day, Stalingrad and the Battle of Britain.

Now I will address a very personal wish of mine—which I expect will surprise you. You see, I have for many years made a study of the Shakespeare authorship controversy, and I have come to believe that the man from Stratford was not the author of the many plays and poetry published under the pen name "Shakespeare." I was led to this conclusion, principally, by the many circumstantial factors that indicate the real author was Edward de Vere, Seventeenth Earl of Oxford. Much of the evidence for this radical proposition is circumstantial, and yet every day we imprison men for decades of harsh punishment based upon nothing stronger than "circumstances." For example, does it seem likely to you (knowing what you know of human nature) that the man from Stratford—whose mother was illiterate, whose wife was illiterate, and both of whose daughters were illiterate—was the greatest poet and playwright who has ever written in the English language? Really! Who believes that?

So I look forward to the opportunity to go back and see the lives of the author—and the non-authors, of whom there are several—including the lives of Queen Elizabeth, Lord Burghley, and so many other notables of that time. This is my personal quest, for how could I rest, in my eternity, not knowing the answer to this controversy?

The Universal Pageant
I hope my giddiness has abated enough for me to approach this subject in a more orderly and thoughtful way. Now having put aside my own personal enthusiasms, and having given this next stop in my journey more calm and measured consideration, I need to address some important factors I have identified.

When I have passed away, I shall take with me all my memories and learning concerning the events of human history. No need for examples—it's what I've studied in high school, college and throughout my remaining years. Living a full and inquisitive life, I have heard stories recounting bits and pieces of our shared past history, most of such stories being, I am sure, only imperfectly recorded and communicated and only dimly remembered by me.

But those events once were real and vital. They were once the "now" in which all alive at the time partook. And in His wisdom, they exist in some realm of universal truth and fact. Yes, we will have truth someday—and for eternity—the truth which was the authentic life lived by each person throughout history. And so, we shall have the authentic events of the life of the true author of Shakespeare's works. Not because it disposes of some historical controversy, but because it represents a life lived by a man with an immortal soul: His moral choices, challenges, successes and failures, for which answerable to God, not for our amusement or base curiosity.

So what might any person expect, upon passing, of this universal pageant of human striving, folly and confusion? This ungraspable plenty? How can my one mind, limited as it is, make sense of so much? Throwing all of my powers of concentration, discernment and reasoning into one effort, I soon discover that this one faultless archive of the world has no apt or easy diagram. It has no one story of which I might turn to the first page and thereby (maintaining a well-ordered narrative) keep the characters and action well in mind. Seeking one thing, I am led off in some other direction where I find amazement, wonder and delight (but not what I was looking for). As grateful as I am to have this bounteous land before me, nevertheless I know that even here I may become lost.

Standing rapt before this universal library, I pause and wonder: Who is it keeps this record? Totals up the score? Who all things seeing never yet forbears to write it out complete, nor ever yet omitting any shame or error that we do? What is that hand He tasks that never tiring, ever pressing on, it writes the never-ending record of our world, that only here we know enduring truth abides? And then I see. In this, the one eternal archive of the world, there is collected every Echo of a universe of Times Gone By, where every moment … one time going out in life, returning brings us memory.

I ask myself, what compass might I find that shows me where my journey lies when all imagination fails? He gives me leave to wander childlike up and down the aisles, where I am free to seek whatever record of the past I wish. But where to start and how to find my way?

I pause and think and see I only need to do what I would do were I among the living. I search among those endless aisles that place that serves a map to every student lost, bewildered and confused. I seek of this, His one eternal Book of Life, that one and faultless Index which the Author here engraves. Now knowing what I seek, I quickly find among those stacks that all-inclusive, comprehensive Catalogue. And if from time to time my concentration fails, I find this comfort here: That turning to those pages dark and worn with use, I trust His all-embracing catalogue (of every moment's going-out and coming-back) will help me find my way.

Thus I begin. Music: I hear the works of Beethoven and Mozart first performed. Billie Holliday records "God Bless the Child." The Beatles play the Cavern in Liverpool, Jimi Hendrix performs at the Fillmore East. And voices not in performance: Union soldiers encamped outside Appomattox sing "The Battle Hymn of the Republic." Mahalia Jackson sings "Amazing Grace." Joni Mitchell sings anything, anytime.

Art: I watch Leonardo da Vinci paint the Mona Lisa and The Last Supper. Michelangelo paints the ceiling of the Sistine Chapel and then sculpts David and The Pieta. Picasso at work during his Blue Period. Cezanne and Gauguin create their masterpieces.

Architecture: The design and building of the Parthenon. The Sphinx—to know what was its original form and purpose. I see the Coliseum built and the great Roman temples of the time. The Taj Mahal, Angkor Watt and the Forbidden City. Finally, St. Paul's in London—from conception to completion—and the greatest of all, the Cathedral of Chartres.

Science: I see Archimedes at work. Darwin on board ship, making notes on his study of the finches. The Curies, Copernicus and Galileo. Isaac Newton, James Maxwell and Edison. And Einstein, Crick and Hubbell in the physical sciences.

Mathematics: An interest of mine. I see and hear Euclid teach. I watch Descartes, Gauss, Leibniz and Newton. I attend the lecture where Gödel first explained his proof of formally undecidable propositions. I listen to Hardy teach, and I hear Cantor explain the many kinds of infinity.

And where should I go from here?

Engineering? The Golden Gate Bridge. The first assembly line. Roman roads and aqueducts. The Temple at Dendera. The Osirion and Machu Picchu. The obelisks of Egypt and its great statues, halls and temples, constructed entirely by human hands.

Shipbuilding? I watch the three little ships of Columbus being built. And the even smaller Mayflower. I see Cleopatra's "barge" (never was a word so unequal to the reality!). I see the whale ship Essex built (and I see it sink)!

Sports? Why not? Isn't this one of the crowing jewels of human achievement? I see the first Olympics in Greece. Then the "games" in the Roman Coliseum. I want to, if I can, see every performance in that cruel stadium. Executions and staged conflicts. Sport? Spectacle? There has never been anything like it!

Theatre? Of course! I see the plays of Aeschylus and Euripides in their original performances. And—no matter who the author—I see Shakespeare's plays first performed. I attend a performance at the Globe—should I go as a groundling or sit with the nobles? And what is more, I see the plays first performed before the Queen. Did she compliment the author? Then Moliere, Ibsen, Strindberg and Shaw. And if you think I'm ignoring America, I want to see *Our Town* with Henry Fonda in the role of the Stage Manager.

This is where I stop. It is too fatiguing to go on. You see what lies before me—before us. The universal pageant of human life. People. All the people. One by one. The kings, generals and leaders. The warriors, farmers and builders. Every mother. Every young woman who labored in lonely bondage in a world made by men. Every child who died of sickness, starvation or war. Every one.

We Count the Universal Pageant

How shall we count these names in eternity? How much time must I allow for this exhaustive examination of the universal human story? How many souls? Let us take the number of our human ancestors – who now live or ever have lived—at 6 trillion. Written out, this is 6,000,000,000,000. Then as we have seen, I have fixed the number of one life at 50,000,000 (moments). Of course, so many of that 6 trillion died far before the age of 85 (which is my measuring stick), but as we know, these numbers are only rough estimates. So to multiply these out, we have 6,000,000,000,000 (names) multiplied by 50,000,000 (moments)—which we must feel is a large number—but you see I can write it in but one line of my meditation: 300,000,000,000,000,000,000.

I see I have further to go in my quest to understand my place in eternity.

My Journey to This Point

My life	44,676,000
Family/friends	4,467,600,000
Others	10,000,000,000
Famous names	50,000,000,000
Mysteries	5,000,000,000
Helped/hurt	15,000,000,000
Afterlife	15,000,000,000
Pageant	300,000,000,000,000,000,000

CHAPTER 10
The Natural World

These are my interests: I enjoy history, literature, the Shakespeare authorship controversy, some sports, current events, and a dab of politics. So up to now my meditation has been focused on people: On the history of humanity, our achievements, our failures, our triumphs and tragedies. But if my father were in charge of this project, it would be very different indeed. For all his life he was a devoted outdoorsman. He loved nature. When he was a boy, he loved to hunt and fish, and when he got older, he became a committed naturalist. He spent his every spare moment in the out of doors, usually bird watching, but really just being part of nature. He got along fine with people, but take them all away and he'd have been just as happy sharing the world, all by himself, with all the animals, birds, fish and reptiles of the world.

Where I am going with these observations? That we know "people" are only a story of the past 2 million years or so of our planet's history. Before then, the story of the world went by the name of "evolution" and "survival of the fittest." I've read that our Earth is about 2.2 billion years old, and for the first half of that period, there weren't even any multi-celled organisms in existence. Then, after more multi-millions of years had elapsed, came the reptiles, who ruled the world for another 100 million years. Then came the dinosaurs—those emblems of the far-distant pre-historic world—which existed on Earth for the next 80 million years or so. After the dinosaurs another 100 million years were given over to various other forms of life, and then at the end of that period, we humans finally made our arrival. Thus, our little 2 million years looks pretty insignificant when compared to the life spans of so many other evolved species.

So even though it's nothing to do with people—and I'm not my dad—nevertheless I, too, would like to see the endless variety of creatures that have

When Once I Lived

lived on this planet. My own body—mostly carbon and water—is no doubt made up of water that was once swum in by some oceanic lizard or pissed on a rock by some fearsome flesh-eating monster. My carbon was probably a large and tasty fern in some long-ago Triassic rain forest or perhaps temporarily metabolized into the tail muscles of a Brontosaurus grazing his way across a field of Jurassic palms.

I would like to witness the inception of life upon this planet. Let me see it. The very first thing that drew breath (or whatever it did to sustain life). Let me see the first species that reproduced sexually. I bet I owe that first brave couple more than I know. (And with every orgasm, I should say a silent prayer of thanks that they survived to pass on the exhilaration of sex to countless grateful couples up to this very day!)

Show me the lives of these creatures. How they gave birth, learned, fought, struggled and finally died out. And not just the land animals but those who dwelt in the sea and those that flew or burrowed under the ground or lived wherever life was possible. And show me, too, the inanimate world—the seas, the mountains, the sky and weather. The stones that weathered down to soil and those layers of rock formed of the bodies of countless living creatures inhabiting ancient reefs and waters.

I want to see the whole long pageant of living creatures. Stretched out across the boundless years, and then to see our ancient ancestors—first the vertebrates, then the mammals, and finally the primates—leading up to that day when we humans start the clock ticking on our 2 million years.

Now all of this natural history would have pleased my father, but let me tell you what he would have enjoyed the most: To see the beauty of the natural world and especially the way it was when men first experienced it. To see again the great eastern forests of North America, stretching from the Atlantic to the Mississippi, as they existed when the Pilgrims first arrived. They say a squirrel could have made that journey jumping from branch to branch without ever touching the ground. To see the Great Plains—a limitless expanse of chest-high grass sustaining herds of buffalo so large that when they traveled, it took days for the herd to pass a given point. The Atlantic, teeming with fish, so many you could scoop them up in buckets. The near shore of Cape Cod, with so many lobsters you could wade in to your waist, reach down and grab eight pounders with each hand.

To see the world before the cities intervened. To see Manhattan Island as it looked before the first European ship arrived. To see London when it still belonged to deer and bear and wolves. To see Rome when it boasted not one

The Natural World

rock placed upon another by human hands. The Nile Delta before man—before the Pyramids, before boats, before herds of cattle, before any farm. To see all the world newly released from the grip of glaciers, thawed out and dried out, fresh and new, before any words of human history were written there. To see such a world is to be uplifted in spirit. There would be no room in our souls for great schemes or bold imagination unless we were first awed by the grandeur of His natural world.

I need to count up the time I will want to devote to my reliving of the natural world. They say our Earth is about 2 billion years old, and I expect I will not need to witness those long eons before living creatures arrived and only selected periods from the interval after. On the other hand, I can't be sure how much time I will actually wish to set aside to enjoy (and be refreshed by) the beauty and serenity of the natural world. So perhaps I will end up needing a good part of this time after all.

Since there is no penalty for over-estimating the amount of time I will need in my eternity to witness all that I wish, it would make sense to at least count this time as available to me should I need it. Let us start with some basic numbers. Two billion years is 2,000,000,000 (years). Then, one year in minutes (our measure) is about 500,000; so 2,000,000,000 (years) multiplied by 500,000 (minutes) is: 1,000,000,000,000,000 (moments). Does it seem possible that that number which expresses the entire lifetime of our planet should be so succinctly and efficiently inscribed? How equally inexpressible is the beauty of the Earth and its awesome majesty.

My Journey to This Point

My life	44,676,000
Family/friends	4,467,600,000
Others	10,000,000,000
Famous names	50,000,000,000
Mysteries	5,000,000,000
Helped/hurt	15,000,000,000
Afterlife	15,000,000,000
Pageant	300,000,000,000,000,000,000
Earth	1,000,000,000,000,000

CHAPTER 11
The World of Intangibles

Now I come to a category that is almost as exciting to me as learning about Bigfoot, UFOs and the Loch Ness Monster. In contrast to the other categories of moments we have already considered, this is a part of our world that is, in many ways, just as accessible to me now as it will be in my eternity. This is the world of literature, scholarship, history, scientific theories and written expressions of every description. It includes the wisdom taught by all the great teachers, the theories of all the great scientists, the observations and truths distilled by all the great philosophers.

For example, William Faulkner is one of the world's great writers, but I expect that, by the time of my death, I will not have had the time or strength of mind to read through all of his works. I have several books by Dickens, but I do not expect to have read them all. And, it goes without saying, there are many, many works in foreign languages which are now inaccessible to me but which, in my eternity, I might enjoy.

This category includes all the novels, other works of fiction and nonfiction, and every creative work ever printed in any language that is or ever was. It includes every work of creativity in philosophy, the arts, science, scholarship, history, the social sciences and religion. And included in this list are the oral lessons of history's great philosophers (whose words, we may be sure, have been only poorly transmitted down to us): the lectures of Socrates, the speeches of Plato, the proofs discovered by Euclid. (I have read speculation that Euclid was aware of hyperbolic geometry—now I will know if he was!)

There are the works of the great scholars of the ancient world. What do you suppose the ancient Egyptians really believed? What knowledge of engineering, physics and mathematics did they have? In eternity I will have quiet time to read the Koran, to read the Torah, to read and contemplate all of the

The World of Intangibles

great religions and philosophical texts of mankind. The Bhagavad-Gita. The sermons of Buddha. The Book of the Dead. The Dharmapada. And including, as well, the learned commentaries on all of these great works written by the greatest saints and scholars in each religion.

(Here I must tell you a cruel joke that just occurred to me. I am, of course, a lawyer, and I assume you know that I, like every other lawyer in this country, spent three years in law school. Most of that time I spent sitting glued to a chair in the law library, reading law books and judicial decisions. So it occurs to me that I am destined—doomed, actually—to experience that mind-numbing drudgery at least three times! Once when I was in law school, the second time when I review the events of my life, and the third time when I am given the opportunity to experience all forms of wisdom available in written form. And if I should experience the similar efforts of my law school classmates and friends, perhaps I'll be lucky enough to review the same dry and dusty law books several times more! I'm beginning to wish I'd gone off to join the circus. Now there's a life worth re-living, and as much fun the third time around as the first!)

Coming back to the subject of intangibles, I see that I must add, in addition to works in written form, all similar intangible works consisting of musical and theatrical performances (both recorded and performed live) as well as movies, TV shows, video games, internet programs and other as yet undreamed of works in electronic media.

There are paintings by all the great masters, and religious works of limitless number—every work by Leonardo, every Tibetan Buddhist scroll, every ancient votive statue in the full flower of its original authentic form, shape and color (including those religious truths expressed and every hidden hint of symbolism). Let me hear the secret doctrines of the Egyptian mysteries. The secret meaning of the Kabala and the Gnostic Gospels. The secret mysteries of the Knights Templar, the Rosicrucians and the Masons. Let every secret be told. Great is His wisdom, and there is nothing hid from His sight thereof.

How much time should I allow for my experience of this subject area? All the written works of history, all the art, music, theater, science and religion? Our recorded history dates back, in written form, something like 5,000 years. I recognize there is much that was contemporaneous and much that would be time-consuming to take in. So what I think I'll do is multiply that 5,000 years by a factor of 1,000,000. This number—1,000,000—acknowledges that there was considerable overlap of expression. That those myriad examples of human creativity which I have just identified were brought into being with explosive speed and mind-numbing variety, competing with each other over a relatively short span of time, influencing those who were able to read, listen and think. So we have 5,000 (years) multiplied by 1,000,000 (expressing the very great richness of these creations), so my total is 5,000,000 (years), which when converted into my standard measure (moments) is:

3,000,000,000,000,000 (moments).

My Journey to This Point

My life	44,676,000
Family/friends	4,467,600,000
Others	10,000,000,000
Famous names	50,000,000,000
Mysteries	5,000,000,000
Helped/hurt	15,000,000,000
Afterlife	15,000,000,000
Pageant	300,000,000,000,000,000
Earth	1,000,000,000,000,000
Intangibles	3,000,000,000,000,000

CHAPTER 12
The World of the Senses

Now I have come to a point in my journey where the road ahead seems impassable. By definition, I will have passed away, and I will then have no body or bodily sensations. No heat or cold. No hunger or thirst. And yet, to fully appreciate the truth of our world, it would seem I should have some experience of the sensations that are so important to human life. How could I take stock of the actions of some person from history if I could not feel the overwhelming hunger that might have been motivating that person at that moment? How could I understand anything about the human choices made by young men and women at critical times in their lives, without feeling the loneliness, lust or love that drove them? No, I will need to experience these essential sensations if I am to gain a deeper understanding of human choices.

So here is what I want to experience: All feelings perceptible to the bodily senses. All the sensuality that a person can experience. Start with food: Delicious meals, desserts and drink. To taste the food served at the great feasts and banquets of the past; the best meats and roasts, fish and fowl, pies and sweets. The best sushi and the best barbeque. With no limitations of time or place, no doubt I will experience foods from ancient times and foreign lands that I cannot imagine. How did wooly mammoth taste, roasted over a roaring fire during the Pleistocene? I'll find out. And 1,000 year old eggs that actually are 1,000 years old! To share a meal with Kubla Khan … and Lewis and Clark. To taste the rations of a Roman soldier standing guard at the Crucifixion. The taste of passenger pigeon—once so common. The taste of the wine in His cup at the Last Supper.

Let me go on to the next realm of sensation—intoxicants. You know I have never been much of a drinker. Oh, I overdid it a few times in college and law school, but I was never much attracted to the way it made me feel. But

When Once I Lived

that is not a common experience. The history of mankind would be impossible to understand without knowing the history of alcohol. Whatever men could manage to distill, using whatever they had at hand, they would drink. And, if they had it to drink, they would drink too much of it. So I guess I have to allow myself the experience of seeing the world through an alcohol fog—and a hangover!

Besides drink, I believe it will be enlightening to experience all of the mind-altering drugs which have fascinated men and women throughout history. I will be able to perceive the hold that heroin—and cocaine, crack and marijuana—has on an addict. And not just addicts who have no other life, but also those (like Edgar Allan Poe) who indulged but who still lived productive lives. Also there are those religious ceremonies involving the use of drugs (for example, peyote, and others, used by the Aztecs, Olmecs and Mayans). The Oracle at Delphi—what was the potion they drank that released the prophesies uttered by the priestesses? And of those who were addicted but who gave up the drug, what strength did they have that allowed them to overcome their addiction, and among those who failed, what did they lack?

(A confession: I was in college during the Sixties, and I smoked hashish and marijuana but I never had the nerve to take LSD. A classmate across the hall did, during the first semester of our freshman year, and he spent years after heavily medicated in a psychiatric ward. So I never took it. Now, in my afterlife, I want to join in on every LSD trip ever taken. Was it worth it? Was there some deeper truth? Another reality? Meaningless hallucinations? Now I will know.)

Here I come at last to the greatest of the sensual experiences: Sexuality. How could anyone possibly understand human choice without experiencing every aspect of human sexuality? The urgency of a man's desires. The aching loneliness a woman is capable of feeling. The intensity of sexual passion. The profound serenity of orgasmic satisfaction. How could I understand the mistakes young people make without knowing how clouded is their judgment? Who could follow the flights of a young girl's emotions without knowing the strong gusts rising up from her developing body? What did I miss out on? What pleasures did others experience—others who were more passionate, less inhibited or more daring? Was Cleopatra a great lover? Marilyn Monroe? The Dark Lady of the Sonnets? Was the Virgin Queen true to her name? If not, who were her lovers? The mistresses and courtesans. The geisha, queens and princesses. Can I see their beauty, their faces, and their naked bodies, revealed to me? Their charms, seductions and wanton sexuality? The secret perversions and sexual abuses they endured in the name of love or fear or obligation? If I am human, there is nothing of the body foreign to me. Let me see it, touch it, feel it. There is no final truth without it.

CHAPTER 13
I Accept His Guidance

I feel the need to pause and evaluate where I am in my journey. Putting aside the numbers, I have planned my journey to include the entirety of human history—lived one life at a time—and the entire unfolding of natural history from the formation of the world until a reasonable time after my death. Also, I have the intention of experiencing every intangible creation of the human mind and spirit and every sensual experience of every person who ever lived.

There will be much overlap and duplication. For example, let us imagine how I might observe the life of the first Queen Elizabeth. To begin with, we have seen that I expect to witness the Earthly events in which she participates as a silent, unobserved observer: Present in the room with her but not perceived by her or anyone else in any way. Here you might think back on *A Christmas Carol* by Charles Dickens. The second ghost took Scrooge to visit a Christmas party where Scrooge and the ghost were omniscient observers. They could see and hear the games and gaiety of the party, but were invisible to those present.

This I imagine would illustrate the broad scope of freedoms offered to me when I witness these events from the past. We might describe it as a sort of universal, three-dimensional movie, and I, the single member of the audience, am not restricted to a seat in the theater but can walk unimpeded and un-noticed through the action, observing and experiencing the natural, authentic acting out of the lives before me.

But this is not the sole means by which I might have access to these events. With the first Queen Elizabeth, for example, in addition to hearing the words she speaks, there is also the continuous living transcript of her internal monologue. When, for example, the Spanish ambassador speaks to her and tells her such-and-so, what does she think? What words go through

I Accept His Guidance

her mind before she speaks? What thoughts, emotions and impressions, conscious and unconscious, occupy her mind? There is not just the universal movie of the world which we might attend, but also to be experienced is the deeper and more complex inner monologue that each person generates from waking to sleeping.

How it might be that I experience this uninhibited, unfiltered expression of human perceptions, reasoning and choices, I do not know. It must be a kind of immediate, sympathetic apprehension of that emotional and sometimes verbal monologue. I just know that I must hear it—feel it—if I am to rightly understand each person's conflicts and reasoning. If I observe Thomas Jefferson composing the Declaration of Independence, I want to apprehend every motive, every passion, every choice of words in the instant he created the text of that immortal document. I want to be there when Shakespeare (whoever he was) wrote the Sonnets. I want to know who was the Fair Youth, the Dark Lady and the Rival Poet and why did he feel about each of them as he did? To follow along as Lincoln wrote the Gettysburg Address, and then to be there to experience how he felt about the reaction of the crowd. And to be there when each of the books of the Bible was written—to feel the emotion, faith and devotion to God that generated those words. These experiences I want to have.

Part of me wants—expects—eternity to work like this: I wake up every morning and ask myself "What part of the Universal Movie would I like to see today? An event from the natural world? Some highlight from history? A book I always meant to read? A woman I never had the opportunity to embrace? Or, perhaps, some mystery still not revealed to me?" Putting it like this, I have to say, rather pushes me further in the direction I have been tending, here, these last few pages.

I suppose the most charitable way of describing where I have come this moment is to say that I had forgotten my purpose. No doubt excited by the prospect of experiencing the abundant variety of human history, I forgot the purpose of that review, which is: To deepen my faith. To elevate my moral and spiritual impulses. To develop in me a truer compassion and a more sympathetic tolerance for the mistakes and limitations of others.

So here is what I imagine must be the case: That my review will not be self-directed. That it will not be I who is primarily responsible to decide who, what and when I will witness. Instead, I believe that these choices will be made for me by my guide. Yes, I expect I shall be judged, and part of that judgment will be His evaluation of where I am most deficient and where I most need help in perfecting my spirit.

Am I especially selfish or egotistical? If so, I expect I will be led to witness those certain people or events which, if I could only see, would nudge me out of that pitfall. Am I intolerant or uncharitable toward those less fortunate or less blessed with talents? Then no doubt my guide will choose carefully (from the entirety of human history) the most apt and instructive examples of this failing. Was this not the original purpose that I identified for my time to be spent as an unobserved observer? The man who beats and starves his horse in life, in death he feels the very pain and privation that he caused. So let him feel himself under the same whip, the same burden, and the same oaths. What is the phrase? "The least of them." No, He is not mocked.

Is my guide just? Yes, everything I have seen of him tells me that he is. Is he strict? Perhaps, in the future, I will see that he can be, but what is most important is that I expect him to have for me lessons of a loving, sympathetic teacher. I trust that there is time—indeed, an eternity—to satisfy a student's curiosity (Yes! Loch Ness!) while not neglecting what it is that I must learn.

My Lesson Plan
What might I expect from my guide? First is companionship. Who of us wishes to be lonely? Would there be any pleasure in the experiences I have described if there was no one to share them with? If I see Bigfoot or the Loch Ness Monster, who can I yell to "There he is!"? If there is no one to whom I can say "I knew it!" then where's the fun? And if I do learn a moral lesson, isn't it the case that I won't truly understand that lesson unless I share that outcome with my teacher? The best way to gain mastery of some lesson is to teach it, and sharing my lessons with my guide will serve that purpose.

Now what might be included in my guide's "Lesson Plan"? Perhaps a series of experiences designed to underscore the folly of the seven deadly sins and then the seven lesser sins. Or perhaps something tied more closely to my personal, individual faults. Or perhaps it all starts with a long period of contact only with the natural world—to develop a proper sense of distance from the day-to-day travails of human life. One thing I know: We have available to us as much time as we need. We can approach any subject directly and immediately or get around to it slowly, by the back door, so that whatever best teaches His message is not hurried to its intended conclusion.

I have given this matter some thought. If I were preparing a lesson plan for my soul in eternity, what would I include at the beginning? This is not the whole plan. Not the part of the plan that I'm not competent to formulate—

the deficiencies of my soul that need to be corrected. No, I'm talking about the preliminaries, like an athlete who prepares for the big game by going through some warm-ups. Well, I've identified a few "warm-ups" for my time most nearly after I have passed. Let us see what those might be.

First the most basic: I am a male. So let me have the experiences of a female. Let me know what it's like to be (in turn) a girl, a young woman, a mother, a grandmother. Let me know what it's like to suffer the monthly curse, loneliness, anxiety and childbirth. (I can hear you now, Molly, laughing, and see your amused expression, thinking how poorly I'll be able to tolerate the pain of childbirth! I will be brave, for your sake!) But also, I will have the chance to feel the joy of nursing, the power of a mother's love, and the satisfaction that comes from bringing a new life into the world.

I won't stop there. Don't be shocked, but I want to have the experiences of a gay man and a gay woman. What does it feel like to be gay? I don't know, but how can I appreciate the variety of His creation without understanding the place of gay sexuality in the world? He made it, and however difficult or uncomfortable it is for me to confront, I have to trust His wisdom and His compassion. Yes. The world is His, and He made it. And he made gay men and women, and who am I to say that they do not bear a greater burden, or have a greater claim on His compassion, than I?

Next, I am able-bodied and have never suffered any incapacitating injury. But what is it like to be born with some debilitating defect in mind or body? To be born blind, deaf or in some other way profoundly damaged? Or to be crippled in my limbs, spirit or emotions? What is it like to suffer the dispiriting agony of a childhood fatal disease? What is it like to have health and vitality and then to be struck down, paralyzed or incapacitated? To suffer injury in war, accident or crime? To know that pain and to feel the resulting despondency, depression and despair? How lucky I have been, and I hope I will be to the end of my days, but that is not the common lot of mankind. I want to know, see and feel it all, however much I fear it in life.

It must also be among my lessons to experience the intangible infirmities to which we are all susceptible, including, for example, anxiety, melancholy, phobias and paranoia and the clouds of delusion, schizophrenia, hysteria and obsession. What is it like to have multiple personalities or to be (what is it they call it?) an "idiot savant?" Or (I'll come back to these later) a psychopath or sociopath? How could I judge the limits of the moral responsibility of these persons without knowing the infirmities which they suffer? Let me walk a mile in their shoes; no doubt my guide will assign this lesson early on.

Coming back to the most basic: I'm a white guy. A Caucasian. I've lived my whole life as a favored person in our country. A white male heterosexual who is not physically or mentally impaired and who is of above-average intelligence. So taking some of this in reverse order, I suppose it might help me to know what it is like to be of below-average intelligence. What if I had had trouble in school? What if I just wasn't very smart? What would the world—what would other people—look like to me if I were always two steps behind? I don't think I'd be anything like the man I am today if I were always struggling to figure out the world or if I were always at a disadvantage with those around me.

Here the more profound lesson is the reality of being a member of a disfavored race or class. I grew up and came of age in the Sixties, so I was sensitized at an early age to race, and I have always tried to live up to the aspirations of the time: Equality, Tolerance and Acceptance. But for me, it's all from the outside in. How can I know what it is like to be black? Or poor? Or Hispanic? Or uneducated, in 21st Century America? My parents were educated, and they felt comfortable and accepted in this country. What would it be like to have ancestors who were kidnapped by force from their homeland, transported against their will to a foreign land, and forced into slavery for generation after generation? How can such suffering and oppression be imagined? I have to feel the very chains around my ankles, feel the whip, and experience the agony of having my spouse or children taken away, never to be seen by me again. If there is any lesson that a favored white American needs to learn, it is how American men and women of another race see the world.

What is the rest of my guide's lesson plan? There are so many other nationalities and cultures that are foreign to me. So many other religions and traditions that I can't know (and some that I should know, but which, by the passage of time, no longer exist). Once the world was almost universally pagan. Now almost no one is. What was that world like? Once the world was what they call "pre-scientific." What was that like? Once there was a world before Jesus, before Moses, before Abraham, Muhammad and Buddha. Before even Adam (at least, before his story was recorded or passed down). What was that world like? Show me His gifts, then, to those living at that time. These are lessons I want to learn.

Some Basic Lessons
The next lesson which I expect to receive is one which might surprise you. I think that as my next lesson, I will be given the opportunity to experience

power over other men. Although I have lived a full and happy life as a lawyer, it may surprise you to learn (if you entertain any illusions about the legal profession) that I have never been granted (or exercised) any form of power over others. I have never run any large corporation or been elected to high office, never served on any important court of this country or any of its States, never elevated to any position of leadership in any other way. You must understand, this is a lesson I want to learn, not just some form of egotistical wish fulfillment. We all might see something exciting and intoxicating in the idea of great power, but the purpose of this lesson is to bring out the other side of such (apparent) good fortune.

Yes, to be the President of our country and to feel that unequaled, ostentatious vanity, but also to know the heavy burden of bearing the hopes of an entire nation, perhaps facing an economic or military crisis. To be a king, an absolute monarch, empowered to order the execution of my enemies but also to know that every sword has two edges and that assassination may await a king who abuses his authority. No doubt my guide will have this lesson well researched: First he shows me a great king who, in solitary grandeur, stood high above the common mob but who also served them well; then next, another noble prince, but this time a man who let his appetites rule and who brought his people down to suffering and ruin.

Now let us turn the page to the next lesson. From the palaces and offices of the powerful, I see my guide takes me to the huts and shanties of the poor. On our planet, he will have much to choose from. What might he select for me? The life of a starving peasant in Europe during the Middle Ages? The place of a Roman slave? A Chinese farmer in ancient times, facing yet another famine caused by yet another flood of the Yangtze River? A young African man, captive on board a slave ship bound for North America? A Ukrainian peasant who has just had all of his grain confiscated by the local Communist Party soldiers in the beginning of the great famine of 1932–33 ordered by Stalin? What about orphan children who live today in the garbage dumps of great South American cities? For once I feel at a loss. I wish I could more easily reel off examples of poverty, anguish and despair. But then, it is natural that these episodes are not well-remembered. The history books I studied devoted many pages to the wars and tyrants of history but very little space to the common prevalence of misery, hardship and despair. Study history and you will soon conclude: The commonplaces of the world are neither remarked upon nor remembered.

While we are on the subject of the poorest and weakest, why not include the innocent victims of war? Now there's a subject calculated to occupy my time in eternity! Let us go back, say, to the Bible, to all those cryptic descriptions of how so-and-so king or general captured such-and-so city, where it says little more than "he slew them." That's all the Bible spares, but we might helpfully supply the following, more complete version: "All the city he took captive - men, women and children. All the men, above a given age, whether soldiers or not, he killed. Then of the women, he (his soldiers) raped many, killed some. The women not killed he made slaves or servants. The children he took as slaves. All the cattle and other possessions, he looted. What was left, he burned. Then, when he was done, he glorified God."

Following this, we move on to wars of Greek against Greek (many cities burned). Invasions of Greece by the Turks (many cities burned). Then the Roman conquests (many cities looted and burned). Oops, I didn't mean to skip over the wars of the Egyptians, Assyrians, Romans, Mongols, Chinese, Japanese, Aztecs and Mayans—so many looted, enslaved, raped and burned. Then the Middle Ages with constant wars and Crusades, and finally coming into the most recent centuries.

Let us take note, for example, of Napoleon's invasion of Russia. Oh, what glory! The mere mention of his name must bring unspeakable joy to the hearts of all those who were killed, starved, looted, raped, made homeless and burned in the name of … (get ready for it) … "The Glory of France!" Oh, my heart! Oh, the rapture! But the first invasion of Russia was a casual, holiday outing compared to the second invasion (occurring 100 years to the hour later). But here I must take care not to pass too lightly over our First World War, that useless, purposeless slaughter and that never-to-be forgotten high point of early 20th Century civilization—the unrestricted use of poison gas.

Of the Second World War, Korean War, Vietnam War, War in Iraq (and there will be more) I will not speak here. Hitler approached the acting out of his hatred of Jews in a most early-20th Century manner: He first dehumanized his intended victims, denying them basic acknowledgement as fellow human beings, then devised an assembly-line system to construct their complete annihilation. But before him—and also after him—Stalin to the east approached his job as merciless tyrant in a more traditional way. When he identified anyone as an enemy, he would have a label ready to place on his victim: "Wrecker," "Spy," "Saboteur," "Kulak," "Petty Bourgeois," and many more. Then parading each victim before a phony judge, the defendant (guilty of nothing) was made to confess (they always confessed), and (completing this shameless parody of a just trial) the prisoner was invariably sentenced to many years in a "re-education camp" (a slave labor camp) in the Gulag.

I Accept His Guidance

I'm sorry. I'm spending too much time and getting into too much detail reviewing the bloodshed, carnage and conflicts of our recent history. I admit it. If you go to the library or a good bookstore, you will see shelf after shelf of history books documenting every detail of the Second World War, the Holocaust, and even Stalin's reign of terror. Sadly, you won't see much about the Communist Revolution in China, even though tens of millions died. And you will find very little, indeed, concerning the Japanese occupation of China from 1931 through to the end in 1945. Because those additional millions starved or raped or killed are not writing books, and those who did the starving, raping and killing are (I am sad to say) not writing books, either. But there will come a time. In eternity, there is a guide waiting patiently, making notes as it pleases Him (for He knows "our secret faults"), and when the time comes, and his student arrives, there will be lessons—and time enough that nothing will be overlooked.

CHAPTER 14
A Subtle Lesson

Making a casual survey of the probable outline of the lesson plan I expect my guide to have for me, I notice one common element. My viewpoint is always that of either myself or another. I am myself witness to some event of history or sometimes I take the place of another, as I experience the emotions or the inner dialogue of some king or prince or other famous person. But in all cases I reflect the bias central to human life—that lives are lived one at a time—one life to each, no more, no less. As omniscient observer, I bring my subjective viewpoint to situations involving everything from one person observed (I witness Joan of Arc struggle with her faith) to seeing many tens of thousands (I witness Mao Tse-tung and the Chinese Communist armies begin the Great March). There seems always to be just one observer. One point of view.

But on reflection, I see this is not adequate to understand the world. Here is an example. Let us go back to the Pleistocene. We are observing a hunting party of early humans (cavemen actually). They are closing in on one wooly mammoth, and with their spears and practiced hunting techniques, success in the hunt is assured. But what is special about this hunt is that this particular wooly mammoth is the last living female of her species. After the hunt, wooly mammoths will be extinct. So this is a significant, albeit tragic, moment. If I, the observer, am present at this event, then indeed I will learn a powerful lesson, witnessing this final, decisive act; pivotal both in the history of our human world and in the natural world.

But this is only part of the picture. I could just as easily visit with my guide a modern-day slaughterhouse, taking in, perhaps, cattle, pigs or chickens. These are places where no one goes—no one who doesn't work there, anyway. In one sense, there's nothing to see—nothing so dramatic as our wooly mammoth. Just one animal after another, taken in and "processed" into meat of one kind or another. The same routine, hour after hour, day after day. We live our lives knowing what goes on there—at some level of awareness—but never delving too deeply into what it all might mean. They are domesticated animals, after all, food animals. They won't go extinct, and they're nobody's pets. Why dwell on them? Weren't they put on this Earth to be used or consumed by people?

Now my guide takes me to a different place. A place of universal perspective. Instead of my solitary viewpoint, seeing animals taken one by one into the processing line, I am permitted to look out over the widest possible horizon to see these things as my guide sees them. I see not just this one slaughterhouse (where we have first paused on our journey), but every other such place that is or was or ever will be. All of them I perceive, all at once, and not just this one day, but every such day. We see the sun—rising with ripe promise of life and growth—now stagger, shouldering its heavy burden of uncountable deaths.

Then ... on my own initiative, and using the tools of mathematics with which we are all familiar, I calculate the sum total of all such living things which have ever been brought to such a place. Having done so, and having paused awhile in an attempt to understand such a number, I find that there has arisen an unbridgeable gap. A gap between—on the one hand—that total which I have just calculated, and—on the other—the largest possible number which my mind can grasp. What do such numbers mean to me? I, being a solitary individual and, in the natural order of things, not sharing in any heavenly perspective, am hardly any better in my perceptions than the caveman, who, when he counted great numbers, counted in this way: "One ... two ... three ... many."

This limitation I believe my guide will overcome. When I with heavenly perspective observe and sum up all these herds and flocks—all the many living things put to our use—and every one of them as privileged as I to have drawn breath and seen the sun and known to God as well as I, then I trust that I will experience this fact with as much emotion as I do the tragic fate of the wooly mammoth. Now I do keenly feel it is not just the incidental details of my life that are limited in time and place, and gender, race, abilities and class, but also that I am always and everywhere in this world just this one—my own self and no more.

But this world is a great and wide place indeed. How to experience, except with His help, the unceasing tide of slaughter all around us? How else to perceive the ocean, in which there are no great schools of Cod, or the great North American continent, where there are no longer endless expanses of forests, or (very shortly, I have read) the great Amazon basin, where there is no longer tropical life in endless lush variety? They say a fish is not conscious of the water in which he swims. But this can't be true. Of course he is well aware of the conditions of the water where he is swimming at the moment. What he is unaware of is: The greatness of the ocean. The multitude of all the life which shares those waters. And the many of his own number—being born, living and dying—uncounted and near uncountable, except to Him.

It is recorded that Stalin once said, "One death is a tragedy. One million deaths a statistic." In this world I have seen this is true, but I have no fear that this limitation will accompany us into the next world.

CHAPTER 15
His First Prophet

Once there was a time before words ... before promises, proverbs, judgments and lies. Once I lived a life entirely unexpressed, silent and unacknowledged. For each of us there were those many months of our young (infant) lives when, as yet unknowing any greeting, warning or command, we dwelt within a world comprising only our most unadorned perceptions, some unbroken chain of transitory moments ... having in it not a hint of memory. If I, coming at last to the afterlife, expect to meet with any time or place or person in my life that shows itself entirely unexplored and new, it must be here and now, from among those months before my mind and body found those faculties which gave me speech.

If I were to go to that time when I existed voiceless, would I not find the world as mute as were those years when our still-infant species did wait-out some endless intermission (being, thus, upon the stage, but lacking any lines to speak). And if, going there, I wished to speak of it, would I dare to break such a silence—wherein prayers were not yet heard, stories not yet told, His wisdom not yet parceled out in words? And when that one, long expectant silence was at last broken, and words beginning shared, piled up, parsed out and rearranged, who was that first prophet whereof all those within hearing could apprehend not just the first words ... but the first truth as well?

Thus, I, like anyone abiding in that time of quiet, called out my needs in cries and squalls (revealing all my joys in some melodic coo). And who was there to hear but that one soul whose voice became for me the sound of angels' harps and hymns and wings: My own mother, of whom I was so recently her flesh, and whose heartbeats were for me the only sure sounds promising warmth and love and sustenance. Who but her the first, sure and faultless prophet of His truth? What words did she speak that were not Truth itself? What sounds of comfort did she whisper that did not fall soft and healing upon my wound or hurt or fear? And when, in time, she shared with me those stories, poems and rhymes which came readily to her lips, was there ever any part of it that I did not take in, embrace and copy out in full across my heart's one transcript of reveal'd truth?

Yes, once there was no true thing. There was the world, and I new to it, but knowing no truth (and in all ways unresistant to error, of which this same world abounds), and if not for that one voice which spoke no falsehood, and wished for me no misfortune, and would have fallen forever silent if ever compelled to speak to me any harsh or hurtful words, or to say to me anything untruthful, I would have gone my way friendless and ignorant in the world, and no doubt quickly come to some convenient grief.

But this was not the case. I had in my life (as I have no doubt that you, too, had in yours) a mother loving, wise and in all thing good. Now, you visiting with me in my afterlife as I patiently observe those many occasions when my mother read to me, you may perhaps object that such poems, rhymes and stories as she favored contained very little Truth compared to what was Whimsy, Humor, Fancy and Delight. We see ... wizards and talking animals, fairies and elves, witches, wishes and fairytale princes, and everywhere the power of magic spells and fairy dust and perfect innocence.

"You see! These things she tells cannot be true!" you say. "This world (we know) is bare of witches, devoid of magic and altogether lacking any animal which ... being spoken to in words might answer back the same. Where is the Truth in that?" you demand.

Seeming to take your point (but all the while conspiring to show you your error), I then suggest, "Let us hear my mother's voice once more. Let us listen to some rhyme or poem which she loved, and hear again that voice I held in such regard." Then, going back to that innocent time, and hearing with ears undisturbed by any inner dialogue (and unconcerned with common circumstance), I grasp what then her voice expressed. Not any one true thing revealed (nor any falsehood now exposed), nor yet any self-evident truism (which we do all agree is so), but this: That in her pace and gait of voice, the rhythm of her gentle breath, the tone and tempo of her words, I have the measure, now, of Truth, itself.

Thus, I, being shown from the first those tempos, tones and cadences which unfailingly denote the Truth, I cannot afterwards be misled or mistaken when spoken to in words not altogether clear. In this I see ... I am as if some tender youth who, at the encouragement of his loving mother, does

His First Prophet

learn to ride some swiftest horse with joy and skill. Of such a man, we know, he will be the master of his own Fate; he will not later fail to tame the heart of that unbroken steed which—overtaking him on his way—he strives to harness to his own purpose, making that beast's ungovernable will bend to the one will which is his life's destiny.

Now, taking stock of those tender occasions when my mother read to me, I search for that special naptime or bedtime when she shared with me that one poem which most bestirred my imagination. There was such a poem, which I will share with you, now, and which, in time, you will see had more to teach than anyone might have guessed. The poem she read to me is an old one—I doubt I could find it, now—but it went something like this:

> *If all the trees were one tree, what a great tree it would be,*
> *And if all the seas were one sea, what a great sea it would be,*
> *And if all the men were one man, what a great man he would be,*
> *And if all the axes were one ax, what a great ax it would be,*
> *And if the great man took the great ax and cut down the great*
> > *tree,*
> *And the great tree fell into the great sea,*
> *What a great Splash it would make!*

You! Pridefully reserving in your heart a place for His words given to you in some incomparable Scripture of reveal'd truth, leave off for a moment your hallelujahs and hosannas to that righteousness which you (so ardently) patronize. Pause and look down beneath that marble altar upon which you have set up your one, perfect idol of Eternal Truth. You see, you would not have Truth itself, nor any soil deep enough to bear up those unshakable stones of your faith's foundation, had your mother not read to you of Rat and Mole and Mr. Toad, of the Hundred Acre Wood and honey pots, of the Three Little Kittens and the Little Red Hen.

CHAPTER 16
Hidden Treasure

I remember reading in some old history book that in ancient Rome there once existed a temple, devoid of decoration on the outside, and on the inside similarly devoid of any art or inscription, but having an altar. And on the side of the altar were written the words: "To the Unknown God." Now, Rome at the time had many other temples to well-known gods—to Athena, Zeus, Aphrodite, Apollo, and others. And these others were great temples, rich with worshippers and priests. The Romans were no less pious than are we today.

But here is what I find particularly admirable about the Romans, and it is a trait I wish we would emulate. They had their gods, but they were also humble enough to see that their devotion might be less than what the gods expected. So they erected a temple to worship that god or gods that they, in their human frailty, might have overlooked. Perhaps their nearness in time to the great Greek philosophers led them to be more familiar with the concept of "hubris" than are we.

What am I leading up to? That I want to keep ever fresh in my mind the example of the Romans and recognize that my guide will have for me lessons that I cannot anticipate. I am well aware of the various broad categories of history, nature, science and art which have been briefly alluded to in this meditation. And I am likewise well acquainted with those other well-known mysteries also touched upon. But what I now want to recognize is that there will be other lessons - lessons which I could never anticipate and which are beyond my imagining. How could I give examples of mysteries which are now unknown to me but which, in my eternity, will be revealed?

I am going to try to identify a few of these "unknowns" by picking a random subject heading from among those available in the universal catalogue.

Hidden Treasure

Let us say … "Hidden Treasure." That might be fun! So let's proceed by imagining a few examples of the "mysteries" that might be found under that heading. No doubt these mysteries will show us what sort of exciting, unforeseeable secrets will be revealed to me in my afterlife. Let us start with this:

❧ ❧ ❧

Before the walls of Troy, the great Greek warrior Achilles does battle with Hector, prince of Troy. Each is armed with a sword, helmet, shield, and armor covering chest and legs. We see that the sword and helmet of Achilles are particularly striking (their polished copper color flashing brilliant in the sun), reassuring his fellow Greeks that brave Achilles still wields his sword with energy and skill. And here is what more we see: We follow the weapons of Achilles back in time to see their manufacture. Some forge and smithy in some port city of ancient Greece, where skill in metals was early learned. Then we go back before that time to see the very copper of these bronze weapons mined from the earth.

And this, we agree, is the mystery: For we see a trading ship—Phoenician—arrive in that Greek port, and we see its voyage, which had as its starting point a crude harbor in what is now Quebec, North America, on the St. Lawrence River. This copper, extracted by Phoenician laborers (each sworn to keep this place—and all its riches—secret) has as its source wide, copper-bearing veins of metal visible in rocks located in the watershed of the Ontonagon River, where it flows into Lake Superior on the shores of what is now the Upper Peninsula of Michigan.

Once beaten from the rocks and smelted into bars, this native copper is carried by canoe and portage to waiting ships, which take it then to Greece. There, far from its place of origin (a now far-off, secret land, destined to be lost and unknown for more than two thousand years), this ore, after being fashioned into weapons, spear points and arrowheads, becomes the stuff of legend. This metal, in the form of armor and weapons of every type, is carried onto that storied battlefield—before the gates of Troy—by a great assemblage of immortal Greek heroes, whose names we know even today.

Let us also observe that these weapons, manufactured of beaten bronze, each one bearing on its surface some dedication to its owner (some crest or mark or symbol), has among their number some one sword, helmet and breastplate worn by that one man whose name is uniquely famous among men—a man revered throughout history for his own heroic journey, equally long and perilous—Odysseus. Even in our modern day there are still storytellers who honor him and tell his story—this Ulysses, who by his life and journey gave us a thrilling tale of bravery, cunning and determination, which moves us even now.

You may be one of those who might someday visit northern Michigan, on the shores of the Ontonagon, on a pleasant August day. Perhaps your only purpose is a restful summer vacation … fishing, camping and hiking in this calm and lovely place. There, if you, walking on the shore, were to reach down and pick up some few small stones (some worn and rounded copper pebbles), and if you were to hold them up into the light, you would see their polished copper color flashing brilliant in the sun. Before this moment, you might have thought this place a wilderness, bare of mystery, and having no ancient story to tell. But that is not the case. No. Look down beneath your feet and know that these are the stones that once produced the sword and shield of Ulysses.

His shield: that once in single combat did many times deflect the sword of Hector, prince of Troy. His sword: having its birthplace within the earth (in some secret, sunless cavity in the rock) that did later endure concealment in another dark and sunless place—within the body of the horse, clutched tight in the hand of Ulysses, waiting for that moment when it might be reborn into the light … and into history.

Shall we imagine another mystery—more "Hidden Treasure?" Now we travel to Sacsayhuaman, the Fortress of the King, in the capital city of the Inca Empire, high in the Andes Mountains. Here the king is meeting with his generals and advisors. They tell him of soldiers who have just reached the border of his kingdom. These strangers (the Spanish, under the command of Pizarro) are few in number but have superior weapons and, what is most worrisome, have already heard tales of a vast storehouse of gold possessed by the Inca king. These ruthless thieves, the king knows, will only be the first among many such men who will come, and he ponders how to rid himself and his kingdom of these plunderers. (The king, not knowing of the several European diseases the Spanish bring, has no idea that he and his people will be more decimated by disease than by any Spanish weapons.) After much consideration, the Inca king formulates his plan which he puts into motion and which, despite the devastating plague his people will suffer, will be fully and successfully carried out.

Here then his plan (and the mystery): The king orders that some small part of his treasure—some trivial portion of his gold, and some few, poor gems—should be brought out of the storehouse and taken to a place where the Spanish might easily find it. Then he orders the storehouse door be tightly sealed and all visible evidence of its location erased. All preparations completed, the king waits for the invaders to arrive.

Pizarro, reaching the fortress of the Inca king, is granted entry without opposition. Going directly to the throne room, he and his men find there the Inca king and all his greatest soldiers, meek and acquiescent. Now Pizarro, seeing that he has met no outward resistance, rightly concludes that the Inca, on the surface seeming to withhold nothing, in secret must have closed and walled up the king's storehouse with such cunning that no searching by his men could find the door. His greed knowing no bounds, and heedless of the slaughter that his plan entails, Pizarro immediately takes the Inca king prisoner.

Now is the moment when Pizarro (having seized his hostage) must name his price for release of the Inca king. The Spaniard ponders this question briefly, then, looking in the direction of one of the royal audience chambers adjacent to the throne room, declares to the assembled Inca soldiers that he, being a great man (and any such great man being due the appropriate tribute), it is their duty to offer up to him that tribute which a man as great as he might claim. Pointing with his sword to the audience chamber, he tells the Inca soldiers that … if they will fill that room with gold (his proper tribute, and the ransom of the Inca king), he will (upon his honor) set free the king unharmed.

Now in this, Pizarro is as cunning as the Inca king. Having taken the king hostage, he well knows that in order to keep their king alive, the Inca soldiers will let nothing prevent them from filling that room with gold. Any other person, pondering to formulate such a plan, would have taken into account such factors as: the loyalty of the king's soldiers, the wealth and power of the Inca nation, and the degree of devotion which the Inca people had for god and king. But this is not the calculation which Pizarro makes. No. He, being a kind of "alchemist" in gold, we see that for him this rarest element is more alive (having more vital energy, and of more intrinsic worth) than any people living in a place where gold might dwell. An earnest, humble student of this blackest art, Pizarro has spent a lifetime in the study of this precious metal: seeing how it has distributed itself among the nations of the Earth, noting its characteristic tendency to gather itself into bars and plates and vessels, and observing that powerful instinct which it exhibits (after it has first transformed itself into crowns and coins and idols) to conceal itself in hiding places deep within the Earth. Having all these things in mind, and with the calm and studied calculation of a man of reason, Pizarro thinks himself well justified to predict that the Inca (if they wish to fill that royal chamber with gold) cannot avoid having to break into the king's golden storehouse. Pizarro's plan is simple: he will set his men to watching, listening and spying all about the royal fortress. As soon as the Inca soldiers open the storehouse door, his men will learn its secret, and all the Inca gold will then be his. Or so the Spaniard thinks.

Shall we—upon these facts—judge him (as he judged himself) a failure? That he was wanting in vanity, greed or lust for gold? Would we be correct to conclude that even Pizarro's unquenchable thirst for gold was—in this one instance—deficient? For we know what happened next. The Inca soldiers, gathering up that small quantity of gold and those few, poor jewels taken earlier from the storehouse, easily fill the royal chamber. No need is there to open up the storehouse door, no need to show the hiding place. Can we imagine how Pizarro felt? Here is a chamber filled with gold—a plunder which the greed of a thousand lifetimes could not exhaust. But still ... he knows ... if only he had asked for more! For more! The storehouse would be his! The hiding place exposed! The golden treasure in his hands!

The rest we know as history teaches: The king is killed and many of his soldiers and retainers slaughtered. The remainder of the Inca people are soon brought to ruin by famine and disease. The golden tribute of the royal chamber becomes a kingly burden for the Spaniards' mules. The royal hostage unredeemed, the plunderers move on. The Inca fortress left behind (its gates unmanned and open). But still, the Inca king achieves his purpose. His plan complete, the strangers now are gone and never will return.

And of Pizarro? If we, now wishing to honor this man of science, this humble student of the alchemy of gold (despite that he, in this one instance, did misjudge the power of that ore), yet still we see that he, in spirit of regret, rebukes himself! He blames himself that in this forge ... this furnace ... this fortress with its golden charge (which all was his), he had sufficient metal, and he added to it all the death and slaughter that he knows this precious ore requires (to drive off all impurities and dross) that he might seize it for himself. Yet now he sees his failing all the clearer (his chemistry corrected and improved) that what was lacking was the quantity of catalyst (he knows) bestows the gleam and glitter on the gold—tincture of greed!

Of alchemy (that most arcane of sciences) we know its highest goal and deepest art a single transmutation: Basest lead transformed to purest gold. But

Hidden Treasure

Pizarro, great alchemist of misery and loss, here in this place of looting, rape and murder, and in the presence of that greater Inca treasure (its hiding place so near ...) a yet more subtle transmutation brings about: He takes a Moment of miscalculation ... and from it produces an Eternity of regret.

Our science lesson now concluded, and by this mystery revealed, we see that in that ruined fortress ... that golden smithy of eternal loss ... we might still find that hidden Inca treasure, untouched by human hands and destined to be so for countless years to come. The storehouse door unknown to any now alive and unsuspected by the world.

When Once I Lived

❧ ❧ ❧

Do you have energy for one further speculation in mystery? Let us imagine this: An ancient time, in Egypt, far before any era of which we are familiar. A great fleet of ships sails up the Nile. These are the few who fled the island of Atlantis when it suffered its tragic fate (when it broke apart and fell into the sea). These survivors carry with them all the treasure of their homeland—which, to them, the word "treasure" signifies all their books and knowledge, their history, science, philosophy and art—the fruits of many generations distilled in this, their precious archive. Not merely written out on animal skins or paper, but the words engraved on sheets of purest gold and rolled up into scrolls of fabulous worth (much more so for the words recorded than for any mere metal).

Then, in time wishing to build for themselves a sure memorial, proof against any natural cataclysm, war or plunder, these survivors construct, first, a great and impregnable vault of stone (of many layers), buried deep within the earth and sealed up tight with lead (that no corrosion should these walls impair). There, sealing in it all their treasure (those words and signs and symbols, writ out complete and etched in gold, well fortified against time's eventual decay), they next construct above it a great memorial of stone, one of a pair (each a representation of the funerary god Anubis—the dog headed god—who they knew to be "God of the Afterlife").

It is the intention of these survivors that hereafter, any person coming up the Nile might see in this place two great markers—one on the west bank of the Nile (facing east), the other on the east bank (facing west). And having seen these two great signposts of eternity, anyone might immediately know that here, beside the Nile, those few survivors of Atlantis (a people rich in learning, piety and art) did sanctify a final resting place for their eternal legacy.

Let us imagine that we, too, have traveled up the Nile, and we, too, have reached this place where we might pause and, falling silent, gaze upon these two great totems of the desert, recumbent, silent watchers of the endless flood (passing now between them), as they, untiring, keep eternal vigil over golden treasure buried here beneath.

But we see (this the mystery) that there being only *one* precious archive of Atlantis, and there being *two* great stone images of Anubis, there can be only one such stone image beneath which we might find the treasure—the other image only watch in silence, no treasure there to guard.

So, today, we see Anubis of the Western shore (his head long ago re-carved in the image of some certain Pharaoh) sitting in silent watchfulness. He sees (or if his image as Anubis yet remained, he might see) that place on the Eastern shore where his twin once waited. The mystery (being now revealed) we see that long ago (so long that none remember), his brother—Anubis of the Eastern shore—was over time so worn and weathered by the desert winds and sands that now no trace of him (but shifting sands and shapeless stone) remains above the ground.

Witness, then, the pity of that people who lived so long and well and labored in their hope to share with us the story of their journey through this world. That on the *Eastern* shore, at that still-secret place where lies entombed the greatest treasure yet concealed (the precious, golden Archive of Atlantis), no memorial is found. While on the *Western* shore, that patient, loyal brother, watchful, is waiting still.

> *Treasure hunters!!*
> *All who lust after gold and fame!*
> *Hear me!*
> *Have you not heard the promise of that ancient legend, that rumor of a priceless hoard of gold, bestowing wealth undreamed of, and fame eternal for the name of him who finds its secret cache?*
> *Have you not heard of that prophetic dream, telling of an ancient map, some fragmentary hint of unknown treasure trove, foretelling much?*
> *Is that—of immortality and gold—not promise enough?*
> *Come! Our destiny at hand!*
> *Let us dig!*
> *Heedless of risk, cost or history bespoiled …*
> *Behold! The prophecy fulfilled!*
> *This the ancient landmark which the dream foretold!*
> *This the hiding place revealed!*

Or so my fevered mind does urge me on, with ever more dramatic fantasies of wealth and honor. And so the years pass by, each giving place in sequence to the next, while I and others hearing of these things, and finding in these

When Once I Lived

words a prophecy or ancient legend (with its core of truth) and never losing heart, might even now scratch and search and dig, believing that under the outstretched paws of that most faithful brother—who in our day we call the Sphinx—might yet be found that ancient, golden treasure.

But this, we know, is nothing but a vain desire. The day of its discovery is not yet come. Nor shall it ever. And so that transcript of immortal art and eloquence, engraved on golden tablets, its truth undimmed by time's elapse, will ever yet await, reposing still across the flood, its resting place as lost to us today as it shall be for all the endless ages yet to come.

CHAPTER 17
A Brief Diversion

Once again let me acknowledge that, being a lawyer, my focus always seems to be on people—their motivations, choices and destinies. However, I have always had an affinity for mathematics—an unlawyerly discipline. In the law, there are no final answers, just today's answers to today's questions. In the world of mathematics, however, there are final answers—absolute proofs. And likewise there exist perplexing questions that mathematicians have struggled with through the ages, many of which remain unanswered to this day. Like mathematics, there are other disciplines where truth is truth because it is testable and where, sometimes, progress is made only because of an insight achieved by some individual genius who sees the solution where others could not. If my guide is thorough, which I believe he will be, then one of my lessons must be to have the solutions of these as-yet-unanswered problems and questions revealed to me.

First, perhaps, will be the proof that Fermat had in mind when he wrote the formula for his famous problem in mathematics—what we now call "Fermat's Last Theorem." He said in his famous marginal notation: "I have a proof of this, but have not the space here to give it." Without meaning to embarrass Fermat, I would be grateful to know if he truly had a proof or, if not, to know where his error was. Next would be Hilbert's Ten Challenges. Of those not already solved, which of those have solutions, and what are they? Next, obviously, is Cantor's Continuum Hypothesis. He went mad seeking a solution, so … is there one? If so, show me the one (or best) solution. Does Riemann's Hypothesis have a solution? Let me see it. Are there theorems or proofs which mathematicians believe are proved but which have a hidden flaw?

Moving on to science, what might my guide show me? The actual origin of the universe (we now think it was the "Big Bang") and the formation of our solar system and our Earth. What, too, will be its final destiny? And what collisions, catastrophes and upheavals has it—will it—suffer? Is there a "Theory of Everything" which physicists are now seeking? What are the fundamental building blocks of the universe and the links between gravity, electromagnetism and the strong and weak forces? How is it that the fundamental constants of physics are "just so" to permit the sun to shine and life to be sustained?

What was the source of life? What drives the transformation of one form of life into another? Now the conflict between Evolution and Design can be resolved. The origin of the eye, of DNA, the brain, and more. Why do we sleep? Why do we yawn? How is it that our bodies (substance) respond to our will (an intangible impulse)? Is it possible to travel faster than light? (Yes, I did watch more than a few episodes of Star Trek!) Could a spaceship be made and powered that could travel to other planets and back? What about "transporters," "phasers" and all the rest? Science fiction fantasy? Or real possibilities?

Will the era of homo sapiens on Earth come to an end? What will be the cause? And if so, who or what will inherit our world? What forms of life? And will there be any world worth having? Finally, has the world under this sun a foreordained end? Let me see. Let me know where it all rolls up. And the universe, too. Does it have an end? Perhaps it is better just to hear about it, and not to see such a thing.

Now that I have my "scientist" cap on, let me suggest one further aspect of my lessons. Going back to one of my favorite areas—the mysteries of UFOs, the Loch Ness Monster, Bigfoot, and others—once we establish the truth of these "fringe" topics, if there are any that have a basis in reality, there remain many honest scientific questions. If UFOs exist, who makes them? Are they from one planet or many? What is the source of their energy? What are their motives and intentions? If there is an unknown aquatic creature in Loch Ness or Lake Champlain or other such lake, what is its ancestry? How could it survive down to today? How has it remained so secret? And the same questions for Bigfoot. If there really was an Atlantis, where was it? How did its people live and govern themselves? What was their science? And Lemuria? And elves, fairies and trolls? Are they only folklore, or was there some element of truth at their origin? I'm just asking. Can you imagine spending an eternity in the hereafter, and others know these answers, but they won't tell? Maybe that's the proverbial "hell." The universal library, but you forgot your library card.

CHAPTER 18
Duck Duck Goose

You have seen that I have spent considerable time reliving the lives of others, where doing so brought me greater perspective and a deeper understanding of the challenges which others face. Each of those lives I saw in the form of a theatrical movie, where I had the patience to sit down at the beginning and watch the story of that life unroll through to its final ending credits. Then, my guide showed me a new and different way of seeing these things.

He came to me and said, "You have learned much from your observation of the lives of others (different from yourself). It was good for you to see those lives unfold, as they did in life, day by day. Now I want you to look at those lives – and your own – in a completely different way."

"Here is what I want you to do" he said. "I want you to review several of the lives you have recently relived and select from among all of the events of each person's allotted time, first, that moment which you feel was the 'happiest moment' in that man or woman's life. Next, look over all those moments given to each person and determine what was the moment when he or she felt 'most hopeless, friendless, and in despair.' Finally, I want you to determine what was that moment when this man or woman most saw life as 'something full of hope and promise, offering a multitude of happy, optimistic choices.'

Taking him up on his request, I devoted myself to the task of learning to see the lives which I reviewed in this more instructive way. Where before the pivotal moments of a life might have been hidden from me in a thicket of routine habits and daily chores, now I saw those moments which define a person's fate (and which have a more permanent place in that person's memory) standing out, with all due prominence.

As I approached more and more lives in this way, I became more skilled at identifying those most important moments which my guide had named for me. Taking them in no particular order, and giving to each the short title which its contents recommended, there were "That Happiest Moment" and "That Moment of Despair" and "That Moment of Most Hope" and then some other moments. (Of any other, darker, moments I will not give them any place in this meditation, where I labor to be uplifted and not be dragged down to anger or regret.)

For example, I soon saw that each life has that moment when we feel the deepest sadness, loss and grief (at having lost a love, a child, a parent or a friend). I'll call this "That Moment of Our Greatest Loss." Then, too, I saw that moment which, were I not in the afterlife and heir to all the wisdom and perception which it brings, I could not have anticipated or understood. This was that one moment, coming latest in that unbroken chain of moments which defines a "life," in which that man or woman last enjoyed the innocence of youth (or, in some few cases, briefly regained, only to be lost again and never more be found). That last moment when … the cares and toils of an adult as yet unknown, his eyes last saw the joys a child might see, her heart last felt that perfect love that only childhood knows. This last moment of childhood's sweet morning I will call that "Moment of Last Innocence."

Now having crafted all these apt repositories, each having a carefully prepared and well-thought-out label on its side, I could not long delay in filling these receptacles with their rightful contents. Thus I started with the more cheerful moments, finding, first, that most joyful of them all, "That Happiest Moment." This I quickly learned was (for my life) not difficult to find—the moment of my daughter's birth (after which a lifetime of greater joy I found).

Next was "That Moment of Most Hope." This, likewise, was not difficult to discover, although I was gratified to see there were several from which I could choose. The one I selected was the moment I got my first job after college, through which, by the people I met and the habits that I learned, I was set on my path to my profession, leading then to spouse, to children and to years of productive work.

I will tell you about one additional important moment from my life. This was "That Moment of Last Innocence." I was surprised at how advanced in age I was to have this moment come.

It was a time when my daughter Emily had only just started going to school. It was winter, and I (each day) accompanied her to her school bus stop before I went to work. That day, I recall, there were several inches of new snow on the ground, and when we arrived at the bus stop, we saw the next-door field as if it were a smooth, unbroken canvas tempting us to soon commence our game. (A snowbound pasture for a merry chase!)

We instantly (together) cried out that we should play a kind of two-man game of "Duck Duck Goose." First, I ran into the field to some random spot and proclaimed "Here is the Center!" Next, she ran around the field, stamping out with her footprints a great circle, having my Center as the axis about which her Great Wheel might turn. Then, together we stamped out some spokes—perhaps six or eight—which tied together the axis (at equal intervals) to the Great Wheel of Fun that we had now described.

Now watch us! See the joy with which my heart is filled as I (the Evil Fox) do chase and try to catch that Clever Goose who spins the Wheel! Is this not Innocence itself? That runs and laughs and cheats and promises to never more the corners cut?

Now watch the Goose! She runs from wheel to spoke and spoke to wheel, and Never-Slowing-Down, she dares the Fox (with laughter) "Close the gap!" (between her speed and his), while all the while we see the Fox (his aged limbs retard his pace); and though he reels and slips and strives, he never will that Gap reduce—between his decades on this Earth ... that Clever Goose (in years) she knows no more than eight.

Behold this Moment! Which evermore will have in memory its honored place. Until that Farmer comes – he bringing, now, his yellow cart that takes away the Clever Goose – but leaving still the Wheel which we (with childlike joy) will spin again the next day and the next ... until that day the sun must come and take away forever more that Final Innocence which I will ever know in this the only life which I will ever live.

Some Greater Number
When I had completed the task of finding all of those expressive moments of my life, my guide came to me to show me more. He said, "You have seen that there are certain Moments of our lives which exercise some irresistible, compelling power over us. Of any other (less compelling) Moments, we naturally expect that they will go along quietly (keeping, always, single file in line) to the very threshold of His unending and all-unabridged compendium where (such moments being well-recorded there) we might see them all again in our eternal rest. But of those other, compelling Moments, having in them yet some fascination for us, we know this is seldom their fate.

"Not granting to them any leave to go, we often keep them with us, fresh and yet (to us) alive. We bid them show us once again that word or look or sigh that made our heart to race or gave us hope or honor, balm or joy. And are these not those Moments Well-Remembered, Gathered Close and Many Times Rehearsed, that in our quiet hours, or having need of loving words, or in that final time when nothing else we have, we hold them up before our inner sight and noting, now, each glimmer which these jewels reflect, we have our life's one treasure trove of Moments dear to us, and true?"

"I have been watching you keep count," he said, "of how much time you will need in the afterlife to see all the truth which the world offers. I see you have set aside some very great number of moments which you must allow if your purpose is to relive the life of every person who has ever lived. Let me help you. Let me suggest some additions you will wish to make."

He continued, "Of every life lived, there is one 'That Happiest Moment,' one 'Moment of Most Hope,' one 'Moment of Last Innocence' and one 'That Moment of Greatest Loss.' Thus, taking your estimate of the number of persons who have ever lived at 6,000,000,000,000 we see that your total (if it is to be complete) must include all of those well-noted Moments for all such persons. Accordingly, we see that of that 'Moment of Most Hope' we will have 6,000,000,000,000 entries; of 'That Moment of Greatest Loss' another 6,000,000,000,000 examples, and so on. Let us write these out in this way: First we write the number of lives to which our sum refers (6,000,000,000,000) and then we note each Moment by its name. So we have (6,000,000,000,000 / That Happiest) and (6,000,000,000,000 / Most Hope) and then (6,000,000,000,000 / That Last Innocence) and (6,000,000,000,000 / That Despair) and finally (6,000,000,000,000 / That Greatest Loss).

"But all this counting-up gets still more complicated," he said. "Recognize that you will already have witnessed all these moments when you followed out each life in its entire duration. But here I want you to recognize a deeper truth. You look and see (of some one man) that Moment of Despair and then, that Moment of his Greatest Loss, and so you think him finished, broken, all worn down. But no, you see that Moment of his Greatest Hope, That Moment of His Fierce Determination, and then you see that greater truth, That Moment when he Trusts his Maker ("That Moment Never Giving Up") and so, in time, you see That Moment When He Conquers All … and in the further distance … That Moment when he Evermore must trust his Maker's love, and having, then, no time for any further Moments."

"You see," my guide said, "if you wish to experience all the truth which resides here, you must witness not just any one Moment (as true as it might be), but all of those Moments placed in combination with each other, each combination having its own truth to tell. Unless you see these Moments brought together (one with another) in ways you cannot anticipate, you will never see all the truth which they record."

"I know you enjoy math," he said, "so let me tell you what you must do. Do you remember the formula for computing all possible combinations of some group of things? It is this (taking the number '12' as my example): 12! (we say 'twelve factorial') which we compute as follows: $12 \times 11 \times 10 \times 9 \times 8 \times 7 \times 6 \times 5 \times 4 \times 2 \times 1$ (which we read as 'Twelve times Eleven times Ten times Nine times Eight …' and the answer is some very large number)."

"So here is what you must allow (in your afterlife) to witness all the truth which these combinations of Moments will show: We take the number of 'That Happiest Moment' for every person of the world (6,000,000,000,000 / That Happiest) and we multiply that number by the number of 'That Moment of Most Hope' (which, again, is 6,000,000,000,000 / Most Hope) and then we multiply that product by the number of 'That Greatest Despair' and by the number of 'That Moment of Greatest Loss' (of all the world), and so on, multiplying each by each by each until we have by computation written out that one exhaustive and entire expression of those Moments (landmarks) of this world. Thus, in the end you will have before you every group and multiple of moments you must set aside to see that truth which all these 'Moments of …' might tell."

Thus, my guide showed me how the tally which I had accumulated to this point now increased greatly in size.

My Journey to This Point

My life	44,676,000
Family/friends	4,467,600,000
Others	10,000,000,000
Famous names	50,000,000,000
Mysteries	5,000,000,000
Helped/hurt	15,000,000,000
Afterlife	15,000,000,000
Pageant	300,000,000,000,000,000,000
Earth	1,000,000,000,000,000
Intangibles	3,000,000,000,000

Moments   (6,000,000,000,000 / That Happiest Moment) × (6,000,000,000,000 / That Moment of Most Hope) × (6,000,000,000,000 / That Moment of Last Innocence) × (6,000,000,000,000 / That Moment of Despair) × (6,000,000,000,000 / That Greatest Loss) × (6,000,000,000,000 / That Trusting Him) × (6,000,000,000,000 / That Greatest Love) × (6,000,000,000,000 / That Never Giving Up) × (6,000,000,000,000 / That Greatest Suffering) × (6,000,000,000,000 / That Most Patient) × (6,000,000,000,000 / That Most Caring) × (6,000,000,000,000 / That Never Falling Short) × (6,000,000,000,000

When Once I Lived

/ That Most Joyous Humor) × (6,000,000,000,000 / That Sympathetic Prayer) × (6,000,000,000,000 / That Highest Striving) × (6,000,000,000,000 / That Unexpected Moment) × (6,000,000,000,000 / That Forgiveness) × (6,000,000,000,000 / That One Regret) × (6,000,000,000,000 / That Sincere Repentance) × (6,000,000,000,000 / That Greatest Sacrifice) × (6,000,000,000,000 / Most Pious Wish) × (6,000,000,000,000 / That Dearest Friend) × (6,000,000,000,000 / That Darkest Hour) × (6,000,000,000,000 / That Farthest Journey) × (6,000,000,000,000 / Most Lonely Moment) × (6,000,000,000,000 / That Implacable Foe) × (6,000,000,000,000 / That Urgent Desire) × (6,000,000,000,000 / That Caring Effort) × (6,000,000,000,000 / That Unredeemable Cruelty) × (6,000,000,000,000 / That Naked Evil) × (6,000,000,000,000 / That Heart's Delight) × (6,000,000,000,000 / That True Repose) × (6,000,000,000,000 / Most Loyal Service) × (6,000,000,000,000 / Those Hurtful Words Unspoken) × (6,000,000,000,000 / That Gentle Caress) × (6,000,000,000,000 / Those Honest Tears) × (6,000,000, 000,000 / That Most Lusty Hour) × (6,000,000,000,000 / That Basest Flattery) × (6,000,000,000,000 / Those Words Most False) × (6,000,000,000,000 / Those Cruel Acts Forborne) × (6,000,000,000,000 / By All the World Reviled) × (6,000,000,000,000 / That Ungrateful Child) × (6,000,000,000,000 / That Giving Up Too Soon) × (6,000,000,000,000 / That Thankless Toil) × (6,000,000,000,000 / That Unacknowledged Generosity) × (6,000,000,000,000 / More Sinned Against) × (6,000,000,000,000 / That Unrequited Love) × (6,000,000,000,0 00 / That Granted Wish) × (6,000,000,000,000 / That Childish Fear) × (6,000,000,000,000 / That Undeserved Honor) × (6,000,000,000,000 / That Hidden Anger) × (6,000,000,000,000 / That Greatest Failing) × (6,000,000,000,000 / That Unforgivable Error) × (6,000,000,000,000 / That Unbearable Shame) × (6,000,000,000,000 / That Feeling Him Near) × (6,000,000,000,000 / That Cheating Death) × (6,000,000,000,000 / That Unexpected Help) × (6,000,000,000,000 / That Grievous Injury) × (6,000,000,000,000 / That Unnecessary Harm) × (6,000,000,000,000 / Those Wrongs Revealed) × (6,000,000,000,000 / That Most Tender Beauty) × (6,000,000,000,000 / Most Heartfelt Words) × (6,000,000,000,000 / Those Errors Once Foresworn) × (6,000,000,000,000 / That Nothing Now Remains) × (6,000,000,000,000 / That Verdict Overturned) × (6,000,000,000,000 / That Selfless Bravest Act) × (6,000,000,000,000 / That Gravest Falsehood) × (6,000,000,000,000 / That Deepest Grief) × (6,000,000 0,000,000 / That Careless Hurt) × (6,000,000,000,000 / That Goal Achieved) × (6,000,000,0 00,000 / That Dares New Life) × (6,000,000,000,000 / That Fear Overthrown) × (6,000,000,000,000 / That Victorious Struggle) × (6,000,000,000,000 / That Finding No Forgiveness) × (6,000,000,000,000 / That More We Cannot Bear) × (6,000,000,000,000 / That Unlikely Friend) × (6,000,000,000,000 / That Ventures Bravely On) × (6,000,000,000,0 00 / That Most Bitter Defeat) × (6,000,000,000,000 / That Unjust Punishment) × (6,000,000,000,000 / That Joyless Fate) × (6,000,000,000,000 / That Greatest Injustice) × (6,000,000,00 0,000 / That Stolen Moment) × (6,000,000,000,000 / Whom No One Mourns) × (6,000,000,000,000 / That No Forgiveness Knows) × (6,000,000,000, 000 / That Honor Shining Bright)

Above, you have seen are those Moments we have set apart individually and which we believe will—if taken one-by-one—in each case show us something unique. But we can go on.

Let us now combine these Moments into groups of two, each group having its own message which it suggests. (And hereafter, in order to make these lists easier to read, I will forego writing out that number—6,000,000,000,000—which we have agreed is the total of all the lives this world has ever seen.)

Duck Duck Goose

Here is that list of groups of two:

(That Moment of Most Hope × That Moment of Last Innocence) (That Moment of Despair × That Greatest Loss) (That Trusting Him × That Greatest Love) (That Never Giving Up × That Greatest Suffering) (That Most Patient × That Most Caring) (That Never Falling Short × That Most Joyous Humor) (That Sympathetic Prayer × That Highest Striving) (That Unexpected Moment × That Forgiveness) (That One Regret × That Sincere Repentance) (That Greatest Sacrifice × Most Pious Wish) (That Dearest Friend × That Darkest Hour) (That Farthest Journey × Most Lonely Moment) (That Implacable Foe × That Urgent Desire) (That Caring Effort × That Unredeemable Cruelty)(That Naked Evil × That Heart's Delight) (That True Repose × Most Loyal Service) (Those Hurtful Words Unspoken × That Gentle Caress) (Those Honest Tears × That Most Lusty Hour)(That Basest Flattery × Those Words Most False) (Those Cruel Acts Forborne × By All the World Reviled)(That Ungrateful Child × That Giving Up Too Soon) (That Thankless Toil x That Unacknowledged Generosity)(More Sinned Against × That Unrequited Love) (That Granted Wish × That Childish Fear) (That Undeserved Honor × That Hidden Anger) (That Greatest Failing × That Unforgivable Error)(That Unbearable Shame × That Feeling Him Near)(That Cheating Death × That Unexpected Help) (That Grievous Injury × That Unnecessary Harm)(Those Wrongs Revealed × That Most Tender Beauty)(Most Heartfelt Words × Those Errors Once Foresworn) (That Nothing Now Remains × That Verdict Overturned) (That Selfless Bravest Act × That Gravest Falsehood)(That Deepest Grief × That Careless Hurt) (That Goal Achieved × That Dares New Life)(That Fear Overthrown × That Victorious Struggle)(That Wounded Soul Repaired × That Finding No Forgiveness) (That More We Cannot Bear × That Unlikely Friend)(Who Ventures Bravely On × That Most Bitter Defeat)(That Unjust Punishment × That Joyless Fate)(That Greatest Injustice × That Stolen Moment)(Whom No One Mourns × That No Forgiveness Knows)(That Honor Shining Bright × That Moment of Despair) (That Moment of Last Innocence × That Moment of Despair (That Greatest Loss × That Trusting Him) (That Greatest Love × That Never Giving Up) (That Greatest Suffering × That Most Patient) (That Most Caring × That Never Falling Short) (That Most Joyous Humor × That Sympathetic Prayer) (That Highest Striving × That Unexpected Moment) (That Forgiveness × That One Regret) (That Sincere Repentance × That Greatest Sacrifice) (Most Pious Wish × That Dearest Friend) (That Darkest Hour × That Farthest Journey) (Most Lonely Moment × That Implacable Foe) (That Urgent Desire × That Caring Effort)(That Unredeemable Cruelty × That Naked Evil) (That Heart's Delight × That True Repose) (Most Loyal Service × Those Hurtful Words Unspoken) (That Gentle Caress × Those Honest Tears) (That Most Lusty Hour × That Basest Flattery) (Those Words Most False × Those Cruel Acts Forborne) (By All the World Reviled × That Ungrateful Child)(That Giving Up Too Soon × That Thankless Toil)(That Unacknowledged Generosity × More Sinned Against) (That Unrequited Love × That Granted Wish) (That Childish Fear × That Undeserved Honor)(That Hidden Anger × That Greatest Failing)(That Unforgivable Error × That Unbearable Shame)(That Feeling Him Near × That Cheating Death)(That Unexpected Help × That Grievous Injury)(That Unnecessary Harm × Those Wrongs Revealed) (That Most Tender Beauty × Most Heartfelt Words)(Those Errors Once Foresworn × That Nothing Now Remains)(That Verdict Overturned × That Selfless Bravest Act)(That Gravest Falsehood × That Deepest Grief)(That Careless Hurt × That Goal Achieved)(That Dares New Life × That Fear Overthrown)(That Victorious Struggle × That Wounded Soul Repaired) (That Finding No Forgiveness × That More We Cannot Bear)(That Unlikely Friend × Who Ventures Bravely On) (That Most Bitter Defeat × That Unjust Punishment) (That Joyless Fate × That Greatest Injustice)(That Stolen Moment × Whom No One Mourns)(That No Forgiveness Knows × That Honor Shining Bright)

Will I have time to witness all of these harmonic pairs? Where of the first, we hear the note it makes, and then the next, in sympathetic key, replies? Yes, I expect to hear all of them, and keep a record of them all, as well.

When Once I Lived

Going on, now, to yet more combinations, I will set forth those groups of three.

(That Moment of Most Hope × That Moment of Last Innocence × That Moment of Despair)(That Greatest Loss × That Trusting Him × That Greatest Love)(That Never Giving Up × That Greatest Suffering × That Most Patient)(That Most Caring × That Never Falling Short × That Most Joyous Humor)(That Sympathetic Prayer × That Highest Striving × That Unexpected Moment)(That Forgiveness × That One Regret × That Sincere Repentance) (That Greatest Sacrifice × Most Pious Wish × That Dearest Friend) (That Darkest Hour × That Farthest Journey × Most Lonely Moment)(That Implacable Foe × That Urgent Desire × That Caring Effort)(That Unredeemable Cruelty × That Naked Evil × That Heart's Delight) (That True Repose × Most Loyal Service × Those Hurtful Words Unspoken) (That Gentle Caress × Those Honest Tears × That Most Lusty Hour) (That Basest Flattery × Those Words Most False × Those Cruel Acts Forborne) (By All the World Reviled × That Ungrateful Child × That Giving Up Too Soon)(That Thankless Toil × That Unacknowledged Generosity × More Sinned Against) (That Unrequited Love × That Granted Wish × That Childish Fear) (That Undeserved Honor × That Hidden Anger × That Greatest Failing)(That Unforgivable Error × That Unbearable Shame × That Feeling Him Near)(That Cheating Death × That Unexpected Help × That Grievous Injury)(That Unnecessary Harm × Those Wrongs Revealed × That Most Tender Beauty)(Most Heartfelt Words × Those Errors Once Foresworn x That Nothing Now Remains)(That Verdict Overturned x That Selfless Bravest Act × That Gravest Falsehood)(That Deepest Grief × That Careless Hurt × That Goal Achieved)(That Dares New Life × That Fear Overthrown × That Victorious Struggle)(That Wounded Soul Repaired × That Finding No Forgiveness × That More We Cannot Bear)(That Unlikely Friend × Who Ventures Bravely On × That Most Bitter Defeat)(That Unjust Punishment × That Joyless Fate × That Greatest Injustice)(That Stolen Moment × Whom No One Mourns × That No Forgiveness Knows × That Honor Shining Bright)(That Moment of Last Innocence × That Moment of Despair × That Greatest Loss) (That Trusting Him × That Greatest Love × That Never Giving Up) (That Greatest Suffering × That Most Patient × That Most Caring) (That Never Falling Short × That Most Joyous Humor × That Sympathetic Prayer) (That Highest Striving × That Unexpected Moment × That Forgiveness) (That One Regret × That Sincere Repentance × That Greatest Sacrifice) (Most Pious Wish × That Dearest Friend × That Darkest Hour) (That Farthest Journey × Most Lonely Moment × That Implacable Foe) (That Urgent Desire × That Caring Effort × That Unredeemable Cruelty)(That Naked Evil × That Heart's Delight × That True Repose) (Most Loyal Service × Those Hurtful Words Unspoken × That Gentle Caress)(Those Honest Tears × That Most Lusty Hour × That Basest Flattery) (Those Words Most False × Those Cruel Acts Forborne × By All the World Reviled)(That Ungrateful Child × That Giving Up Too Soon × That Thankless Toil)(That Unacknowledged Generosity More Sinned Against × That Unrequited Love) (That Granted Wish × That Childish Fear × That Undeserved Honor)(That Hidden Anger × That Greatest Failing × That Unforgivable Error)(That Unbearable Shame × That Feeling Him Near × That Cheating Death)(That Unexpected Help × That Grievous Injury × That Unnecessary Harm)(Those Wrongs Revealed × That Most Tender Beauty × Most Heartfelt Words)(Those Errors Once Foresworn × That Nothing Now Remains × That Verdict Overturned)(That Selfless Bravest Act × That Gravest Falsehood × That Deepest Grief)(That Careless Hurt × That Goal Achieved × That Dares New Life)(That Fear Overthrown × That Victorious Struggle × That Wounded Soul Repaired) (That Finding No Forgiveness × That More We Cannot Bear × That Unlikely Friend)(Who Ventures Bravely On × That Most Bitter Defeat × That Unjust Punishment)(That Joyless Fate × That Greatest Injustice × That Stolen Moment)(Whom No One Mourns × That No Forgiveness Knows × That Honor Shining Bright × That Moment of Most Hope)(That Moment of Despair × That Greatest Loss × That Trusting Him) (That Greatest Love × That Never Giving Up × That Greatest Suffering) (That Most Patient × That Most Caring × That Never Falling Short) (That Most Joyous Humor × That Sympathetic Prayer × That Highest Striving) (That Unexpected Moment × That Forgiveness × That One Regret) (That Sincere Repentance × That Greatest Sacrifice × Most Pious Wish) (That Dearest Friend × That Darkest Hour × That Farthest Journey) (Most Lonely Moment × That Implacable Foe × That Urgent Desire) (That Caring Effort × That Unredeemable Cruelty × That Naked Evil)(That Heart's Delight × That True Repose × Most Loyal Service) (Those Hurtful Words Unspoken × That Gentle Caress × Those Honest Tears) (That Most Lusty Hour × That Basest Flattery × Those Words Most False) (Those Cruel Acts Forborne × By All the World Reviled × That Ungrateful Child)(That Giving Up Too Soon × That Thankless Toil × That Unacknowledged Generosity)(More Sinned Against × That Unrequited Love × That Granted Wish)(That Childish Fear × That Undeserved Honor × That Hidden Anger)(That Greatest Failing × That Unforgivable Error × That Unbearable Shame)(That Feeling Him Near × That Cheating Death × That Unexpected Help) (That Grievous Injury × That Unnecessary Harm × Those Wrongs Revealed)(That Most Tender Beauty × Most Heartfelt Words × Those Errors Once Foresworn)(That Nothing Now Remains × That Verdict Overturned × That Selfless Bravest Act)(That Gravest Falsehood × That Deepest Grief × That Careless Hurt)(That Goal Achieved × That Dares New Life × That Fear Overthrown)(That Victorious Struggle × That Wounded Soul Repaired × That Finding No Forgiveness)(That More We Cannot Bear × That Unlikely Friend × Who

Duck Duck Goose

Ventures Bravely On)(That Most Bitter Defeat × That Unjust Punishment × That Joyless Fate)(That Greatest Injustice × That Stolen Moment × Whom No One Mourns)(That No Forgiveness Knows x That Honor Shining Bright × That Moment of Most Hope × That Moment of Last Innocence)

(No doubt you have noticed that, these groups and combinations growing with impulsive and irresistible quickness, I have taken the precaution of writing them out in smaller and smaller letters, so that our total remains as manageable as we can make it.)

Shall we go on? Yes, why not? Let us next see those further combinations (groups of four) where, given but a few minutes and imagination enough, we discern some story, mystery or moral which (by our geometry informed) we see each group subtends (first "Starting Out" then "Conflict and Confusion" and then in time, "Haphazard Fortune, Fate and Insight," and finally "Coming Home"). Here are those groups:

(That Moment of Last Innocence × That Moment of Despair That Greatest Loss × That Trusting Him)(That Greatest Love × That Never Giving Up × That Greatest Suffering × That Most Patient)(That Most Caring × That Never Falling Short × That Most Joyous Humor × That Sympathetic Prayer)(That Highest Striving × That Unexpected Moment × That Forgiveness × That One Regret)(That Sincere Repentance × That Greatest Sacrifice × Most Pious Wish × That Dearest Friend)(That Darkest Hour × That Farthest Journey × Most Lonely Moment × That Implacable Foe)(That Urgent Desire × That Caring Effort × That Unredeemable Cruelty × That Naked Evil)(That Heart's Delight × That True Repose × Most Loyal Service × Those Hurtful Words Unspoken) (That Gentle Caress × Those Honest Tears × That Most Lusty Hour × That Basest Flattery) (Those Words Most False × Those Cruel Acts Forborne × By All the World Reviled × That Ungrateful Child)(That Giving Up Too Soon × That Thankless Toil × That Unacknowledged Generosity × More Sinned Against)(That Unrequited Love × That Granted Wish × That Childish Fear × That Undeserved Honor)(That Hidden Anger × That Greatest Failing × That Unforgivable Error × That Unbearable Shame)(That Feeling Him Near × That Cheating Death × That Unexpected Help × That Grievous Injury)(That Unnecessary Harm × Those Wrongs Revealed × That Most Tender Beauty × Most Heartfelt Words)(Those Errors Once Foresworn × That Nothing Now Remains × That Verdict Overturned × That Selfless Bravest Act)(That Gravest Falsehood × That Deepest Grief × That Careless Hurt × That Goal Achieved)(That Dares New Life × That Fear Overthrown × That Victorious Struggle × That Wounded Soul Repaired) (That Finding No Forgiveness × That More We Cannot Bear × That Unlikely Friend × Who Ventures Bravely On) (That Most Bitter Defeat × That Unjust Punishment × That Joyless Fate × That Greatest Injustice)(That Stolen Moment × Whom No One Mourn × That No Forgiveness Knows × That Honor Shining Bright)(That Moment of Most Hope × That Moment of Last Innocence × That Moment of Despair × That Greatest Loss) (That Trusting Him x That Greatest Love × That Never Giving Up × That Greatest Suffering) (That Most Patient × That Most Caring × That Never Falling Short × That Most Joyous Humor) (That Sympathetic Prayer × That Highest Striving × That Unexpected Moment × That Forgiveness) (That One Regret × That Sincere Repentance × That Greatest Sacrifice × Most Pious Wish) (That Dearest Friend × That Darkest Hour × That Farthest Journey × Most Lonely Moment) (That Implacable Foe × That Urgent Desire × That Caring Effort × That Unredeemable Cruelty)(That Naked Evil × That Heart's Delight × That True Repose × Most Loyal Service) (Those Hurtful Words Unspoken × That Gentle Caress × Those Honest Tears × That Most Lusty Hour)(That Basest Flattery × Those Words Most False × Those Cruel Acts Forborne × By All the World Reviled) (That Ungrateful Child × That Giving Up Too Soon × That Thankless Toil × That Unacknowledged Generosity)(More Sinned Against × That Unrequited Love × That Granted Wish × That Childish Fear) (That Undeserved Honor × That Hidden Anger × That Greatest Failing × That Unforgivable Error) (That Unbearable Shame × That Feeling Him Near × That Cheating Death × That Unexpected Help)(That Grievous Injury × That Unnecessary Harm × Those Wrongs Revealed × That Most Tender Beauty)(Most Heartfelt Words × Those Errors Once Foresworn × That Nothing Now Remains × That Verdict Overturned)(That Selfless Bravest Act × That Gravest Falsehood × That Deepest Grief × That Careless Hurt)(That Goal Achieved × That Dares New Life × That Fear Overthrown × That Victorious Struggle)(That Wounded Soul Repaired × That Finding No Forgiveness × That More We Cannot Bear × That Unlikely Friend)(Who Ventures Bravely On × That Most Bitter Defeat × That Unjust Punishment × That Joyless Fate)(That Greatest Injustice × That Stolen Moment × Whom No One Mourns × That No Forgiveness Knows × That Honor Shining Bright)(That Moment of Despair × That Greatest Loss × That Trusting Him × That Greatest Love) (That Never Giving Up × That Greatest Suffering × That Most Patient × That Most Caring) (That Never Falling Short × That Most Joyous Humor × That Sympathetic Prayer × That Highest Striving) (That Unexpected Moment × That Forgiveness × That One Regret × That Sincere Repentance) (That Greatest Sacrifice × Most Pious Wish × That Dearest Friend × That Darkest Hour) (That Farthest Journey × Most Lonely Moment × That Implacable Foe × That Urgent Desire) (That Caring Effort × That Unredeemable Cruelty × That Naked Evil × That Heart's Delight) (That True Repose × Most Loyal Service × Those Hurtful Words Unspoken × That Gentle Caress)(Those Honest Tears × That Most Lusty Hour × That Basest Flattery × Those Words Most False)(Those Cruel Acts Forborne × By All the World Reviled × That Ungrateful Child × That Givi

When Once I Lived

ng Up Too Soon)(That Thankless Toil × That Unacknowledged Generosity × More Sinned Against × That Unrequited Love)(That Granted Wish × That Childish Fear × That Undeserved Honor × That Hidden Anger)(That Greatest Failing × That Unforgivable Error × That Unbearable Shame × That Feeling Him Near)(That Cheating Death × That Unexpected Help × That Grievous Injury × That Unnecessary Harm)(Those Wrongs Revealed × That Most Tender Beauty × Most Heartfelt Words × Those Errors Once Foresworn)(That Nothing Now Remains × That Verdict Overturned × That Selfless Bravest Act × That Gravest Falsehood)(That Deepest Grief × That Careless Hurt × That Goal Achieved × That Dares New Life)(That Fear Overthrown × That Victorious Struggle × That Wounded Soul Repaired × That Finding No Forgiveness) (That More We Cannot Bear × That Unlikely Friend × Who Ventures Bravely On × That Most Bitter Defeat)(That Unjust Punishment × That Joyless Fate × That Greatest Injustice × That Stolen Moment × Whom No One Mourns)(That No Forgiveness Knows × That Honor Shining Bright × That Moment of Most Hope × That Moment of Last Innocence)(That Greatest Loss × That Trusting Him × That Greatest Love × That Never Giving Up) (That Greatest Suffering × That Most Patient × That Most Caring × That Never Falling Short) (That Most Joyous Humor × That Sympathetic Prayer × That Highest Striving × That Unexpected Moment)(That Forgiveness × That One Regret × That Sincere Repentance × That Greatest Sacrifice)(Most Pious Wish × That Dearest Friend × That Darkest Hour × That Farthest Journey)(Most Lonely Moment × That Implacable Foe × That Urgent Desire × That Caring Effort)(That Unredeemable Cruelty × That Naked Evil × That Heart's Delight × That True Repose)(Most Loyal Service × Those Hurtful Words Unspoken × That Gentle Caress × Those Honest Tears)(That Most Lusty Hour × That Basest Flattery × Those Words Most False × Those Cruel Acts Forborne)(By All the World Reviled × That Ungrateful Child × That Giving Up Too Soon × That Thankless Toil)(That Unacknowledged Generosity × More Sinned Against × That Unrequited Love × That Granted Wish) (That Childish Fear × That Undeserved Honor × That Hidden Anger × That Greatest Failing)(That Unforgivable Error × That Unbearable Shame × That Feeling Him Near × That Cheating Death)(That Unexpected Help × That Grievous Injury × That Unnecessary Harm × Those Wrongs Revealed)(That Most Tender Beauty × Most Heartfelt Words × Those Errors Once Foresworn × That Nothing Now Remains)(That Verdict Overturned × That Selfless Bravest Act × That Gravest Falsehood × That Deepest Grief)(That Careless Hurt × That Goal Achieved × That Dares New Life × That Fear Overthrown) (That Victorious Struggle × That Wounded Soul Repaired × That Finding No Forgiveness × That More We Cannot Bear) (That Unlikely Friend × Who Ventures Bravely On × That Most Bitter Defeat × That Unjust Punishment)(That Joyless Fate × That Greatest Injustice × That Stolen Moment × Whom No One Mourns)(That No Forgiveness Knows × That Honor Shining Bright × That Moment of Most Hope × That Moment of Last Innocence × That Moment of Despair)

Shall we press on? What greater truth can we find here, in this wilderness of groups? Where once, thinking we knew and understood each Moment as we might an old, dear friend, now we come to a place where, by this cacophony of groups, we no longer hear any single, intelligible human voice. How, then, do they speak to us?

Witness now, below, those groups of five: Combinations having in them each a story which, if we should set aside some group of Moments gathered solely from your life, will taken (then) together … tell your story, teach your moral, or (to all) reveal the mystery which is your fate.

(That Moment of Most Hope × That Moment of Last Innocence × That Moment of Despair × That Greatest Loss × That Trusting Him) (That Greatest Love × That Never Giving Up × That Greatest Suffering × That Most Patient × That Most Caring)(That Never Falling Short × That Most Joyous Humor × That Sympathetic Prayer × That Highest Striving × That Unexpected Moment)(That Forgiveness × That One Regret × That Sincere Repentance × That Greatest Sacrifice × Most Pious Wish)(That Dearest Friend × That Darkest Hour × That Farthest Journey × Most Lonely Moment × That Implacable Foe)(That Urgent Desire × That Caring Effort × That Unredeemable Cruelty × That Naked Evil × That Heart's Delight)(That True Repose × Most Loyal Service × Those Hurtful Words Unspoken × That Gentle Caress × Those Honest Tears)(That Most Lusty Hour × That Basest Flattery × Those Words Most False × Those Cruel Acts Forborne × By All the World Reviled)(That Ungrateful Child × That Giving Up Too Soon × That Thankless Toil × That Unacknowledged Generosity × More Sinned Against) (That Unrequited Love × That Granted Wish × That Childish Fear × That Undeserved Honor × That Hidden Anger)(That Greatest Failing × That Unforgivable Error × That Unbearable Shame × That Feeling Him Near × That Cheating Death)(That Unexpected Help × That Grievous Injury × That Unnecessary Harm × Those Wrongs Revealed × That Most Tender Beauty)(Most Heartfelt Words × Those Errors Once Foresworn × That Nothing Now Remains × That Verdict Overturned × That Selfless Bravest Act)(That Gravest Falsehood × That Deepest Grief × That Careless Hurt × That Goal Achieved × That Dares New Life)(That Fear Overthrown × That Victorious Struggle × That Wounded Soul Repaired × That Finding No Forgiveness × That More We Cannot Bear)(That Unlikely Friend × Who Ventures Bravely On × That Most Bitter Defeat × That Unjust Punishment × That Joyless Fate)(That Greatest Injustice × That Stolen Moment × Whom No One Mourns × That No Forgiveness Knows × That Honor Shining Bright)(That Moment of Last Innocence × That Moment of Despair × That Greatest Loss × That Trusting Him × That Greatest Love) (That Never Giving Up × That Greatest Suffering × That Most Patient × That Most Caring × That Never Falling Short)(That Most Joyous Humor × That Sympathetic Prayer × That Highest Striving × That Unexpected Moment × That Forgiveness)(That One Regret × That Sincere Repentance × That Greatest Sacrifice × Most Pious Wish × That Dearest Friend)(That Darkest Hour × That Farthest Journey × Most Lonely Moment × That Implacable Foe × That Urgent Desire)(That Caring Effort × That Unredeemable Cruelty × That Naked Evil × That Heart's Delight × That True Repose)(Most Loyal Service × Those Hurtful Words Unspoken × That Gentle Caress ×

Duck Duck Goose

Those Honest Tears × That Most Lusty Hour (That Basest Flattery × Those Words Most False × Those Cruel Acts Forborne × By All the World Reviled × That Ungrateful Child)(That Giving Up Too Soon × That Thankless Toil × That Unacknowledged Generosity × More Sinned Against × That Unrequited Love)(That Granted Wish × That Childish Fear × That Undeserved Honor × That Hidden Anger × That Greatest Failing)(That Unforgivable Error × That Unbearable Shame × That Feeling Him Near × That Cheating Death × That Unexpected Help)(That Grievous Injury × That Unnecessary Harm × Those Wrongs Revealed × That Most Tender Beauty × Most Heartfelt Words)(Those Errors Once Foresworn × That Nothing Now Remains × Th at Verdict Overturned × That Selfless Bravest Act × That Gravest Falsehood)(That Deepest Grief × That Careless Hurt × That Goal Achieved × That Dares New Life × That Fear Ov erthrown)(That Victorious Struggle × That Wounded Soul Repaired × That Finding No Forgiveness × That More We Cannot Bear × T hat Unlikely Friend)(Who Ventures Bravely On × That Most Bitter Defeat × That Unjust Punishment × That Joyless Fate × That Grea test Injustice)(That Stolen Moment × Whom No One Mourns × That No Forgiveness Knows × That Honor Shining Bright × That Moment of Most Hope)(That Moment of Despair × That Greatest Loss × That Trusting Him × That Greatest Love × That Never Giving Up)(That Greatest Suffering × That Most Patient × That Most Caring × That Never Falling Short × That Most Joyous Humor)(That Sympathetic Prayer × That Highest Striving × That Unexpected Moment × That Forgiveness × That One Regret)(That Sincere Rep entance × That Greatest Sacrifice × Most Pious Wish × That Dearest Friend × That Darkest Hour)(That Farthest Journ ey × Most Lonel y Moment × That Implacable Foe × That Urgent Desire × That Caring Effort)(That Unredeemable Cruelty × That Naked Evil × That Heart's Delight × That True Repose × Most Loyal Service)(Those Hurtful Words Unspoken × That Gentle Caress × Those H onest Tear s × That Most Lusty Hour × That Basest Flattery)(Those Words Most False × Those Cruel Acts Forborne × By All the World Re viled × That Ungrateful Child × That Giving Up Too Soon)(That Thankless Toil × That Unacknowledged Generosity × Mo re Sinned A gainst × That Unrequited Love × That Granted Wish)(That Childish Fear × That Undeserved Honor × That Hidden Anger × That Greatest Failing × That Unforgivable Error)(That Unbearable Shame × That Feeling Him Near × That Cheating Death × That Unexpected Help × That Grievous Injury)(That Unnecessary Harm × Those Wrongs Revealed × That Most Tender Beauty × Most Heart felt Words × Th ose Errors Once Foresworn)(That Nothing Now Remains × That Verdict Over turned × That Selfless Bravest Act × That Gravest Fal sehood × That Deepest Grief)(That Careless Hurt × That Goal Achieved × That Dares New Life × That Fear Overthrown × That V ictorious Struggle)(That Wounded Soul Repaired × That Finding No Forgiveness × That More We Cannot Bear × That Unlikely Friend × Who Ventures Bravely On)(That Most Bitter Defeat × That Unjust Punishment × That Joyless Fate × That Greatest Injustice × That Stolen Moment)(Whom No One Mourns × That No Forgiveness Knows × That Honor Shining Bright × That Moment of Most Hope × That Moment of Last Innocence)(That Greatest Loss × That Trusting Him × That Gre atest Love × That Never Giving Up × That G reatest Suffering)(That Most Patient × That Most Caring × That Never Falling Short × That Most Joyous Humor × That Sympathetic Prayer)(That Highest Striv ing × That Unexpected Moment × That Forgiveness × That One Regret × That Sincere Repentance)(That Greatest Sacrifice × Most Pious Wish × That Dearest Friend × That Darkest Hour × That F arthest Journey)(Most Lonely Moment × Th at Implacable Foe × That Urgent Desire × That Caring Effort × That Unredeemable Cruelty)(That Naked Evil × That Heart's Delight × That True Repose × Most Loyal Service × Those Hurtful Words Unspoken)(That Gentle Caress × Those Honest Tears × That Most Lus ty Hour × That Basest Flattery × Those Words Most False)(Those Cruel Acts Forborne × By All the World Reviled × That Ungrateful Child × That Giving Up Too Soon × That Thankless Toil)(That Unacknowledged Generos ity × More Sinned Against × That Un requited Love × That Granted Wish × That Childish Fear)(That Undeserved Honor × That Hidd en Anger × That Greatest Failing × That Unforgivable Error × That Unbearable Shame)(That Feeling Him Near × That Cheating Death × That Unexpected Help × That Grievous Injury × That Unnecessary Harm)(Those Wrongs Revealed × That Most Tender Beauty × M ost Heartfelt Words × Those Errors Once Foresworn × That Nothing Now Remains)(That Verdict Overturned × That Selfless Bravest A ct × That Gravest Falsehood × That D eepest Grief × That Careless Hurt)(That Goal Achieved × That Dares New Life × That Fear Ove rthrown × That Victorious Struggle × That Wounded Soul Repaired) (That Finding No Forgiveness × That More We Cannot Bear × Th at Unlikely Friend × Who Ventures Bravely On × That Most Bitter Defeat)(That Unjust Punishment × That Joyless Fate × That Greates t Injustice × That Stolen Moment × Whom No One Mourns)(That No Forgiveness Knows × That Honor Shining Bright × That Momen t of Most Hope × That Moment of Last Innocence × That Moment of Despair)(That Trusting Him × That Greatest Love × That Never Giving Up × That Greatest Suffering × That Most Patient)(That Most Caring × That Never Falling Short × That Most Joyous Humor × That Sympathetic Prayer × That H ighest Striving)(That Unexpected Moment × That Forgiveness × That One Regret × That Sincere Repentance × That Greatest Sacrific e)(Most Pious Wish × That Dearest Friend × That Darkest Hour × That Farthest Journey × Most Lonely Moment)(That Implacable Foe × That Urgent Desire × That Caring Effort × That Unredeemable Cruelty × That Naked Evil) (That Heart's Delight × That True Repose × Most Loyal Service × Those Hurtful Words Unspoken × That Gentle Caress)(Those Hones t Tears × That Most Lusty Hour × That Bas est Flattery × Those Words Most False × Those Cruel Acts Forborne)(By All the World R eviled × That Ungrateful Child × That Giving Up Too Soon × That Thankless Toil × That Unacknowledged Generosity)(More Sinned Against × That Unrequited Love × That G ranted Wish × That Childish Fear × That Undeserved Honor)(That Hidden Anger × That Greatest Failing × That Unforgivable Error × That Unbearable Shame × That Feeling Him Near)(That Cheating Death × That Un expected Help × That Grievous Injury × That Unnecessary Harm × Those Wrongs Revealed)(That Most Tender Beauty × Most Heartfe lt Words × Those Errors Once Foresworn × T hat Nothing Now Remains × That Verdict Overturned)(That Selfless Bravest Act × That Gravest Falsehood × That Deepest Grief × Th at Careless Hurt × That Goal Achieved)(That Dares New Life × That Fear Overthrown × That Victorious Struggle × That Wounded So ul Repaired × That Finding No Forgiveness)(That More We Cannot Bear × That Unlikely Friend × Who Ventures Bravely On × That Most Bitter Defeat × That Unjust Punishment)(That Joyless Fate × That Greatest Injustice × That Stolen Moment × Whom No One Mourns × That No Forgiveness Knows)(That Honor Shining Bright × That Moment of Most Hope × That Moment of Last Innocence × That Moment of Despair × That Greatest Loss)

Once again, we see that the time which I must allow in my eternity grows very great.

That Higher Power
Had it been my choice, I would have abandoned all this "higher math" at this point. (I do have sympathy for you, dear reader, who is not likely to find any very accessible "truth" in large and complex numbers. Nevertheless, my guide was not finished with my mathematics lesson.)

"We have already come this far," he said, "and we have only a little further to go to see something you will want to learn." I shrugged my shoulders; he was the boss.

"Now observe," he said, as he wrote in the space before me, where we could both see. He wrote '5 × 5 × 5 × 5'. This is easy to read, and easy to understand and calculate. It is 'five times five times five times five' (the answer being 625). Now you know, in mathematics, we can also write this as:

$$5^4$$

The '4' above and to the right of the 5 we call the 'power.' It means we write out '5' four (4) times, then multiply those numbers out to get the final product. So we would pronounce this 'five to the power of four' or perhaps 'five to the fourth (power)' (but we do not say the word 'power,' we just say 'five to the fourth' which is shorter).

Mathematicians being lovers of complexity, they (of course) allow further, even more complicated (and confusing) expressions. They allow us to write:

$$5^{4^6} \quad \text{and} \quad 5^{4^{6^{10}}} \quad \text{and} \quad 5^{4^{6^{10^{12}}}}$$

The first expression we would read by saying: '5 to the 4th to the 6th.' The second and third expressions (which I have included only to show to what extremes these numbers can take us) we would read by saying (for the second): '5 to the 4th … 6th … 10th' and then (for the third): '5 to the 4th … 6th … 10th … 12th.'

To compute the value of the first expression, we would first calculate '4 to the 6th' which is 1,024. Then we calculate '5 to the $1,024^{th}$' which if you have a computer, you can calculate if you wish. You get the idea. We can take some 'power' of a number; then (if we want) we can take some further 'power' of that 'power,' and this we count a deeper, hidden secret, which without this skill our minds could not this greater sum compute.

I said to my guide, "I can tell you where you have brought me: To the absolute limit of my tolerance for frustration! What am I supposed to make of all these 'powers'? I admit, the 'truths' of mathematics are no less true for being ungraspable by my poor mind, but, having said I want to hear all the truths of the afterlife, do I have to suffer any more of these impenetrable numbers?"

"No, no," he laughed. "We are about to give up numbers in favor of something the human mind can more easily comprehend. Let me just point out one or two aspects of these things which you may not have recognized. We have in our previous examples used numbers which are easily understood by anyone. We saw the expression:

$$5^4$$

(5 to the 4th) which is made up entirely of whole numbers. But we can also write:

$$5^\pi \quad \text{or even} \quad 5^{\sqrt{-2}}$$

The first is '5 to the power of π' (and you know that "π"—the Greek letter 'Pi'—is a number which has an infinite number of digits: 3.141592… never coming to an end). Then the next is '5 to the square root of negative 2.' The first expression (5 to the π) we can understand (in a rough and ready sort of way). We know that π is about 3.14159…, so we feel we have some sort of grasp on this expression. It is the number 5 raised to some power more than 3.1415 but less than 3.1416.

"The other expression," he continued, "we cannot grasp with our minds. We know in mathematics the symbol $\sqrt{-2}$ must have some meaning, but we have no way to understand how we might raise the number 5 to the 'power' of such an irrational, imaginary quantity. So, once again (as is our endlessly repeated grievance with the science of mathematics) we can write some symbols on a page (and all alike will read them in the same way), but neither we nor any soul alive can guess what quantity these symbols mean.

"Now," he said, "there is one more step you must take when you think about these things. Try this. Start with our most simple example: 5 to the 4th. Now, we cannot help but marvel (knowing the strong and independent nature of our friend, the '5') that he could ever be induced to involve himself in any higher computation, which would only threaten to disturb his peace of mind and possibly lead him into confusion or despair. But no, this '4'—insinuating himself into this place of power—he casts a kind of spell of magic over our steadfast and trustworthy friend, such that now, by some power of hypnosis or magic or (for all we know) some 'evil eye,' our friend is led to multiply himself three times, and thereby calculate this power (his 4th) which he (without this spell) would never in this world have done."

"Do you see it, now? That coming into such relation with some given quantity (the 'base'), the power that we specify does cast its spell, and by this universal force (which none resist) it so extends and amplifies its elemental nature, giving to that nature, now, the power which it has.

"Look here," he said. And then he wrote:

$$\text{Moments of Wrongdoing}^{\text{Moments of Repentence}}$$

"By this, we specify those Moments (which you have been diligent to identify, set apart and contemplate) in which you were guilty of some wrongdoing. Then, those Moments, as if subject to some invisible force, or spell of magic, or alchemy, are put into relation as the base to which the power, now, we see, is those Moments of Repentance (in which, with honest eyes down turned, you feel that sadness which your wrongs gave birth).

"And here you find is truth. That though you see your wrongs revealed, you see them, too, that they a Greater Power must respect. That you did wrong (which all might see) but yet (by this a power which we calculate and know) we also see repentance brought to bear (that heals the pain you feel for all that wrong).

"And let us express this other additional truth, as well," he said, and then he wrote:

$$\text{Moments of Wrongdoing}^{\text{Moments of Regret}^{\text{Moments of Forgiveness}}}$$

"And we can calculate it all like this: Of all those Moments of Regret (which I, in sadness, feel myself at fault), these all I see are by my Moments of Forgiveness healed, and so all this (my guilt, of which Forgiveness salves) it casts its spell of bitter-sweet regard upon those acts which all will call them 'Wrong,' yet still by bringing all these Moments here, together, in this place, and in this one relation (having in it power), I feel my Wrongs a little less; it takes away some part of my Despair.

"Shall we explore further? Let us examine the following expressive Moments, seeing all that 'power' which within these three resides:

$$\text{That Honor Shining Bright}^{\text{That Selfless Bravest Act}^{\text{That Nothing Now Remains}}}$$

"Of that young man we knew ... a soldier (son, a spouse, a friend), let us now calculate his worth (if that we must) in just this way: We see his single bravest act (of sacrifice) by which he gave his all, and now that 'all' (that 'nothing' which by one account we see is all remains of every precious gift entrusted by his Maker at his birth) is by the power of that Giver sanctified. We see that 'all' he gave transfigured by his selfless act to Purest Gold, where fashioned in the image of this man (his true Memorial ... untarnished to the end of time), it but reflects undimmed that ever-shining light of his undying honor."

"Now let us look at another expression, reflecting Moments of the most common, every-day and general variety, where, notwithstanding the hidden power which this group partakes, we do not expect to find any story personal or unique to any one person:

That Trusting Him
Those Fears Overthrown
That Dares New Life

"If, of some young woman we were to see this written, and if we were to take these Moments all together, draw them out and sum them up, what 'power' might these words unloose? We witness this: That seeing all her fears ... of loneliness and want, of poverty ... abandonment, she gathers all her apprehensions in a single vial (and seeing then the black and odious concoction which it brews) she adds the merest pinch of what her witchery prescribes (a smidge of 'Trusting Him, Complete'), and so that mixture (which before she turned away her eyes) she sees anew, that sparkles, lights the way, and says to her 'The time is right!' his eyes (by her illumination led) she Trusts will evermore her safety—and her child's—seek out."

It took me some time to become familiar with this lesson my guide had taught me. Here was a simple and yet powerful tool to bring two or more collections of Moments into relation with each other. These events and occurrences of all the world (not being numbers), they cannot be brought into combination with each other except by some act of imagination, or effort of our understanding, memory or will. Should it be any surprise to us to learn that, only by bringing these Moments into some more powerful relationship with each other, we might finally understand those truths wherein we find His greatest power lies?

My guide gave me a considerable period of time to explore these ever greater powers which we (by this simple device) might invoke. Then once again my guide came to me and said: "If I were to ask you to write down in one place that true expression of all the innocent joy which you were privileged to have experienced in your life, what would you write?"

I gave this problem much deep consideration; then finally wrote my answer, thus:

                                            Goose
                                    Duck
                         Duck
My daughter is born

CHAPTER 19
I Come to a Crossroads

Up to this moment, I have considered my life as if it were a movie which (after my death) I might attend, watching it over and over again to my moral and ethical betterment. I have also supposed that there will be other movies that I might choose to attend—the lives of family, friends, influential persons, and events of every description. I imagine I am the ultimate omniscient observer, present at the side of every person who has ever lived, witness at the creation of the universe, silently observant from that moment long ago until this day.

Everything I have imagined up to now has been founded on one assumption, and it is one that I must now recognize and address. It is an assumption that, it would seem, must underlie every religion and nearly every philosophical system ever devised by human creativity. It is this: That we have free will, and that all of the events and occurrences of the world might have been different.

This seems not really a question at all. How could we not have free will? Our lives seem to consist of one choice after another, from morning to night. Our perception is that we—and all others—are (within the limits of our culture, language and nationality, animated always by our innate desires, and ever expressive of our unique personality) free to choose what we will do and say and think.

Now there seem to be varying degrees of predetermination, among those who so believe. There are those who adopt the philosophy of astrology—that "the stars impel, they do not compel." That is, that we each have a fate, which is expressed in general terms. Perhaps that I was fated to be successful in some learned profession. Or of someone else, that he was fated "to come to no good end" (and so he goes to prison). And so on. That the panoramic, over-arching story of each life is predetermination and, of any other details, that our familiar, routine, daily choices will fill these in.

I have never given credence to this view of predetermination. I think it merely stands for the proposition that an individual, having a unique, God-given array of talents and a unique personality (with whatever elements it has), is indeed "impelled" in one direction or another. A person who is lazy, unfocused, self-involved, impatient and insensitive is not so much "fated" to come to no good end as he is "designed and built" to reach that destiny. No doubt those around him, being acquainted with him and the attributes of his personality, might say, in a casual sort of way, that this young man is "fated" to come to such an end, but this is merely a short-hand way of speaking.

No, when I talk about the theory that our lives are predetermined, what I mean is the hypothesis (nearly impossible for our minds to entertain) that all of the events of this world have been preordained by our Heavenly Father. All such events: Every natural occurrence, every wave in the ocean, every breath of wind, every raindrop of every storm—from the inception of the universe until now until the end of time. (And all your speech, emotions, dreams and unconfessed desires; your most creative works of all-unbounded fancy, these things we see long-foreordained by His expressive Will; your greatest failing, which you hide within that secret vault of your still-burning shame, by Him foredoomed).

No doubt you are one of the many who do not find this view of the world credible. After all, we seem to have free will. We feel as if we do. And although we may easily believe that our Heavenly Father, if it pleased Him, could so arrange the world that it unfolds precisely according to some pre-arranged plan (after all, it is said the world "is His, and He made it"), nevertheless such a theory goes against all the evidence of our senses, and our deepest acquaintance with the world.

Life feels to us chaotic, random and unplanned. Certainly we are aware of the laws of nature, and that both we and the natural world operate in ways often predetermined by natural scientific processes. Despite this, much seems left to chance. So why would anyone—why do I—give so much attention to this theory which seems to have so little to recommend it?

Here is the reason, or rather, one of the reasons. There are stories told from time to time throughout history of children who are born and who remember their prior life. Not cases of some vague memories that cannot be connected to any certain time or place. No, these are cases where the child says, "I was a man and my name was such-and-so, living in a village named so-and-so, and my wife was this name, and I died because of such-and-so reason." And the parents of the child at first do not believe but later investigate the story, and it's all true. All the important parts of his story turn out to be true, even details no one could easily anticipate. And although these cases are not common, they are not as rare as you might think.

Now these stories are a kind of "trout in the milk" that seem to confirm reincarnation and by themselves constitute powerful evidence of predestination. But often there is more to the story. Sometimes the child will say, "And after I died, I went somewhere, and then I was shown my life that I will lead, and I was shown the job I will have and my wife and children and where I will live. And then I chose my new life and now I'm here." Of such stories there are also multiple examples. So it seems, if these stories are true, that each of us enters this life "forgetting" and, if that divinely inspired predisposition to "forgetting" fails, that we can remember not just a prior life but more besides: Some facts about this world and our purpose in it and that the course and outcome of our life are (from the first) predestined, but yet we chose them.

I expect you may be thinking, "Why are you going off on this wild tangent with all this talk about the world being predetermined? It's such an outlandish, screwball sort of theory. Why even look at it?"

There is one essential reason, and it is this: That an honest and exhaustive review of all the possibilities of life indicates that it is at least possible that my life, your life, and all the vanity and glory of the wide world are all predestined. In keeping with the nature and purpose of this meditation, I have to consider this proposition. It is at least possible that, upon my passing away, I will learn (or remember) that my life was fated down to the smallest detail. What happens at that point, I do not know. Will I still enjoy our Heavenly Father's promise of eternal life? Will my guide still help me to pursue my lessons? I can't imagine what would be the circumstance of finding the world to be such a place. It seems to me that if I am led to this conclusion, I will have to say that the truth of the world is this: That it serves another purpose, one which is hidden from us.

If all the events of my life were fated, would there be any point in my reviewing those events during my eternal life? How can I learn anything from the mistakes of the past if all those mistakes were not authentically chosen by me but were preordained? On the other hand, why shouldn't my soul see these things and be uplifted? Can I not bear witness to those truths which we might learn from the words and deeds of the past, even if those actions were not the products of free will? I can watch a play on the stage, with every word and action pre-written by the playwright, and yet my heart and soul are moved by the power of the drama.

I am going to stop here giving any further consideration to the possibility of the predetermination of the world, for three reasons. First, because, as a theory and principle, it seems contrary to the integrity of His word. I cannot believe that He has made us free to accept or reject His Holy Word and, at the same time, believe that every detail of our lives is foreordained. It seems nonsensical to believe that some are predetermined to accept His gifts while others are predetermined to reject Him. Trying to think in this way brings to mind that concept which (in mathematics) we know of as a logical inconsistency: Where, for example, having something (equal to itself), from "it" we first subtract "itself" and then we find (upsetting every syllogistic truth) some remnant yet remains.

Next, my experience of the world is that we do have free will. It just feels as if I do actually choose. I think that if my feeling of free will were illusory, I would have very different sensations. Now, earlier I alluded to a powerful predisposition to "forgetting," and perhaps that forgetting is so very complete and profound that I could be completely oblivious to the preordained nature of the world, but I have to say I cannot believe this is true. There is nothing so strong as this perception that I have (that I share with all the souls in this world) that we choose—a thousand times a day, to the end of our days, and that this is the one, universal, shared destiny of men, that we are weak, small and ignorant, and yet we must choose.

And there is one final argument against predetermination: That the world seems to be so arranged that we are intended to live as if we have free will. We each, from birth, have in us that all-pervasive, seldom-failing predisposition to "forgetting." And if this were not enough, it further appears that our faculty of reasoning, our logic and our consciousness (each one operating pursuant to His prearranged design) are built incapable of entertaining any thought that fits within a predetermined world.

Thus we would all agree: If we cannot think in such a world, we cannot live in it. I can only conclude, then, that if it is His intention and desire that I should live as if I have free will, then I will not resist His purpose for me.

CHAPTER 20
I Resume My Journey

I feel refreshed. I have a guide who has a loving, sympathetic plan for me. I perceive the world to be a richer and more "energetic" place than I had known. I can see the past and all the people and events that stretch out over uncountable years, but now I likewise see it all might have been so different. The "givens" of life now take on the appearance of mere happenstance—fortuitous occurrences, sparkling as if under the spell of some whimsical magic (imperfectly remembered and only haphazardly employed).

Here is the lesson which my guide has for me: He takes me to that place where I might learn that skill (requiring aptitude and art) to think about events which might have occurred, but yet did not. I find immediately that I am thrown back in utter confusion. Up to now I have busied myself making plans to experience the entirety of human history (and good parts of natural history, as well), which seems a time-consuming task. But now I am forced to recognize that I must also be a witness to those even more numerous events of history that "might have happened" but did not.

Think about that. At any given moment, there are "x" number of events and circumstances that "are." Whatever choices were made in the past, they have given us a world which is just this one certain world. But if we acknowledge that any of those choices might have been made differently—and all the apparently random events of the world might have occurred differently—then we see there are as many "might-have-been" worlds as there were choices. Now, granted, many of those other worlds would be different in only trivial ways, but many others would be profoundly different, even unrecognizable to us.

When Once I Lived

Let us start with: "Events that were tragic and, we now see, might 'not have happened' but for some trivial cause." Here I list a few such events:
- In Dallas, JFK, at just the right moment, leans over to say something to Jackie.
- Lincoln's bodyguard is not absent from his post at Ford's Theater.
- John Lennon decides not to go out that night.
- Jimi Hendrix, having trouble getting to sleep, decides to go out for something to eat; he never takes the sleeping pill.
- James Earl Ray gets drunk, is arrested and spends the night in the Memphis City jail.
- Mozart does not die of the plague; he lives many more years.
- The ancient Library of Alexandria is not burned.
- An oil leak in the engine room of the Titanic forces it to reduce speed; it makes port in New York City one day late.
- The captain of the Exxon Valdez decides to have one more drink before the ship sails. He falls asleep in his cabin; the second in command takes the ship safely out to sea.

Here is what we might observe about this list. That "what has to be different" seems trifling and insignificant in comparison to the horrific event which would have been averted. We feel wistfully sad that, but for the non-occurrence of some slight and incidental event, a very great tragedy could have been avoided. So we naturally feel that our Heavenly Father, who first made and now sustains the world, might, without the slightest exertion, have caused those trivial actions to come about. And, too, that in His wisdom, He well knows what would have been the outcome of such tragedies being averted.

- Lincoln is not shot. What further acts of compassion and mercy might he have won for the former slaves?
- JFK is not shot. Would the U.S. have fought on for so long in Vietnam?
- Martin Luther King, Jr. is not shot. What wider and stronger bridges of understanding might he have built between the races?
- Jimi Hendrix does not die of an accidental overdose. What music might he have played?
- John Lennon is not shot. What might he have created?
- The Library of Alexandria does not burn. Does Europe still suffer the Dark Ages? Does it end sooner? What achievements are not lost to us?

I believe my guide will have these answers for me: Here the tragic events that we well know; there the world that would have been but for such tragedy.

I Resume My Journey

Here I must pause to deliver one of those grandfatherly reminiscences that have been the burden of children and grandchildren throughout history. Even without addressing what I might learn in the afterlife, I can share with you—if you will indulge me one moment—a lesson that has already been impressed upon me, merely from my having lived to my present age. That is, that as hard as you might work and however much you might believe that you are the author of your fate, I can tell you there is more, much more, that you owe to chance.

If you look at the great men and women of history, it seems self-evident—inevitable—that they would take up those roles history has assigned to them. But this is not so. Every great man was once 13 ... then 14 ... and then 15 years of age. And if you remember those years, was there anything that looked inevitable to you at that time?

Let us look back at the historical record where we might see some young man who (we think) was destined be a great painter. Yes, well, but we also see there were those who recognized his talent and who singled him out so that he might learn the disciplines of his art. Was there another young man who (we believe) was destined to be a great author? Yes, but observe that he received years of tutoring in Latin, Greek and history. Finally, you might name a young man who—all would agree—was destined to be a great leader. But once again we see he achieved this position only after coming into contact with others who, while he was still young, kindled in his heart the flame of ambition and a thirst for justice.

Every age has its special blindness. While still young, a man cannot see the limitations of his knowledge or experience. Every teenager knows more—in his own estimation—than the blind and foolish older generation. Then, in middle age, he looks over his accomplishments, and he thinks, "I did this." But once again, he does not stand upon a place sufficiently lofty. Let him age two more decades and he thinks, "How grateful I am that I was permitted to do so much." He stands in wonder at the generosity of his Maker that so many trivial events could have come together in so beneficial a manner that he could achieve so much in one lifetime.

There, now I have given the lecture. What, exactly, is the moral of this fable? It is this: Be humble. Be modest Do not be proud. The fate of even the greatest among us is driven by forces beyond our understanding or control.

CHAPTER 21
What Fools

An Unmerited Affront

Passing the time in my eternity, I chance to read, again, that play by the immortal Bard entitled *A Midsummer Night's Dream*. Thus coming to one of the scenes involving Puck (that mischievous woodland fairy), I read again that line which is so well-known among those who love this play. Puck says (after marveling at some folly by one of the human characters) "What fools these mortals be."

Now, I have heard this line before, and, taken in the context of the story (and not forgetting the dry humor which Shakespeare often displayed) I had previously found this comment amusing, apt and well-deserved (by we who often play Love's fool). But, on this occasion, for some unaccountable reason, I find this line infuriating—indeed dripping with some malevolent condescension. Feeling that my reaction is in some way unnatural, I go to my guide to obtain an explanation of this inexplicable result.

I first give him an account of the event, and then I wait for his explanation, which is not long coming. "I perceive," my guide says, "that you have developed an oversensitivity to criticism. If you have grown so thin of skin that some casual jest by a mere woodland fairy produces such a wound, then we need to find some exercise that will build up your resistance. Come, let us go and find that rude and upstart fairy, so you can have it out with him and get your just revenge."

Now, had I been anywhere else but in my afterlife I would have interpreted his words as humor, fantasy or metaphor, but having already observed my guide's unbounded power to go to any place or time or person in the universe, I well expect soon to be face-to-face with Puck himself. My guide takes me by the arm, and, gesturing with his other hand, we soon find ourselves present in some lovely wooded glen, all framed about with flowers, ivy vines and leafy branches.

Looking around that lush and fragrant woodland shelter, I prepare myself to confront my green-clad fairy antagonist. But there is no one there. I look to my guide, who whispers, "We must wait just a moment … She is coming, but we must be patient." I am sure my expression betrays my puzzlement that, though I expected I would be meeting Puck (a male), my guide now promises me to meet some female. But before I can speak, my questions are answered.

A soft and luminescent glow invades the clearing where we stand, and immediately I see coming toward me out of that light a tall and beautiful female, her figure (slim and womanly) draped in spotless white, her gaze fixed upon me with an expression of gentle amusement. She turns to my guide, who I see nods his head, not just in greeting, but deeply, as if to acknowledge some sovereign dignity of which she is possessed.

My guide speaks, "If it please Your Grace, I have brought this man … who has a grievance with one of your retainers who (although fictional) I know is well-beloved of you and ever dear to all your subjects. Thus, he demanded of me that I bring him here that he might revenge himself upon that one who slanders mortal men (himself among them).

Now, even were we not—plainly—standing (uninvited) in the presence of some undoubted Queen (of Time or Space or Nature, I know not which), I think that I (were I not already dead) must certainly expire of mortification, brought on by my own precipitous and ill-considered words. How could I have predicted that my guide, taking my words at their plainest and most unadorned aspect, would turn them against me, making them the source of my now unconcealable shame before this mighty Queen?

Turning to me, my guide (seeing the redness in my cheeks) speaks with gentle reassurance. "Do not be embarrassed. I have brought you here to meet someone who knows you well, though you do not know her. She is well-acquainted with you and all the events of your life. I only wanted (speaking as I have in front of her) to let her see how red your cheeks might be (and so, how thin your skin). You asked to confront Puck. But seeing that your grievance is with fairies—generally—I had no choice but to bring you to their Queen, that she (no doubt intending to apologize for the intemperate words uttered by her subject) might satisfy the honor of your mortal state.

I see that my two companions wait on my reply, but I am too over-awed and thunderstruck to speak. At last my own discomfort at my loss for words breaks the logjam in my mind, and I hasten to explain—and justify—myself.

"You see," I finally choke out, "of course ... I know the words spoken by your subject—Puck—are all too true. Many have observed that, in the grip of love or lust or even mere infatuation, we humans do the greater part of all our logic, wit and reason then mislay. And well it might be noted (even by a creature as bereft of culture as a woodland fairy) that humans do from time-to-time, when acting out some great romantic part, wear the costume of the "Fool."

"But, if it please Your Majesty, and with all my deepest reverence to your exalted eminence, I have, still, one grievance which troubles me. Trusting in your sympathetic wisdom, I ask your leave, now, to explain to you my honest and sincere complaint." Having previously cast down my eyes before her, I now glance up from by bowed head to see her reply. Smiling with a gentle grace, she replies, "Yes, please, tell me. It will do me good to hear and you to tell."

I begin. "Your Majesty, for the moment setting aside your subject's comment (as it might relate to "Love") there yet remains the matter of his words as if applied to humans in their common, un-romantic state. If I take his words at face value, he slanders us, derides our greatest efforts, and demeans himself (that by his words so little charity bestows).

I hasten to complete my thought. "You are, I have no doubt, well-acquainted with the state of mortals. Our lives are all too brief, and by such time that we have gained some meager store of learning, tact and skill, we are cast out into the world to make our fortune (which, in all too many cases, hardly justifies that word suggesting "wealth"). Instead we labor many decades (with some small rewards along the way), till stealing on us in our unawares, we find our end delivers not reward nor fame nor honor, but no more than that one soundest sleep which does this waking dream enshroud.

"Thus I feel, Your Majesty, that calling men and women 'fools' who to such destiny are bound is hurtful, low and out of touch with what our Maker asks of us."

The Fairy Queen Replies
There is silence, as it seems each of us hesitates to break the spell of what (I hope) this story of those burdens which we humans bear must sure have cast. But I see, to my surprise, that far from reacting with sympathy to my complaint, the Queen only collects herself to (with added energy) rejoin the fray.

"I see," she begins (exhibiting, I perceive, a certain, ill-defined coldness). "You feel that humans are deservingly entitled to our pity, pardon and solicitude." She pauses a moment in silent thought, then continues, "Since I do not expect that you yet understand my position—or that of my subjects in this, the Fairy Realm—let me tell you of the world of fairies. It is, after all, the role assigned to us in that great play of which our Maker casts the parts." Looking around us, she spies some large flat rocks half-sunken in the ground, and turning to them, we soon find ourselves seated in a pleasant, shady circle, of which the Queen occupies the highest and most honored stone (my guide and I assembled on the ground).

"It is," she says, "the universal opinion of your species [as it would be of all your brother species (who live on land or sea or sky) and of your sister species (who occupy dimensions small as they might be)] that all the 'substance' of the world [excepting only (briefly) living flesh] is dead-to-all—that basest, lifeless matter which our Maker gave the name of 'clay.' You know yourselves to be but frail, imperfect transients (who, thrust out on this Earthly stage without your lines, you struggle all to improvise) and having suffered, now, that universal "Fall," you wander nameless, numberless and naked through that world of lifeless dross.

"We have also seen that humans (having, among all living creatures, the keenest instinct for turning the adversities of life to their own advantage) have come to understand and put to use those many vital forms of energy that move your world. These natural energies (measurable by your science) you see impel the world this way and that according to some undisclosed and slow-unfolding script of our exalted Playwright.

"That then ... the world you know, but not our world. Nor is our Fairy World a world unknown to you (among some certain mortals, living in the ancient past).

"I know that you have heard it said of old that 'Fairies bring the dew.' And 'Fairies put the frost upon the pumpkin.' And even, 'Fairies paint the colors of the autumn leaves.' And so you think these things are merest legend, having in them more of poetry than fact. But legend has this truth to tell: You mortals live within a world both purposeless and dead; we fairies live within a world transparent to His every Wish, which having in it only what His Will desires.

"Here in this Fairy World, you will find no empty, unliving stones or soil or earth, but only His abiding fairy-essence, showing that perfection which it gains by compound of His Will and Wish with fairy-made quiescence (that of such fairy-stuff, each particle is but the handiwork of its upholding fairy). You see, there is a fairy who, by all his effort, gives to 'water' all its 'wet.' And then another, who by going to those places where bright sunlight does not reach, does pitch his tent of cool and dark (to which we give the name of 'shade'). And yet another, whose employment is to make the stones upon the shore wear down (which in your mortal world you credit to the waves and tide), and later (noting that the moon has turned its back) he does but dry that wetness from those very stones and paints upon their surface all the heat of summer's sun.

"In the Fairy World," she continues, "all that you observe with your senses is alive, continuously expressive of the unceasing efforts of uncountable living souls, all of them my subjects and each of them obedient to our one eternal Majesty. You mortals exist as (briefly) living outcasts in a dead and wasting world; we fairies exist (our kind eternal, though we also age and pass away) within a world we feel in all its parts alive, and having each of us our task (eternal), we do but trust that in this Fairy World we serve that greater King.

"So you see," she explains (as if lecturing a child), "we fairies labor ceaselessly, and though it has pleased our Maker to give us inexhaustible energy, long life and bodies constructed (as we naught but suppose) of His very Wish (no doubt the source of all those stories where your kind imagines that, if only you might seize and hold some one of us, you might then get three wishes in return), yet still, you must admit, we labor thanklessly (were we to look to mortals for any gratitude or praise).

"Let me remind you, as well," she continues (her voice rising in exasperation), "that however impoverished and destitute you might imagine your fate to be, still you must acknowledge that from time-to-time throughout history, in many different words and forms and styles, our Heavenly Father has spoken to you, giving to you not just the wisdom and righteousness of His words but also (merely by His having taken notice of your state, and caring to address you where you stood) confirmation that there must exist within His heart some place for all your suffering. You mortals are the undoubted beneficiaries of His special intervention, being comforted even today by those same religious truths which, over the course of your history, He has from time-to-time taught you.

"Only compare your state to that of the fairies! (Her voice betrays the edge of tears.) We trust that in some way we serve His perfect Will, but still we have from Him (as yet) no words or laws ... no precepts or commandments. We live out all our lives encumbered with this solitary lack: That still (despite the countless years our kind has known) He never has of fairy-kind be-sired a Son to share with us our pain (nor yet to take away the sadness of our faults). Speaking, now, as one who wishes you no ill, do you not recognize that you, a mortal, have what any fairy might (with justice) be entitled to describe a privileged, even enviable, position among all the souls of His entire creation?

Had I at this instant the presence of mind to stop and sum up where I'd come in this, my Fairy Audience, I would have said: That from my initial standpoint of awkwardness, uncertainty and peril, I (when then my face was only red) had brought me through that fiery tribulation (with now a face all-drained of color, palest as a corpse) to full disaster, panic and defeat! Having brought my cup of petulance and whine into the presence of this Queen, I find she drinks it down (complete) then pours upon my head that cloudburst of her outrage, indignation, lecture and rebuke! (I pause to make this note to self: "Never argue with a Queen.")

My Grievance Forsaken
I begin looking about the glade for some convenient and ready opportunity to effect my retreat, but the Queen (seeming at last to have herded me into that inescapable trap which she had set for me from the first) undertakes a transformation which (at once) reveals to me: "Indeed, this is a Queen." Now looking at me with inexpressible pity, and smiling but a smile that promises perfect understanding, again she speaks.

"I will show you, now, the reason my subject spoke as he did. There is no mystery about it, and as you will soon see, more sadness in it than envy or spite." She pauses for some moments, and I cannot be sure if she is saying a silent prayer or merely collecting her thoughts. Then I notice emanating from the woods behind the Queen a lovely glow of color lighting up the surrounding trees. Presently the glow resolves itself into the figures of three youthful, fair and luminescent fairies, each rounded about with a soft, receiving light that baths her features in this warming sight.

The three fairies come close to us and, in silent obedience to their Queen, together take up seats there at her feet. The Queen continues, "I have brought here three of my subjects so that they might tell you their stories." At this, the fairy nearest to the Queen stands up and, motioning a little way off, shows us a series of scenes as she tells her story.

"My name," she says, "if I were to pronounce it out in fairy-speech, you could not grasp. So rather, let me tell you what it means: My name is 'Fairy of Those Tears of Lack.' And this my duty, which every day I do: I find some man or woman who some great advantage lacks or which some manly talent … skill … accomplishment, he does not have, or of this woman, all the beauty, grace and shapeliness she knows will not be hers.

Then she shows us this scene: Herself (this first fairy), invisible to a young woman seated before her dressing mirror. We see this woman (now in crisis of despair) berate herself, that still in spite of all her arts, her face remains as plain and featureless as ever woman knew, and, grieving for that beauty which she knows she lacks (and this eternal lack her certain fate), she brings her face up to the mirror. Now, this fairy, doing her (invisible) duty, we see reach out with gentle hand and, bringing her finger up beside that modest cheek, draws out from this young woman's eyes her Tears of Lack (that she no earthly beauty will enjoy).

But this is not all. This fairy, insensible to the image reflected in the dressing mirror (which copies but an earthy, mortal beauty), takes out her fairy mirror (as if to help her see the rest and any other tear the girl had shed). She holds her fairy mirror up before the secret heart of this young girl, and marveling, she shows us all a beauty which my mortal eyes see not: A gentleness of touch. A spirit innocent and sweet. And binding all together in one perfect gift … a love both pure and grateful, living in a healing heart.

Having finished her story, the first fairy returns to her seat at the foot of her Queen. Presently, the second fairy stands up. She is no less graceful and welcoming than the first, as she takes her place in the clearing before us.

"My name," she says, "is 'Fairy of Those Tears of Loss.' I am, if I may say so (she murmurs, nodding obeisance to her Queen) very busy indeed." She motions before her, and immediately we observe another scene. We are present in a hospital room (actually, a room in what we would properly call a 'hospice,' where of its occupant recovery is not expected). In the bed is an older woman, of seasoned years, but not in any sense elderly or frail, and by her side, clutching her hand in his, is her spouse of many years. Stricken with some invariably fatal disease, her spirit retains but the weakest connection to this husk upon which her eternal spirit fed. On her face is the faintest shadow of a smile, of which her husband knows its brightest glow.

Next we see this fairy, with quickness and a practiced gesture, reach out her hand beside this husband's face and so draw out (with patience) all his Tears of Loss (that from this moment, all her love he knows will be from him forever gone). Now if at this point the fairy had departed this scene, I might have found another moral, but instead she shows this more: Taking out her mirror, as if to allow the husband to be sure no stain of tears remains, we see instead this fairy mirror reflect these images his eyes had seen.

His wife when she was young and fair, and of the struggles which they had (of joining two performers in one harmony, in unison to balance life's afflictions with relief). They shared these things between them, sometimes being then a burden (of which she took one end, he took the other—heavy—end). And other times—of joy—they shared. She found them first, then made them wait until his slower wit could catch them up. A life together, adding joy to dread and mirth to sorrow, but not his life alone, nor hers, but only this: a partnership of life's duration, he taking ownership of all their cares, she giving birth to all the joy that two can share.

This Fairy of Those Tears of Loss returns to her place, and my guide and I silently await the story which the third fairy must tell. The Queen, however, turns to the first and second fairies, who have already spoken, and says, "You may leave us now." Then, a greater shock. She motions to my guide and says, "You, too, may go. What next I have to show is for his eyes, alone." Expecting some objection from my guide, I turn to him, but see he bows his head in obedience to the Queen and makes ready to go. "I will rejoin you when you are free," he says to me, then takes his leave.

The Queen grants me a moment to accommodate myself to our more intimate group then speaks to the third fairy, "You may begin." The remaining fairy, as meek and fair as the first two, now stands up before me and speaks. "I have several names. One of them is 'Fairy of Those Tears That Signify a Broken Heart.' The place where I will take you is one familiar to you, though never seen by you in quite this way." She motions to some place before her, and presently we see what she can see.

It is a bedroom (in the dark of night) though we with fairy eyes can see the scene. There is a figure (female) in the bed, the covers pulled up to her face, so that nothing will expose her shame. I have a feeling … sensing some familiar sounds or shape or shades … and then with shock of recognition, I see this place for what it is: The bedroom of our house! When Molly and I still lived there! And there beneath those covers, softly sobbing is my wife.

All of us invisible to the person in the bed, the fairy speaks to me, "You see this room is dark, which in some earlier time, at this hour of the night, would have been bright with conversation, news and loving jests. You see her curled up round your pillow, which at that time she would have rather cuddled close and found your shoulder, there to rest her head. You hear those sobs that rack her dreams (or would, if ever she could sleep, or find within her grief and loss some respite from her broken heart). Now last, the fairy says, you see that in this place of loneliness and hurt, the thing she mourns (of lost) is that Unbroken Vow of which she trusted, keeping faith, and Never Letting Go; it was the rock on which her love did often shelter, from this lonely dark.

The fairy whispers to me, "Of all my names, there is also this, of which perhaps I am better known. It is, 'Fairy of Those Tears that Faithlessness Despairs.'" Then I see her reach out her hand, and bringing her fingers up to my sweetheart's cheek, she draws out (skillfully, betraying, thereby, how all too common is this task) a host of bitter tears that streak my darling's face. Now taking out her fairy-mirror, the third fairy makes ready to show us the source of my sweetheart's misery. But suddenly, before she can call up that scene which would explain all, the Queen speaks up.

"No, that's enough," she says. "There is no need show any more." Then I see this Queen (of all-unrivaled majesty, eternal, good and true) reach out her hand to that of her fairy-servant, and, with skillful motion, efficiency and grace, gather up those very tears my sweetheart shed; then reaching out again she finds my face, and placing those tears upon my reddened cheek, at once I feel those tears confounded with my own.

The Queen looks into my eyes, expressing with her gaze both compassion and a sure promise of the possibility of redemption, and says to me, "Tell me, now, what truth do you confess? What verdict would you render in this fairy court? That judges mortal men according to that weight of Tears, which giving substance to those faults of which our hearts despair, it measures out in judgment all our passions, flaws, deceptions and regrets?

Tasting, still, my sweetheart's bitter tears—and mine—upon my cheek, I bow before the Queen, and this reply, "What fools we mortals be."

CHAPTER 22
Shall We Gather?

Passing the time one day in conversation with my guide, it occurred to me that there was one lesson—touching on religion—that I had not yet learned. I asked my guide, "What about atheists? What happens to them when they die? Do they come here to this place in the afterlife? Or—not believing in God—are they denied eternal life? Can you tell me?"

A broad smile crossed my guide's face, "No, no, they are not denied eternal life. As you ought to know by now (my guide gently reproaches me) the one essential purpose of this afterlife is that those dwelling here are provided experiences by which they might be uplifted in spirit. Our most gracious Maker has plans for us—plans too important to be frustrated by some trivial, childish error such as atheism." He was then silent, so I pressed the point. "Alright, fine. They, too, enjoy eternal life, but is their experience here the same as mine? Certainly there must be some accommodation made for such a strong (and obviously erroneous) belief?"

My guide once more smiled, "Yes, there is a special arrangement made for atheists, which you might learn something by seeing. Let us go. I will show you." He motioned a little way off, and immediately we were on a hillside looking out over a pleasant, green and cozy valley. We could see a goodly number of modest homes, clustered around a village square. A small river flowed through a park adjacent to the center of town. Near us was a worn and narrow path leading down the hill toward the square. We started down the path, and as we walked, my guide explained.

"We call this place 'The Village.' Whenever any man or woman who is an atheist dies, that person comes here. And there are other 'Villages,' so if one location threatens to become too large, another Village is established. Always the intent is the same: That here, these men and women are provided a quiet, restful place of meditation, free of any obligations or interference." Then I asked him, "Are there any special rules for this place? What about those privileges which I have enjoyed—reliving some pivotal events from my life or from the great pageant of history? And are they prisoners here? What if they want to leave?"

"You are getting ahead of me," my guide replied. "Yes, you have guessed one of the 'rules' of the Village. No one can leave—although, actually, the way I would express it is, that no one here knows of any other place than this village. As far as they know, this is the whole and complete afterlife. So no one tries to leave, and no one comes to visit." He stopped. "So let me set the stage. When an atheist dies, that person comes here. The residents here have no guides, and they have no access to (or awareness of) the universal archive of human history. They reside here without any demands being made upon them (as, for example, having to labor to produce what they need) and (with those few exceptions I will explain in a moment) every need or want they have is provided." We were just about to reach the first dwellings, so my guide said, "Let me reassure you. Our presence here will not in any way disturb the people living here. So you need not fear intruding."

He continued, "Now you and I know that in the afterlife, we dwell within a world of spirit, having no longer any flesh or blood or bone by which we feel ourselves alive. Here, however, the people have no perception of the world of spirit. All the evidence of their senses tells them that there is nothing here but material things subject (as they were in life) to those common, natural scientific processes of chemistry and physics and biology. In short, there is nothing 'spiritual' here. Likewise, you will not find any books of Scripture (of any religion) nor any sacred art or music. No place of worship. No objects of religious devotion, nor any provision in any other way (as by, let us say, any prohibition of eating pork) supporting or encouraging any religious observance.

"If we search every home, and every library and bookstore here," my guide said, "we will find no books, music or art recognizing or perpetuating religion, or any other spiritual devotion."

"So that includes ... ," I started to say. "Yes," my guide replied, "no Shakespeare, no Dickens, no Tolstoy, no 'Requiem' by Mozart, no 'Messiah' by Handel, no 'Amazing Grace,' no 'Let It Be,' and of the great monuments to faith, no St. Paul's, no Hagia Sophia and no Cathedral of Chartres. And just so we are clear, this extends even to religions which the people in this village would know only from their history lessons: that is, no *Iliad*, no *Odyssey* and no *Aeneid*. And of the great cities of the ancient world, if we look in books here, we will see nothing telling us of such ancient sanctuaries as … Stonehenge, the Temple of Amun-Ra at Karnak, or the Osirion at Abydos (indeed, nothing concerning Memphis or Dendera or Giza or Thebes … why, practically nothing about Egypt … and of Jerusalem, nothing at all!)

"How could such a place as this exist?!" I cried. "Wait, wait" my guide implored. "There is one more important feature. Also not to be found here are any forms of religious observance … such as … " I interrupted (finishing his sentence)… "Christmas, Easter, Passover, Hanukkah, Ramadan (what else?) … Buddha's birthday."

"Yes," my guide continued, "and also no Sabbath, no Lent, no Mass, no Daily Prayers, no Hallows' Eve, no Yom Kippur."

I was speechless. I could not reply nor think of any further questions to ask. Trying to take in all that my guide had shown me, I wandered silently up and down the streets of that little village, looking in this home or that, pausing to admire some display in the window of a well-kept shop, and struggling to make sense of what I saw.

My guide walked with me, watching me as much as I observed the passing scene. In time I saw that it was a sort of refuge, where men of science might give full scope to all the reason, logic and proof on which their souls depended. Having made no place here for their Maker, nor any words which He might share, nor any celebration of His works, or Him, or of His mercy, this Village was, indeed, a perfect and eternal "Heaven" (for those without a God).

Then something struck me funny, and I started laughing. My guide looked at me with a perplexed expression, waiting for me to share the joke with him. At length I did. "It just occurred to me why you need a place like this. Now if a man, during his lifetime, does not believe in UFOs, or Bigfoot, or the Loch Ness Monster … and then he dies and he comes here (to the afterlife), and he learns: Surprise! That outer space is thick with alien spacecraft. That the deep forests of the earth are overrun with smelly, 8-foot tall, hairy primates with over-sized feet. That Loch Ness is a favorite summer spawning ground for some large (but shy) form of plesiosaur. Why, that man might easily reply, 'Well, I guess that's one on me. Who would have guessed it?' And then he goes about his business, feeling no shame or embarrassment at having been so very, very wrong."

"But if the man we are discussing is an atheist, then what it is he disbelieves is this: The Lord God Eternal. That Great King Above All Gods. The

Lord of Hosts. The All. The One. He Whose Name We May Not Speak. Then this same man, an unbeliever, passes away and comes to the afterlife, and arriving here (feeling, no doubt, lonely, lost and abandoned) the very first thing he learns is that he has been wrong—as wrong as anyone could be—not about some trivial matter, but about The All-Seeing, All-Knowing, Eternally Existing, Sole Architect and Creator of the Universe! Why, we would expect that he feels ... not just wrong, but negligent, at the very least.

"Are you one of those who has had that common dream where you arrive at a fancy dinner party, and you see there are many other guests in attendance, and every one of them is dressed in formal and fashionable attire, and then you look down and see that you are not wearing pants! (Or, if a woman, that you suffer some other humiliating nakedness!). We all know that feeling, but can we imagine how much more humiliated we would feel if we were so spectacularly, conspicuously, preposterously and cataclysmically wrong!"

My guide smiled, appreciating the point I found so humorous. "Next," he said, "we need to spend a little more time observing the people and events in this Village so that you can see the wisdom of its design."

His Gifts

As my guide suggested, I allowed myself more time to witness the passing scene in this, the Village. I saw the routine habits of the day: First breakfast, then the chores to do, and time spent chatting with a neighbor. Next walk the dog, take out the trash, then get the groceries, home by lunch. Then take a nap, bring in the mail, the grass to cut, then cat to feed. When dinner's done, the day allows some time to join with others hearing, now, a stimulating speech or artistic performance. More social time, then come back home, at last to bed (put out the cat).

Speaking as a believer, I wish I could say that this little village harbored some hidden depravity or fell inescapably into chaos or disorder. But this I found was not the case. Perhaps it was that these atheists, being in the main devotees of science, logic and reason, their baser appetites were, if not absent, at least so weakened that a mutual acceptance and tolerance prevailed. I heard music. There were some creating art or telling stories, and from time to time a play produced (but not the Bard).

Despite how hard I looked to see some secret evil, base corruption or pitiless self-centeredness, I saw none. I had to recognize that (but for that one error and omission of which we have already taken notice) these people ... these disbelievers ... were happy, loving, tolerant and good.

Shall We Gather?

My guide and I were standing in the Village square outside the coffee shop. In (not quite) anger and exasperation, I asked my guide, "How can this be? These people—failing to admit the existence of our most loving Maker (and practicing none of His earthly religions)—nevertheless live a life compassionate and just? How can this be? That mocks His loving Word?" My guide suggested we go into the coffee shop, where we soon found a table. I could see he had much to tell me.

"There are three lessons I want you to learn here in the Village," my guide began. "Let me explain the first. You have correctly observed that a belief in God—or the practice of a religion—is not a necessary condition to living a moral life. You see, here, that these people entertain no love of God, nor any piety nor humility before His works, and yet still they love one another and (generally) do good. But this observation is only a pale reflection of a still greater truth which knows no boundaries. Which is this: That while you and I might see in all things the evidence of God's divine hand (who made this earth and seas and sky) yet all these things remain a gift.

"And by 'gift' I mean a thing which He did freely give, no obligation or necessity involved. If by any means of science, logic or reason we wished to show that some one fact or circumstance of this world, or nature, or mankind (that was His gift) just 'had to be' to make some formula complete, or balance out equations to be true, we see this theory proven wrong. Omitting to incorporate in our science any factor specifying His intentional intervention in the world, we see that formulas nevertheless compute—equations balance. Would we, honestly (as believers), find this fact objectionable? Would we prefer the universe was such a place that no common formula of physics or chemistry might find its true balance, except by intervention of Divine Decree? We say our God is Great, but do we thereby wish to imply that He (jealous of any other cause) is likewise Petty? I think not. This life, the world and all you see is all a 'gift'—this truth will not by formula be proved."

My guide continued. "That was the first lesson I wanted you to learn. Now I will explain the second. This is a lesson not about unbelievers but about our Maker, and how patient is His love for us. Observe. Here we are in the afterlife, a place of spirit, where all we see is by His generous will sustained. Yet we see before us a place (the Village) specially given over to those who actively—even violently—disbelieve (and curse) His name. Not that these atheists find anything lacking in His grandeur (other than—in their opinion—that there is no object to which such Eternal Glory might be attached). We see the residents here would (and do) find much to criticize and fault in

His religions (and the many who count themselves believers—as might we all), as if imperfection in religion were some sort of proof of the imperfection of His will or Word or promise (and imperfection being proof He is not Great).

"In fact, as you will come to observe, if you witness the events in this place for a sufficient period, the people here (whatever else we might say of them) do have the integrity and honesty of their non-belief. That is, if while pursuing their studies here they were to come upon some factual or logical proof of the existence of their Maker (which we have already seen will not be found), we would (notwithstanding the other shortcomings we see in them) expect that they would have the courage to give up their unbelief and find a place in all their knowledge for this proof of He who stokes the furnace of the sun. But finding no such tell-tale sign, they miss the greater undivided truth, which is their (temporary) error, but not yet any fault or imperfection in their soul.

"So, despite their continuing stubborn refusal to acknowledge Him or any of His gifts, despite their unrelenting criticism of Him (and all his works) and despite their inability to recognize any proof of Him, or of His love, yet, still, He makes for these people here a kind of paradise, where any evidence of love of God, or God, or of religion, is uniformly excluded (that the people here do not thereby feel discomfort, guilt or shame, to lack in Love for Him). And, furthermore, as you so well pointed out before, this Village, by itself, shields all these men and women from that great truth (which might this painful fact reveal to them) that God exists."

Suddenly an idea occurred to me which I could not help but share with my guide. "I just realized something. Now I understand! Let me explain. When I lived, I had two children. Each of them was as normal a child as any, and my wife and I were privileged to raise both of them from infancy through to adulthood. Now each of them, when they reached a certain age (one of the early teenage years), underwent a sort of mortal transformation which, at the time, I would have been justified to ascribe to Satan, but which, in this afterlife, I clearly see was due to hormones. A child who, before, would pause and listen and answer, now a teenager, would (at best) but sneer and scorn and argue. All that I knew (and might have told them) about life and work and society was instantly transformed into basest falsehood, gross mistake and petty interference. Going out in public, then, with them, my mere existence became a thing repulsive, awkward and abhorrent. This was the case for several years until (by hormones' moderation) my children found in me a person whom they might tolerate and humor"

Now, having made my point, I said, "So! You see! I never stopped loving my children, even when—due to circumstances—they ignored me, rejected everything I said, and elevated their own (uninformed) opinions above the truths I might have shared with them. My love for them was so great that I put aside my temporary feelings of being misused in favor of the greater good. So I went on loving and supporting and caring for them, even when my love for them was neither acknowledged nor returned.

"So now I see our Maker's plan! He, in all His patient wisdom, gives these people here a place where they might see their error play out to its inevitable conclusion. He is patient, indeed, and of His tolerance, no end."

My guide once again smiled, "That's right. I forgot you once had teenagers. Nothing teaches the value of patience, forbearance and humility like raising teenagers." He paused to take a sip of coffee, then continued: "I said before that I would explain the third important lesson which this Village teaches, except that now what I think is … I would rather just let you continue to watch the people and events of this small village, and in time I have no doubt you will see the final point demonstrated." Being more than satisfied with this promise, I thanked my guide, and we left the coffee shop.

Thereupon returning to my previous watchfulness, I spent a considerable period of time observing events in the lives of those residing in the Village. Now that the story has played itself out, I will give you a more complete picture of those people and events and what I learned.

The Impious
Returning to the Village some time later, I crossed over the little bridge spanning that peaceful river near the center of town. I walked to the village square and was immediately reminded of one of the distinguishing characteristics of this gathering of atheists. Here I saw that almost every little lane or byway had some shop offering a place to sit and talk and pass the time. For example, on one corner of the square was the coffee shop where my guide and I had conversed earlier. There was a sign over the door with an image of a caribou (proud and strong) and inside, as with numerous other similar places in the Village, were residents—cheerful, animated and happy—sharing stories, jokes and good-natured gossip (all alike intoxicated by coffee-scented clouds and mists and vapors).

There being no mass media or other empty distractions here, there was that much more time for genuine human conversation and debate. I saw that—these people all sharing one common point of view—there was a natural tendency for them to return again and again in their discussions to the subject of their non-belief. And, there being a wide divergence in the natural talents, abilities and preferences of these people, it soon happened that the whole population divided itself into several more-or-less distinct groups of disbelievers, sorted by their aptitude, interest or enthusiasm for all those things they disbelieved.

Then, in time, I saw that one such group (which was the most vocal in its disbelief) began to find fault with those several other groups who were more inclined to be lazy, passive, casual and weak. Seeing in those other groups (which, in their view, displayed insufficient ardor) a source of weakness or, more worrisome, insincerity or even backsliding, that stronger group (which I will call the "Impious") decided that this fact revealed a "crisis of disbelief." Then, these Impious—feeling that the wisdom, truth and future of their faithlessness was at risk—decided they would meet (in secret) to decide what action they might take to ensure the purity of this, their common, vital purpose.

Gathering together to discuss this threat to their most cherished non-beliefs, the Impious first made an attempt to identify some of the imperfections and inadequacies to which those weaker residents might fall victim. Were there not some among them who, in life, had suffered the loss of a loved one, but even here, in this place of respite, could not be accommodated to their loss? Were there not some who, feeling the shame and guilt of wrongdoing (which in this place of reason, truth and fact, they had freely and honestly admitted) but who, despite the burning flame of their confession, could not be cleansed, nor could they feel forgiven? And were there not some who, having spent a lifetime (and now some greater period here) in ceaseless study of all the lush and bounteous fruits of the material world, now found even that plenty but a thin gruel upon which to sustain a soul immortal and alive?

Taking note of these all-to-human weaknesses among their fellow residents, the Impious first gave this matter much (unprayerful) meditation. Then, at length finding within themselves some new and more powerful enthusiasm for the truth and purity of their non-belief, they concluded that those (weakest) among them might yet be nourished and sustained if only they could have available for study and devotion some one Edition (flawless and entire) of one Compendium of Truth (in words and formulae of faultless irreligion) which they (these most unfaithful) would undertake to write (no help from Him).

Giving to the creation of this document a considerable period of effort, the authors at last completed their task and, after taking one last opportunity to read over and approve its contents, were pleased to see that they had

Shall We Gather?

succeeded in gathering into this one volume a lengthy collection of acceptable opinion, instructive lessons, ancient stories of virtue and accomplishment (in which, you may be sure, He played no part) and many poetic hymns expressing profoundest disinterest in Him (or of His words). All this material they bound together and (for want of any other name) called it their "Book of Truth."

Then, wishing to avoid any misunderstanding or mistake, they likewise produced a list of ten "Articles of Unbelief" which (in their opinion) any man or woman living in the Village must agree (or by refusing, name himself a heretic most vile). This group, then, feeling themselves humbled by what they had accomplished (and unshakeable in their ingratitude to Him) finally agreed upon the contents of these two documents.

Now taking these two writings to every social gathering in the Village, the authors again and again insisted on the importance of the whole population swearing their loyalty to the Articles of Unbelief and likewise studying, learning and daily-applying the lessons of the Book. Not tolerating any opposition or disregard, the authors pressed to have these writings form the core, the essence, of all their social interactions.

The Book of Truth

(For those who are so inclined, I have included in this section a more detailed description of the contents of the Book, so that any person being yet unsatisfied with my previous explanations might appreciate what there was in that compilation that gave comfort and support to the residents of the Village.)

Shall we eavesdrop on these Impious authors as they labor to put into words all the truth they know? Shall we, accustomed to words of piety and grace, and stories of unquenchable faith, find anything of value in these endless, morbid pages (having in them not a hint of that Eternal Life to come)? You will be shocked to hear this, but however little I found in its pages that would be of consolation to any man or woman of flesh and blood, nevertheless I did find evidence that the Book possessed some unearthly, otherworldly, dark and hidden power (as if it were a book of magic, alchemy or spells).

I turned from page to page and saw there evidence of miracles (!) yet not divine. Where in our Scriptures we might see a thing impossible ... yet be! Here in this Book of Truth I see the same! Some words, or fact, or circumstance that no one knows, can say, or by the deepest prophesy foretell ... here in the Book we see ... the Authors know! Proclaim! And by some greater wisdom of the world ... Predict (unfailingly)!

Here is but one example: The Authors, addressing the source or origin of life on Earth, declare (without the slightest hint of doubt) that that (or those) first creatures calling Earth their home arose by act of random chance, bestirring in some goop or goo that spark of life (of which the poets sing). And this—conclusively—the Authors know! Which by itself would be accomplishment enough, but there is more.

The Authors, despite that they cannot specify the process by which life arose nor give the year (within ten million years of its true date) nor tell the history by which this one (or several) creatures changed and grew and came to occupy the seas and land and sky, yet still the Authors know (!) that all this came to pass without His help or by His plan or purpose!

You will recall, once again, that in life I was a lawyer, and, as such, I was exceedingly sensitive to the problem (which presented itself from time to time, in one case or another) of having to "prove a negative" in order to win a case. I cannot tell you with what care and trepidation I approached such issues. Why, even the most experienced lawyer will not attempt such a thing unless there is no other choice, and especially if this issue arises in a case or trial where there is much at stake. So believe me, I stand in awe of any equally rational and competent professionals (such as these Authors) who, despite having to "prove a negative" (in this case: His non-assistance, non-involvement and non-interference in the world) nevertheless maintain an attitude of Perfect, Unambiguous and Absolute Certainty of His profound detachment and indifference.

Along this same line, let me give you an example of one of the miracles which these Authors work within the page of the Book. This miracle, I think, is one of their greatest achievements. I begin the description at a most unusual place. This occurred back when the Soviet Union still existed; when Nikita Khrushchev was its ruler. At the time, the USSR had sent a capsule into orbit around the Earth. Upon its return, in answer to some question asked of Khrushchev, he answered that, having spoken to the cosmonaut, he learned that this earthly spaceman—while visiting the realm of that "so-called Heaven"—had seen no evidence of any elderly man in a long white gown with white hair and white beard. Accordingly, he said, he felt they had all the proof they needed of the non-existence of the Almighty.

I am sure that even the Impious would laugh at such a story, and even they would feel a sense of condescension for such childish literal-mindedness. I would never suggest that the authors of the Book were guilty of any similar form of immaturity or lack of imagination. Nevertheless, there is at work here a rule or theorem of logic which is directly at issue and which, by its contravention, shows that dark and secret power which the Book contains.

So, going back to our story, we need to ask: What was that rule or formula of logic which the exalted General Secretary of the Communist Party so conspicuously violated? Why, just this: That lack of evidence (of some one thing) is not proof of the non-existence (of that thing). That pious cosmonaut (in secret a believer) came home a sadder man that he no Father God could see or touch or worship. Or so we might conclude, if we thought him unskilled in logic (which, of course, we don't).

But do not lose the thread. The authors of the Book were well-acquainted with this simple rule of logic. They do apply it when the formula requires. So keeping that in mind, I will tell you, now, the miracle which we find published, celebrated and established in the Book (which by its cryptic, supernatural power, we will not find in any archive of His word).

Where we and others, having conducted countless scientific experiments, and applying (as we must) that rule of logic we have just identified, might conclude only that we have not (as yet) found incontrovertible evidence of His divine hand, these miracle-workers (the Authors) see a greater truth. Which is: That solely in the case of God … that lack of evidence (of Him) is evidence He cannot be!

And so they look for God today … not finding Him, He cannot be. They master chemistry and math … They dig up fossils, measure out the stars … They bridge great rivers, cure disease … and everywhere and always (though they say they look) … not finding Him, He cannot be.

They make of all those things "Unknown" a single formula of math, which they at length do balance out in final form to read the answer (sure and true), and then they say … not finding Him, He cannot be.

Behold! This perfect Gospel of the Irreligious! Transcript of Un-Sacred Truth! Page after page of miracles! Of elucidations, refutations and pronouncements, unconstrained by any bonds of reason, common sense or logic.

Answers! Which 'till now no man could justify—here, within the Book, we see receive the mantel of Unquestioned Truth!

Opinions! (unsupported) touching on eternal questions which no hand has yet the final chapter written—here, within the Book, become Eternal Verities!

Facts! (most stubborn creatures) which in any other place the iron law of truth respect—here, within the Book, they bend themselves (miraculous) to do or say or be whatever point the Authors wish to make!

At last I perceive: This Book proclaims those things which, even in that one eternal record of the world (of all those things which are, or were, or by His wisdom may yet be), we will not find, nor read, nor see. For in this Book we see collected, written out, preserved … those things which cannot be … could not have been … and notwithstanding all the power of random chance (by which, the Authors say, the gears and levers of this world are made to turn) … shall never in the future come to pass.

Shall We Gather?
I thought at this point it would be helpful to go away from the Village for some period of time, thereby allowing the residents some interval free from observation during which they might reach a general consensus as to how the Book and Articles should be incorporated into the habits of their daily lives. Giving them this opportunity, I went away, only returning some months later when the time seemed right.

Again coming to the Village square, I see several changes have been made. First, in the center of the square (where before had been found a band shell for concerts in the summertime) now stands an imposing, larger-than-life statue. It is a horse, rearing back in energetic power, as if he trampled underfoot his foes, and on his back, a man in military garb, his scowl befitting all the anger which his cause bestirs. His gaze fixed upon the horizon, we imagine that he witnesses his enemies' retreat (as from the armies of unrighteousness, which he—General of the unGodly—commands). This great statue stands upon an imposing pedestal, on the side of which we see are engraved the words "Defender of the Unfaith" and below that, "Charles Darwin."

Feeling a bit bemused by the liberties which the sculptor has taken with his subject (but, after all, this is "art" not journalism), I decide to take a stroll around the square. At first, all seems unchanged. Then I notice: Many of the coffee shops and stores where the residents had previously gathered to sip coffee, argue and converse are now closed. Only one or two remain. I see that many of those shops have been replaced by businesses operated by members of the Impious. For example, a coffee shop has been converted to a bookstore, and, looking in the window, I see (in place of tables and chairs) shelf after shelf of copies of the Book and, on a table in between, stacks and stacks of copies of the Articles. Looking further, I see in that section given over to "New Releases" many new titles offering some commentary or elucidation on one part of the Book or another, or some deeply felt confession of appreciation (but never faith) in the self-evident truths well-documented in the Book.

Shall We Gather?

Is this the reason so many cozy, casual gathering places have closed? Is it possible that even here, where reason, fact and logic are thought supreme, it is no longer permissible to disagree concerning the nature of "truth"? Can it be that, certain elements of truth having been collected and arranged in the Book (as if it were a kind of "Periodic Table of All the Elements of Truth"), that there is no longer any room (nor any other place) for any other "truth" than what is written in the Book? What other reason could there be that conversation, here, has died? Dispute no longer tolerated? Curiosity no longer a healthy, optimistic thing to share? Indeed, we have more to see.

Returning to my observations of the Village, I see another new business. One of the larger stores has been converted to a sort of store-front "Mission." Inside, a member of the Impious gives away cups of coffee (and for those in need, a meal and place of warmth). Then, for those who by some human impulse linger (feeling in their soul some hunger, lack of love or sadness), he opens up his copy of the Book and, reading from it, does his best to give these people (heartsick, lost and lonely) some comfort and support.

Now continuing my tour of the Village, I see across the square a new building, painted white, its doors opening onto the square. At this moment, this new structure is welcoming a crowd of well-dressed residents who are filing in to take their seats. I see that the Impious, having at some point in the past concluded that true devotion to the Book could not be expected unless solemn ceremonies of recognition and affirmation could be conducted, they next realized that such ceremonies would necessarily require the erection of a specially designed meeting place (reflective of their un-exalted purpose). Accordingly, in due course, a suitable building (this building) was erected and to this purpose formally dedicated (but not consecrated).

I see this building, large and graceful, has above its entrance a tall and tapering spire (but most certainly not a steeple) and on either side of the great assembly hall a series of beautiful windows of colored glass (in no way stained) featuring portrayals of brave and famous atheists of ages past (their unfaith unquestioned; their irreligion resolute), which the honor of their martyrdom (but not for God … and probably not for country) these images might show.

Going in the front doors, I see a large room with a multitude of benches. There is an aisle down the middle, and at the very front a raised platform on which the lectern of the speaker is placed. Beside the lectern, in the center of the raised platform (where light from the windows above falls upon it), is a special low table over which has been stretched a pure white cloth, and on the cloth are placed some items of fruit and flowers, of which the whole congregation will soon show its gratitude (but not to Him).

I see that the Impious, having concluded that only regular, repeated and compulsory exposure to the collected wisdom of the Book could ensure its perpetuation, the Authors conduct a weekly ceremony (held, for convenience, on Sunday morning) which I now have the good fortune to witness. At the appointed time all are silent and the speaker (who I see is that same member of the Impious who volunteered at the Mission) opens the ceremonies by speaking a few words of greeting. This man, the speaker … (What title should I give him? Who ministers to the needy? Who seeks the proper words to give these people hope, and love and healing? I can't think of any word.) The speaker invites the members of the congregation to take out their song books and lift their voices in grateful praise (but not to anyone in particular—and especially not to Him). They sing first this song: "How Great Thou Art (Not Very)" and then this other: "Shall We Gather at the River (No, Let's Not)."

Next is a very moving series of responsive readings, led by the speaker. Reading out in order several of the Articles of Unbelief, the congregation speaks responsively, in unison, the words they have become accustomed to recite: "These are the things we disaffirm … that aren't … or can't … or won't … or shan't … that never were … and never will … that we deny ("it's all a lie") … from now until a long, long time … because it's written in the Book."

When this very beautiful (but in no sense uplifting) portion of the ceremony is concluded, the speaker walks over to his place behind the lectern. Momentarily pausing to collect his thoughts (the room, responsively, falling silent), he commences to deliver a short (but stirring) speech, which (leaving aside for the moment his point of view) I find well-crafted, humorous and deep (which fairly and with well-selected words, proclaims the tenets of their common bond). Now using words poetic, beautiful and grand, he tells the truth (the "truth" the Book might tell):

> *Of all those things in which they have no faith,*
> *The attributes of Him (who can't exist),*
> *His life eternal (which He does not live),*
> *The many blessings which His love (does not) bestow,*
> *His perfect justice (which will not be done),*
> *His promises (He does not keep),*

This Lofty Place

His loving kindness (which we will not know),
His mercy and forgiveness (which He does not share),
His everlasting love (which soon runs dry).

Finishing his address, the speaker once again invites his listeners to join in song. This time they sing "I Love to Tell the Story (of His non-existent Glory)" and the final song "When the Roll is Called up Yonder (I'll Be Gone)."

Having come to the conclusion, and wishing to close the ceremony with some appropriate words of suitable finality, the speaker leads the congregation to call upon some Other Power (but not that Higher Power, who is not there) to hear their words of unbelief (of things that happen randomly and never by His Will or Word) and give them strength to disbelieve, from now until … a long, long time (but not "eternally").

Feeling some indefinable sadness that this ceremony has concluded as it did, I watch the disbelievers file out, each one pausing at the front door to shake the hand of the speaker and compliment him on a speech both entertaining and informative (but not in any way inspirational). Then I am joined by my guide. We only smile in greeting, finding on this one occasion that no words are necessary. At last one of us says "Yes, some lessons only time can teach."

CHAPTER 23
We Count Up the Numbers

You have probably noticed that, since that earlier point where I listed out those vital and expressive Moments of our lives, I have not been diligent in keeping an account of the amount of time I will need in eternity to experience all the truth that might be found there. My last "Total to This Point" set forth a very extensive list of Moments (and their combinations), each of which had first to be multiplied by that number of all the lives which have ever been lived (6,000,000,000,000) and then multiplied each by each by each until all such combinations were exhausted. Thus I have, this far, a very long list of numbers, but no ready means of continuing that count.

Let me try another form of record keeping. Here is what I calculated. I took for a starting point my old childhood Bible. It is about six inches by eight inches, and is printed on onionskin paper. Each page is printed in very small type in two columns. Now, if I eliminate the margins at the top, sides and bottom, and fill up each page with zeros (70 zeros from side-to-side and 80 lines of zeros from top to bottom), I can get 5,600 zeros on each page. Now, my old Bible is 1,050 pages, so if I multiply, I get 5,880,000 zeros in a book this size. This is an impressive number, but as we have already seen, I have much to experience: The universal pageant of human history; all the events of the natural world from the creation of the universe until the present day; all the books, music and other intangible creations of all the ages; the full and unedited inner monologue of every person who has ever lived; and so on.

So how might I easily add to my total of necessary zeros? Well, why not just add pages at the end? As we have just seen, every page (with two sides) adds 11,200 zeros to my total. If, for the moment, we assume My Total to This Point has reached 1,050 pages, I can easily double or triple my total simply by doubling or tripling that number of pages. We have seen how easy it is for me to suddenly need many more zeros to accommodate some new calculation.

CHAPTER 24
An Antique Land

Taking some quiet time reading in the archives of the world's great literature, I happened to see, again, that famous poem by Shelley entitled "Ozymandias" (which in gratitude of its beauty, I repeat below):

> *I met a traveler from an antique land*
> *Who said: 'Two vast and trunkless legs of stone*
> *Stand in the desert. Near them, on the sand,*
> *Half sunk, a shattered visage lies, whose frown,*
> *And wrinkled lip, and sneer of cold command,*
> *Tell that its sculptor well those passions read*
> *Which yet survive, stamped on these lifeless things,*
> *The hand that mocked them and the heart that fed.*
> *And on the pedestal these words appear—*
> *"My name is Ozymandias, king of kings:*
> *Look on my works, ye Mighty, and despair!"*
> *Nothing beside remains. Round the decay*
> *Of that colossal wreck, boundless and bare*
> *The lone and level sands stretch far away.'*

Now, I doubt that anyone reading these immortal lines could fail to appreciate those traits of character which the author mocked: The boundless vanity, the arrogant cruelty, the megalomania. We see these as clearly now as when the author wrote.

I visited my guide and, sharing with him these beautiful words and vivid images, I asked him if there might be any truth to what this poem tells. Is it alone a work of fiction, of imagination, or is there any truth of fact and time and place that I might witness? My guide, seeming never to have been asked this question before, gave me leave to search the record of the world to see what greater truth or more compelling moral I might find there.

Thus, searching the archives of the universal pageant, looking through the stories of all the great kings that are or were or might have been, in time I found that one man who (no doubt) Shelley had in mind. Now, meaning no disrespect to the poet, I will set forth as follows a more complete account of all the works of that great king.

My guide and I are standing outside the entrance to the archives, and I motion a little distance off. Immediately, we are witness to an ancient kingdom in the Middle East, its location and identity not entirely clear to me. Nevertheless, we see, off in the distance, what appears to be a tower and walls of a great fortress standing tall above the plain. We travel closer, and, as we do, we cross rivers, canals and ponds in which we see are living a rich bounty of fish. These waters likewise nourish lush crops and green fruit trees, their branches heavy with fruit. What few people we see (this land seeming oddly underpopulated) are cheerful, optimistic and busy with their work and chores. Children play in the grass surrounding pleasant homes (of brick and mud), and here and there we see smoke arising from chimneys of bakeries, workshops and forges. Indeed, we see a peaceful land—or so it would appear.

We travel to that great fortress we saw, the walls of which are many feet thick, its gates large and powerful. Certainly, this must be the citadel of a king inspiring both awe and fear! We enter through the gates and find ourselves in a spacious courtyard where, in the very back, we observe the entrance to a passageway leading to the great king's throne room. This entire courtyard, we see, is crowded with the king's subjects, men and women, farmers, artisans, fishermen, bakers, teachers, priests and so on. Every class and group that we (by our modern science) might identify or name has here its representatives, in numbers.

We see that all these groups and individuals (none pausing to do more than catch his breath) are ceaselessly in heated dispute with those around them. Their voices, now loud and imperative, then soft and disdainful, are practiced, well rehearsed and very like a kind of chant or spell that magic or religion teaches (seeing in the repetition of the words all the power that they might possess). The faces of the people (we see) are equally energetic and expressive, acting out the drama which their arguments expound—now the tragedy that will surely result if their position is not adopted, then the joy and exaltation that the angels will doubtless sing if only they can get their way. On and on in this way, without pausing, unhearing of any other, contrary opinions, we notice the ebb and flow of these voices, now rising to a crescendo of logic and reason ("as … what I have to say … could any not agree?") then falling away to a murmur of despair ("If what I do propose is not accepted … who can say what misery entails?"). Finding all these things confusing, my guide and I travel on, crossing the courtyard to the other side, where we enter that long corridor which leads to the throne room.

There, traveling down this long hallway, we walk between two lines of disputants standing along the walls on either side. Their arguments not in any way muted or subdued by their nearness to the throne, they passionately act out in words and bodily expressions all the injustice which they predict will necessarily befall the kingdom if (by sad miscarriage) their petition is not granted. Then at last we come into the throne room where we see the great king—Ozymandias—this King of Kings, sitting lonely on his throne.

And a great man he is: Tall and strong, with kindly eyes, his hair graying at the temples. His robe, we see, is of finest velvet (as befits a king) but not uncommon rich or gaudy. His throne, not gold, is merely wood, and on its seat, a velvet cushion (which we see is threadbare from so many years of constant use). Before him stand two groups of citizens, each in turn laying before the king their strongest arguments (including basest flattery). First one disputant gives his argument, and then, after the king has nodded his consent, the other speaker commences his own dramatic speech in his own honor, all the while watching closely the visage of the king to gain advantage, and to see what words or reasoning might gain the king's favor.

My guide and I watch this royal audience for some time. Then (in due course tiring), we decide to go away a little while that we might spare ourselves these clamorous disputes. After some hours of restful contemplation, we return, hoping to see what other examples we might observe of this king's work. However … we see that nothing has changed. The king remains where he was before. The disputants have changed (although, at first, I could not be sure), and, looking down the corridor, we see that the line of supplicants for the king's favor has not been reduced in any way.

What could this mean, I ask myself? This endless procession to the feet of the king? What powerful words of wisdom might this one man recite, that by his judgment, alone, so many antagonists might be reconciled? Or by what healing words (that only he might speak), some ancient grievance finally be forgiven? Or by his just decree, what misery thereby be avoided? I decided that I would spend a full day with this king ... this King of Kings ... and learn what was this "work" of his of which the mighty might despair?

Here, then, the record of this great and kingly labor: The farmer claims that of the value of his crop (in this case eggplant), the value lacks one-tenth. The grocer claims, instead, that of the value of such goods, the value is over-priced by one-in-twelve. The artisan and teacher ... they each join in to say the value is over much by one-in-seven. So back and forth the arguments proceed before the king until, in time, by voices failing, and concentration exhausted, the king does finally issue his decree (the value of the crop improved by one-in-fifteen).

And then it starts again. This time, the teachers press their claim that all their effort and their skill are sorely undervalued (by one-in-twenty). At first we think that by the dint of (seeming) anger, fit of passion and childish tantrum, the teachers might get their wish. Instead, we see that others (some elderly) argue: "No, their value is much less, we think. In fact, by comparison with others (midwives, physicians and the like), the actual worth is no more than one-in-fifty undervalued." Thus back and forth the disputation rages. First up, then down, then up again, then (once more) down. The king his royal gaze unwavering, until at length, the last few rays of sunlight glimmering ... he makes his judgment.

Dare we ask? Shall we, no more than common men, by our base curiosity reflect a shadow of disrespect upon his divinely ordained majesty? Shall we, lacking of his deep acquaintance with the worth of kings, and of his concomitant right to reign and rule as he sees fit, anticipate what judgment he might make—like Solomon: perceptive, wise and just?

But wait! We hear him! Now, in voice stentorian and grand, proclaim his most august and sovereign judgment thus: "One-in-thirty undervalued." The rest is silence.

This same unvarying audience we see before the king each day: The worth of fish and bread and wood, of onions, cooking oil and kettles, the worth of clothing washed, of hair to cut and garbage hauled away. And of every lonely farm and cow and hut, the value must be set, alone, by him, this one, this King of Kings.

Looking out over this kingdom, we see that every farmer, when he rises in the morning and emerges into the day, asks not, "What of the weather, the rain, or hail, or drought or weeds?" But instead, "What of the king's breakfast? Was it undercooked? Or burnt? Is he well- or ill-disposed? How might the king decide today, if by some chance he hears a case involving what I make or use or do?" For him, this farmer, as for every man and woman of this kingdom, the value of his labor (his fields, his goods, his services) depends more upon the whimsy of the king than any other fact.

And if I ask this king, "Good sir, what are your works? What power do you claim, in this your earthly kingdom?" Here is how he might answer, "Am I not the greatest of all kings? Look around you. You see, no man might milk a cow or mend a pot or plant a melon except at my royal sufferance and command. The slightest petty labor will not its final value find until, before my throne, its every aspect endlessly debated and untiringly disputed, I with His authority endowed, do by decree establish its true worth."

Hearing the great Ozymandias speaking thus, I saw that in this eyes were tears that he, a man both wise and just, and still with energy of youth (ambition innocent and pure), was brought to this, a soulless, bloodless petty arbiter of every idle appetite and urge. Did not our Maker sculpt this man of flesh and blood? A man of kindness, tolerance and tact who (looking in his soul) I see, indeed, is "great"—or would have been, if only challenge he had found or crisis faced. I see the sadness in his eyes that all around him call him "King" and "King of Kings," while (in his heart), he only sadness, loss and heartbreak knows.

Now I see there is a brief pause in that relentless parade of petitioners coming before the king. It is one of the royal retainers accompanied by a small group of priests, officials and stonecutters, including among their number one sculptor. Standing before the throne, the chief retainer tells the king that his people, wishing to express their sincere and everlasting gratitude for his many works, and wishing likewise to create an imperishable expression of his unequaled glory (as an example to any other king, and so to all the world, now and forever more), they propose to erect an enormous statue of the king and to engrave at the foot of it some words which (for all time) might capture that true and honest judgment on his reign, and his eternal epitaph.

The king, hearing these words, his soul recoiled in revulsion (!) that any other king would think him "great" or find in this, his kingdom, anything to emulate or praise (it being, to him, a pit of endless, petty jealousy, of envy and ingratitude, inconsequential grievances, and selfish grasping for the smallest crumb).

He looked square at the sculptor and spoke these words (with undisguised contempt): "I ... Ozymandias ... a great king?!" (And then in utter disbelief.) "A King of Kings?!" His face contorted in an angry, violent sneer, and then with tone of rank disgust, derision and rebuke, he spoke those timeless words we know so well:

"*Look on my works, ye Mighty, and despair!*"

ઠા ઠા ઠા

Now one last time I stand beside the throne. Taking my place at the shoulder of the king, I look up and see what he sees. Of his youth, his ideals, his ambitions ... nothing else remains. Round the decay of all his hopes which he, in private hours, might mourn, I see this man ... this king ... as were a ship once bound for foreign lands, adventurous and brave ... instead, alone, aground, now but a lost, colossal wreck. And of the years remaining of his life (this well he knows) ... boundless and bare, the endless disputations—lone and level—stretching far away.

CHAPTER 25
My Assignment

Let me share with you one of my lessons. In this way, you will see one of the teaching methods employed by my guide and also something about the wisdom and compassion with which he instructed his pupil.

After I had been for some time absorbed in re-living of the events of my life, my guide came to me and asked me to undertake a particular "homework assignment" (if you will). He said "Your working life was devoted to your profession as a lawyer, and we have seen that you were deeply committed to the goals and procedures of the law as you knew them to be at the time and place where you lived. Now I want you to take on this assignment: I want you to review all of the people, events and occurrences of the criminal trials in which you played a part. Follow each individual defendant through to the end of his or her trial and then through to prison or whatever other punishment was imposed, and see, in the end, what you might learn about the system in which you participated. I want you to estimate, for yourself, how much justice was ultimately done."

Naturally, I was pleased to take on this assignment. Now I would have the chance to look over all the events of my professional life to see what I hoped and expected would be a story of earthly justice uniformly and compassionately dispensed. Having given my whole life and my sincere and honest trust and devotion to this system of regular and impersonal laws, it was not my expectation that I would find any substantial defect or inadequacy.

Here is how my lesson progressed. I first witnessed (in their completeness) all of the criminal trials of which I played any part. I found (as I have previously explained, commenting on the heavenly judgment which I expect) that nearly all such trials were, within the limitations of human frailty, reasonably fair and honest. Yes, there were errors made from time to time, and (in some rare cases), there might have been that greatest of all injustices (an innocent man found guilty of a crime he did not commit), but, even from a heavenly perspective, I felt that something near to justice was usually achieved.

Next, I witnessed those sentences (fines, imprisonments, and so on) handed down by judges and juries, and, once again, but for some few exceptions, the guilty man or woman was, in most cases, sentenced to a punishment well within the confines of the law. In such cases, the sentence, however harsh the defendant might have felt it to be, was in its severity consistent with other punishments imposed upon men guilty of crimes similar in magnitude.

It was at the next step in my assignment that I came to a completely unexpected result. I followed those many defendants (who were found guilty) through the years—and in some cases, the decades—of their imprisonment. Here was the overwhelming reality of our system of justice which I, involved only in trials and appeals, never experienced or understood. But from the standpoint of the man on trial, who is first a defendant (at his trial) and then, being found guilty, becomes a prisoner liable to serve many years in prison, the trial (even if it was entirely fair and just) is but a dim memory by the time his full sentence has been served out.

I saw that the punishment which our system of justice employs is a kind of slow-motion, low-grade torture. Men are locked up in little rooms in large buildings, where they are subjected to years of enforced idleness and mind-numbing boredom, in an environment dirty, claustrophobic and vile. Their living conditions are the minimum necessary to sustain life, and (despite what you would think) their health and physical safety are often endangered both by the circumstances of their imprisonment and by their fellow prisoners.

What is this "prison system" but an enormous engine of misery, its design well calculated to inflict upon its subjects the maximum of human loss, waste and ruin? Its every pulley and lever, when in operation, relentlessly pressing down upon the humanity of the prisoner, reducing him to nothing more than a nameless cipher, a bare collection of irreducible animal necessities (food, shelter, warmth) to be accorded satisfaction only at the very least subsistence level. Any man here, waiting out a sentence of many years, might accurately conclude that what his jailors—and the greater world outside—wants from him is nothing less than that his talents, abilities and ambition should be ground to dust and come to nothing.

What a contrast with those earlier stages in the process of justice! I have seen that the processes of investigation, arrest and trial are carefully controlled (having rules intended to protect the defendant from passion, prejudice and error). However, should he be so unlucky as to come through the system to its final phase (his imprisonment) he sees all the rules revolve so that they now have as their object the complete and utter annihilation of his humanity.

Struggling with the reality of these criminal punishments, I went to my guide. "Here is the conflict I see," I told him. "In contrast to the efforts our justice system makes to provide every defendant with a trial both fair and just, the treatment that prisoners receive during their imprisonment is appalling. It degrades and devalues every human quality of which these men are still possessed. It erodes and damages all the generous, godly qualities that we wish to nurture and encourage in our fellow citizens. Such punishment represents, itself, a kind of societal crime (the "Intentional Infliction of Cruelty, Suffering and Waste, Upon Another Human Soul"), such crime being utterly inconsistent with the ideals and aspirations of a free society having among its principles the equality and brotherhood of all men."

"Yes, you have estimated these things well," said my guide. "But is there any excuse or justification for these punishments? After all, as bad as these punishments may be, we all know that the crimes committed by these men are often at least as savage, hurtful and destructive as any such punishment might be. Let me ask you this: How is it that 'society' ever got into the business of handing out these dreadful punishments in the first place?"

Now, I was not completely unprepared to answer my guide's question. I had been (during my lifetime) enough of a student of the history of the law—and of history, generally—that I could answer his question without any further research or investigation.

"This is something I think I know," I replied. "In ancient times, if a man committed a crime upon his neighbor, it was the responsibility of that neighbor (really, the entire extended family of that neighbor) to apprehend the criminal and administer some punishment (or vengeance) in return. This was so throughout the world and for most of human history. No doubt this was merely an extension of that very ancient and most basic impulse (not limited to our human species) that, if I am done injury, I will strike out against that aggressor, to defend my life and protect those whose lives depend upon me."

I continued, "Then, in somewhat more recent times, some king (I believe it was one of the kings of England in the Middle Ages) decreed that acts of private vengeance were to be proscribed. All retribution, punishments and forfeitures (in recompense for crime) would henceforth be the sole monopoly of the Crown. All acts of private vengeance being thus prohibited, it fell to the State—the authorities, the government—to mete out punishments of every kind.

"So we see it was the natural evolution of the world that that one, powerful law-giver (the king or other all-powerful embodiment of our collective will) who, having a monopoly on the promulgation and enforcement of criminal laws, is also that same pitiless entity which daily imposes brutal and agonizing punishments upon those individuals who have contravened those laws."

Seeing these things, I asked my guide, "What could have motivated that ancient English king—or any other king or similar temporal authority— to issue such a decree? And, such a decree having once been promulgated, what could have caused the many successors of that king, and all the other kings and governments of all the world, to have continued along that same path, from that ancient time until today? Are we—who love the law and seek to do justice—not offended that that same government which labors so tirelessly and (apparently) sincerely to provide the defendant with a fair trial is also that same merciless jailor who breaks the souls of men upon the rack?"

I Research the Question
My guide for a moment pondered the conflict and inconsistency I had found and then replied, "Perhaps this might be a good time for you to do some research. For all we know, this may be the sort of conflict which, seeming real to you at your current stage of understanding, may resolve itself and dissipate entirely if only you could learn some one or a few additional facts. Let me, therefore, suggest that you use the resources which are available to you here; go back to that time and place where the king of whom you spoke issued his decree prohibiting private punishments. Learn what facts and circumstances motivated that great change in theretofore ancient law and custom."

So I did. I resorted to the universal catalogue of human history. I found that place and time and persons where this fundamental change took place, and, watching with sympathetic interest and not solely from some intellectual curiosity, I saw (and learned) what was the impetus and how that king, deeply meditating on these things, finally made the change we know. I saw, as well, that those factors recognized as important by that ancient king are no less prevalent in our contemporary world.

"Tell me now what you have concluded," my guide requested. I was ready to respond. My investigation had been indeed illuminating. The following is what I explained. "There were three principal factors which led to this great change. First, the process of private retribution against crime and the criminal inevitably led to great over-reaching and excess. A crime consisting of only (let us say) simple assault (a beating) might be punished by death. The family of the victim, being angry and aggrieved, might easily repay the wrongdoer with some punishment far in excess of the severity of the crime. Then, the family of the criminal, itself feeling aggrieved over the unjust punishment imposed on their family member, might themselves institute some equally unreasonable punishment upon some other member of the victim's family. You can see how this system of private justice soon led to childishly illogical, tit-for-tat punishments, having no sure end. By the time each instance of crime, retribution, counter-retribution, and counter-counter-retribution had played itself out, great and unnecessary suffering and hardship had been experienced by the king's subjects.

"The second principal factor leading to the prohibition of private justice was this: That it reflected disrespect upon the king and derogated from his natural sovereign authority. If, for example, some crime was committed, and the victim's family apprehended the person responsible (and went on to impose some punishment) then, even if the criminal's family took no further action in response, still, all the community would say that the king permitted and approved this verdict and this punishment. As ... is he not king? Is his not the sole legitimate authority over this, his kingdom? And, if he has knowledge of the crime and its verdict and ensuing punishment, and if he does nothing, is this not evidence of his consent and complicity?

"The third and final factor leading to the king's decree was this: Think of those instances where the criminal, being apprehended and charged with some capital offense, is accordingly executed. Now, even in those cases where the crime was clear and plain to all, and the guilt of the wrongdoer evident (and the punishment—even considering that it was death – not disproportionate to the crime), still, all the community will know that these members of the victim's family (and most prominently, the patriarch of that family) did order, ordain and carry out the execution of a fellow citizen. The king, making no objection, by his silence acquiesces in this, a private power to put a man to death."

"Your reasoning is unassailable," my guide concludes. "No doubt the king reasoned exactly in the manner you describe. And because of that, private acts of retribution, punishment and revenge were no longer permitted among the people of that kingdom. Perhaps as a result, those citizens, even especially those few citizens who (regretfully) committed some crime, were better off for it and suffered less. Now, how would you apply this learning to the conflict you wish to resolve?"

No Earthly King
Feeling as I did that I was at a crossroads in my efforts to find an answer to my confusion, I went off for a while from my guide to meditate upon what I had seen and learned: Not just the story of that king who asserted what was, for him, some indivisible part of his divine right, but also all that I had seen of the suffering and waste daily served up by our prisons as a bitter ration to its countless unfortunate captives.

After a time in quiet meditation, I saw the answer clear as day. Immediately my guide was with me, and I hurried to explain. "Everything that I have said so far is true enough and natural for an earthly king. Who, jealous of his temporal power, forbids the common man to do those things which ancient custom, natural law and holy writ reserve alone to kings. But have we consulted every king whose power and authority we might encroach? Is there not one greater king—that King of Kings, that Great King above all gods—whose decrees we do not yet fully observe? Thus, I asked myself, what does our Heavenly King ask or expect of us? How might these things appear to us (those factors so important to that earthly king) if we were to see them through the prism of His holy law, hearing them (as we do) in that one court where His divine judgment is read out? Is He not the greatest of all kings? And of the waste and loss and ruin of the world, is there any which He does not see?

"Here is what I have concluded: That it is not only an earthly king who might object to wasteful and destructive acts of retribution freely and commonly imposed in this world. That it is not only an earthly king who might wish an early end both to the injury and suffering caused by crime and the no-less agonizing torment resulting from imprisonment.

"And—this the most important point – that it is not any earthly king who is jealous of that power over life and death, that power to impose indescribable suffering (and the waste of life attendant upon these things) which we know is His alone, not to be shared by Him, nor bestowed by Him upon any earthly king.

My guide, obviously pleased at my reasoning, replied "Very true, indeed. You know that He, that first and greatest lawgiver, has said 'Vengeance is mine' and, in the same place, 'Overcome evil with good.'"

It was then that I finally understood that all the punishments and suffering which our prisons inflict, all the waste and loss and ruin of which they are the cause, are, from the standpoint of our Eternal Sovereign, illegitimate, over-reaching and without foundation in His divine law.

My guide, sensing that I had made a breakthrough in my understanding of His greater plan, extended my lesson, giving me yet a further assignment. He said, "Now that you have seen that prisons (notwithstanding that they are authorized by your Constitution and your democratically elected government) ought not to be places of punishment or retribution, I want you to do this: I want you to formulate a proposal showing how these places of imprisonment might be changed so as to be brought into conformance with His word—that they become places where we might 'Overcome evil with good.' I give you free access to the universal catalogue of all the world that is or was or may yet be. Seek widely and freely; then give me that answer which you believe may best please Him."

So it was that I began my search, taking as my compass all that I knew of human nature and ranging far and near among the great number of "causes" and the even more numerous "effects" that are possible to occur in this, our earthly life. I tested many powerful forms of moral enlightenment, seeking always the one that might be most easily and effectively employed in the environment of a prison. What I thought would be merely difficult turned out to be nearly impossible. Nevertheless, after a long period of experimentation and much faithful meditation, at last I felt that I had come to my best answer to this portion of my lesson.

My guide, seeing that I was ready to provide my solution to the problem which he had given me, said "Before you start, let me tell you how I will grade your answer. First, although your purpose is to eliminate from the definition of a 'prison' any activity or effect which constitutes 'punishment' (this having been reserved to our Maker), yet nevertheless knowing what we know of human nature, it will not be a successful reformation of this all-too-common earthly institution unless the victim of the crime (and his family and loved ones) are satisfied that all the disciplines, challenges and tasks imposed upon the prisoner are, if not painful, at least as exhausting, all-consuming and uncompromising (in their demands) as any punishment might be.

"Yes," I hastened to reply, "I think you will agree, when you have seen my proposals, that where before, the prisoner, having forfeited his physical freedom (to be and go wherever he liked), all the while retaining his same unfettered freedom (in his conscience) to remember and regard his crime in whatever way he wished, in this new, reformed institution (which I propose) we make a different bargain: We will inflict upon the prisoner no physical, mental or psychological punishment. We will, instead, expect (indeed, ensure) that each man, following along the lessons which are taught in this place, will set aside in his mind and memory some honored and newly prominent place for what these lessons teach."

"My next expectation of your answer," my guide said, "is that you provide a solution that is well-adapted to the deficiencies which these men suffer. It does us no good to have an answer adequate for prisoners whose moral sense is strong and well-developed; we know our challenge here is to teach and elevate the souls of men who are, in some (moral) sense, weak and lost and lacking.

"Next, I will look for a course of moral improvement that might be available immediately, easily, cheaply and (how should I put this) on an 'idiot-proof' basis to those who would serve as moral instructors. Prisons are staffed by ordinary men. We cannot expect an answer that requires every prison guard and warden to be a Mother Teresa.

"Finally, you must propose a course of moral instruction which is as varied in its voice and message as the human crowd. Men locked up in prison are no less diverse in their modes of expression, their pre-conceived ideas, their prejudices and their reasoning as any man might be. If you are to have any hope of reaching every man and woman so in need (as I believe is your desire) then you must have the widest and most diverse possible language, lessons and technique."

My Proposal in Three Parts

Thus, after having expended a considerable period in diligent effort, and having made constant resort to the resources of the universal catalogue (to test some theory of mine or to investigate some idea which offered itself to me), I felt I had finally come to a place where I had done my best. Now was my time to present my answer to the difficult question presented in this examination: How might our prisons be operated (punishment being eliminated) such that the men incarcerated there might enjoy significant moral, physical and spiritual improvement? I was nervous to be taking upon myself this heavy responsibility (even if only a hypothetical test) to propose some new and, I hoped, improved form of moral education, but I was also exhilarated to be using the resources of the universal catalogue to present my work.

I said to my guide, "As you specified in the assignment which you gave me, I have divided my proposal into three parts, corresponding to the three aspects of each prisoner's character that we wish to improve: the physical, the moral and the spiritual. First I will show the 'physical' dimension of my suggested new regime." As my guide had done so many times before, I motioned for his attention, and pointed a little way off.

There immediately appeared a scene within a prison in our country. Not merely a local jail where the prisoners might stay only a short time, but a State or Federal prison, large, gray and populated by a great number of men whose sentences are, in many cases, measured in decades or, for some, just the one word—"life." We see it is morning and, after breakfast, the men are brought out into an adjoining building—the prison workhouse—where every man faces a similar day of labor. This is not an industrial shop floor where workers operate machinery. No, here every man takes up an implement of hard labor: A shovel, an ax, a saw, a sledge. Each man is put to hard labor cutting or hauling stone or lumber and doing so in the most ancient way—breaking one stone upon another, then carrying off the broken pieces on his back, or cutting up the timbers with only an ax or saw, then lifting up the raw lumber on his back. Each man is compelled to put his body, his muscles, to the test, without mechanical assistance, each laboring against the weight, the size, the burden. Each day every prisoner labors in this way to earn his daily allowance of meat and bread and drink—eights hours entire, no less. Without this daily labor, that day he does not eat (giving him yet more time to appreciate the value of work).

I say to my guide, by way of explanation, "In this way, each man learns that to live is to work and that every man must press his bones against the yoke. Here there is no idleness, no leisure, only the same message that all the world and every man must learn—'If you don't work you die.'"

My guide nodded, indicating his approval of the first part of my proposal. I then explained, "The next part of my proposal is a little unusual, but I hope you will be patient with me and my unfamiliarity with use of the universal catalogue. What I mean is ... well, just watch."

Then once again I motioned to a place a little way off, and my guide and I see that the prisoners have had their mid-day meal, and after a further several hours of labor, it is time for another activity—lasting an hour or so—before the evening meal. Now, the prisoners are brought into another building, this having cages along the walls and a large exercise area in the middle. Each man sprints (that is the only word for it) to a familiar cage where he opens the door and goes in to greet and be greeted by a dog which is his alone. (And who can say which of these two—man or dog—is more possessed with

My Assignment

speechless joy and animal enthusiasm!) The men are given some time for this greeting; then, according to an unvarying schedule rigidly adhered to, each pair (man and his dog) goes out into the exercise yard where each prisoner leads his dog through "walk" and "heel" and "sit" and "come." Never has any animal enjoyed the single-minded devotion of any man as these doubly caged dogs! But you would never believe they feel any such confinement … now that they have their master (!) here (!) to play (!) and pet (!) and love (!).

My guide looks at me in what I believe is an appreciative way, and I say, "There is no greater love to which any man can aspire in this world than that he puts the happiness and welfare of others before his own. These men, who by their inner nature or by their upbringing, may, before this moment, have been blind to this fact, now they see the world complete. Knowing what I know of human nature—and of dogs—I believe that even the coldest and hardest among them will in time be led unerringly to understand this principle (which is the very nature of a man's love for his dog)."

To this moment my guide had not offered any comment, but now he spoke. "I am pleased with what you have suggested so far. You seem to have a natural sense of what might be accomplished with men such as these. Now let us see what you have suggested in the third and final part of your answer."

Once again I motioned some distance away, and the action continued. The same prisoners are present. Now, the time spent in the exercise yard is complete. Every pair has had its opportunity for the man to praise his dog and for the dog to teach his master some greater lessons in patience. Now the guards lead the pairs to another place; each man walking with his companion at his side, and heeling well a point of pride in every heart, both man and dog. They file into yet another room, with a high ceiling and several vantage points from which guards might keep watch over the whole assembled group.

Each man goes to his appointed place—a desk with reading lamp, notebook paper, pens and several binders on either side. Also, on a low shelf above the desk are several volumes of books … novels, generally, but also among them some works of history, philosophy or biography.

Let us look more closely at one of the prisoners. This man is in his early thirties, thin, with tattoos visible on his arms. He sits at his desk, and at his side is his companion, a Springer spaniel, now transported with pleasure that he will have several more hours this evening to sit quietly at his master's feet. The prisoner reaches up and takes down one of the volumes above his writing surface. He places it before him next to a pad of notebook paper.

He finds the bookmark which he placed there the night before, and, checking to see where he left off, he picks up his pen and resumes writing.

The book is *Bleak House*. He holds the book open with his left hand and, using his index finger, he keeps his place on the line as he copies out the text. He moves methodically from line to line, page to page, following along the story, becoming acquainted with the characters, following their tests and trials, feeling rewarded when they are successful or have good fortune and feeling distress when they suffer failure or face apparently insurmountable barriers. Chapter after chapter he copies out, and when he completes the last page of the book, he enters that final chapter into a binder. He then stands up, walks over to the bookcase on the wall, and places this binder next to the others he has filled. Now *Bleak House*, and next to it *To Kill a Mockingbird*, and before that *My Antonia* and *Lincoln: The War Years* (by Carl Sandberg); before that *The Autobiography of Malcolm X*. He returns to his desk, looks up, and finds the next volume (*The House of Mirth*) in this, the judgment of the court. His sentence, which when he stood before the judge was not measured out in years but this, a long list of books, each one representing some immortal achievement of human imagination. Telling some story of hardship, struggle and fierce determination ... having some moral telling the worth of love and loyalty and compassion. So many stories.

Let us look now to the right of this prisoner. There, another man we see; his dog, some mixed breed, and his crime "Assault with a Deadly Weapon; Possession of a Weapon While under Disability." On the desk before him we see: *The Good Man of Nanking* (a story of bravery, compassion and honor). To the right of this prisoner, we see the next man—his dog a Labrador mix— and his crimes: "Trafficking a Controlled Substance; Second Degree Murder." Before him, under the fingers of his left hand, is *Profiles in Courage* and above him, on the shelf next in order, *The Great Terror* (an account of the purges and show trials perpetrated by Stalin, telling stories of those who resisted heroically to the end).

My guide interrupts me, and I am taken aback. "This is most interesting," he says. "Where did you get this idea ... to deal with these prisoners in this manner?"

"For a long time I was at a loss," I told him. "I could not imagine any discipline which could be relied upon to elevate and improve the soul of a man who had suffered a lifetime of deprivation and mistreatment. Then, thinking of my own situation, an idea occurred to me: This prison, having within its walls men who are to all the world dead, their time here is a kind of living afterlife, where everything they knew is gone forever. I, residing in this heavenly place, am grateful to be a beneficiary of that most generous and perceptive plan (design of our most loving Father), which is: That we—being witness here to all the wisdom, compassion and forgiveness of the universal pageant—are thereby in the end uplifted. Thinking along those same lines, it occurred to me that with some small effort, we might (even in an earthly prison) provide each man with a similar opportunity to be a witness. Here each prisoner, by his own labor and attention, copying out the words of the world's immortal authors, might (in time) join his voice to theirs—silently rehearsing along with them those same undying words of hope and love and trust—and be uplifted."

My guide nodded his head in understanding, and he motioned for me to go on. I continued. The final prisoner we will see is a most unusual case—his dog a collie mix, but not his first dog, so long has he been in this place. This man, bearing out to the very end the judgment of the court (his crime "Murder, First Degree, With Specifications of Particular Depravity") has on his desk some volume which we need not trouble ourselves to see. This man, most patient scribe, has before him all the remaining days of this, his earthly afterlife, during which to copy out not just all the volumes we have already witnessed, but many more besides, there being (for his crime) no end to his sentence, and no one final volume in the debt which he must pay.

Now if we look out over this room, this library, we see many more men like these men. Each one in the company of his dog (resting patiently, obedient at his master's feet), while at the desk above, his master, with equal patience, marks out in words and syllables all the truth and learning which is our common heritage. Each man in time translating those many volumes, word by word, page by page, into as many binders as his sentence might require; we see his soul, in turn, uplifted and transformed. Each in the company of his loyal companion, we see each prisoner writing … pausing … and writing—for as long as volumes yet remain unrecorded. And if we could see into the heart of every man in this room—criminals all—we would see that each man has among his most earnest desires this one wish: That on that joyful day when his final binder is complete and he walks out (free) into the world, that by his side will be that same faithful companion who every night has waited, patient and trusting, at his feet.

"I am pleased with your answer," my guide said "You have done well to propose those three remedies which you described. I have no doubt that those proposals, if put into practice, might well bring about improvement in the lives of those men. I see, for example, that your proposal involving 'hard labor' directly addresses physical shortcomings. I can also see that your third proposal—in which each man copies out in his own handwriting some great works of literature—would indeed uplift and refine the spiritual qualities each man possesses. But what I cannot understand is how your second proposal—giving each prisoner a dog to care for—could bring about any change in his moral outlook?"

For once it was my turn to correct my guide. I smiled and answered. "The part about physical labor, you have understood, but as to the rest, you have got it backwards. Let me explain. One remedy is the companionship of a dog—which is a creature created by our Heavenly Father to love us, even when we do not love ourselves; the other remedy consists of some of the truest and most sublime creations of human imagination and inspiration, brought together from every land and time and language. In short, one remedy is the express and purposeful creation of our most loving God; the other, merely so many works of human hands. The conclusion can only be this: That from a dog (who loves us and whom we love), we see and learn our Maker's love for us, which is the foundation of our spiritual self. From the works of others, we learn (or are reminded) of those human qualities which we and others share (this being, then, the basis of all morals, that we love our neighbor as ourselves)."

Looking away from the scene thus presented, I turn to my guide, expecting to receive my final grade. I see his smile and, relieved that my assignment has at last been completed, I notice what may have been a tear in my guide's eye. Then I remember. He, too, once owned a dog.

CHAPTER 26
I Add More to Our Total

I need more numbers. Looking again at my Total to This Point, I see I need many more zeros to calculate where I have come and where my next steps are taking me.

Thinking about my old-fashioned Bible, printed in red and black letters on onionskin paper, it occurred to me that I need not confine myself to the use of those letters – that size type – needed for legibility. For these purposes, and for my use in the afterlife, I need not limit myself to a size that my human eyes can read. If I wish, I can keep my record in as fine a print as I wish.

Here is the next step that I imagine. Each page of my old-fashioned Bible has, as we have seen, 80 lines of text (top to bottom) and 70 characters (left to right). Thus the total is 5,600 characters (zeros) per page. Now, however, writing with some finer hand, I write an entire page of my old Bible in the space previously occupied by a single character. Thereby, instead of 80 lines, I now have 80 times 80 lines of zeros, and where before I had only 70 characters (zeros) left to right, now I have 70 times 70. Thus, previously, I had 5,600 zeros on each page, but now, multiplying 80 by 80 and 70 by 70, I have a new, even more comprehensive total for each page, which is 5,600 times 5,600.

So now my tangible record of time, of the time I will devote in the afterlife to the refinement of my soul, is increased again, and not by a small amount.

CHAPTER 27
That Place of Quietude

We know, in life, that if we strive to hear of notes (we sense) are faint indeed, or if we try to grasp of words not altogether silent (that breathless, whisper some prophetic truth), we must make ourselves as still as our attentiveness allows—suspending for the instant every motion which our will commands. Only now, being present in the afterlife, and no longer subject to those calamitous distractions unceasingly pressed upon me by my earthly appetites, my bodily infirmities and my mental uncertainties, might I (at leisure) hear those truths which only senses motionless might comprehend.

And would we not all agree, that as difficult as it may be for creatures as easily distracted as ourselves to put this theory into practice, this principle is but common knowledge in the world? Indeed, it speaks to us reciting psalms of truth which, being spoken out (aloud) in words of some profoundly deep and penetrating pitch, we cannot help but know that Voice who speaks. Let me share with you, now, one instance where I felt that I (though still residing in this all too cacophonous world) did—for one brief instant—go to some place of so much quietude that I could briefly hear that deepest Voice.

First let me set the stage. When I was younger, I spent several years living in Japan. I was single then and more athletic than I am now. On many weekends I went with some of my co-workers up into the mountains around Tokyo to go mountain climbing. When I say "mountain climbing" I do not mean with ropes and pitons. No, this was more like very challenging hiking—following along trails through the forest with backpacks on our backs, winding back and forth and up and down 'till we got to the top, and then a similar trip back down.

I was happy to be with friends and happy to get exercise, to be out in the forests and mountains, and to experience the beauty of Japan. We would often travel past rice paddies to the foot of some mountain; then pass through groves

That Place of Quietude

of "*meekan*" (tangerine) trees before we climbed into the forests at a higher elevation. Often, we came upon locations of spiritual meaning. There were Buddhist temples in the villages beside the rice paddies and sometimes smaller temples on the path to the mountaintop. But what affected me most deeply was this: Here and there along the way were shrines—Shinto shrines—still active as places of worship by fellow climbers.

Since I don't expect you to know about Shinto, let me be your teacher for a moment. Shinto is a very ancient religion, a form of pagan animism. Shinto has no holy scriptures. No body of ethics or sacred teaching. No doctrines dividing up the world into good and evil. And no prophets, no saints, no Savior and no Satan. No supreme deity, but not no deity at all. No, in Shinto, believers, meditating upon the world, or with their spiritual senses open to places or things that have been especially touched with godly energy, have singled out this place or that where the influence of spiritual energy is most visible.

Perhaps it is an unusual rock formation that speaks of ancient, subtle energies. Or a tree with roots twisted in patterns expressive of elemental, natural forces. We with our scientific minds see only the trivial playing out of chemical, mechanical and biological laws. Those, however, who see with eyes turned to natural spirits see a different world. They see a poetic truth, a wordless, symbolic expression of eternal, transcendent beauty. So here and there along the trail, we would come upon some small shrine, usually with a small offering of a cracker or *meekan* left in commemoration of the spirit present there, and always we would pause to share that spirit and experience the serenity it briefly offered.

Here is my challenge. This is the possibility that has often occupied my thoughts: That just as we might find divinity and sure evidence of a living spirit reflected in the image of a gnarled tree or an oddly fractured rock, we might also discover—in the true account of some few and singular events which have occurred in our world—that same evidence of a transcendent, conscious spirit alive and active in our midst. And just as we might make an offering to the spirit of a place—some rock or pool or tree—we should likewise find it in our hearts to pause and make a silent offering to those few moments—events in our world—that cry out the living spirit of our world. If you will listen, you will hear that ever-active spirit, and you will ask what offering you might give in commemoration.

Here is the moment that stopped me. That gave me this glimpse of the vital spirit of the world, and bade me pause, among all the noise and chaos of the world. It was this (not that I was there to witness it, but still):

When Once I Lived

  This occurred during August 1945, at the end of the Second World War in the Pacific. The first atomic bomb has already been dropped (at Hiroshima), and now a U.S. B-29 bomber is in the air carrying the second atomic bomb to be used against Japan. This plane flies first to its Primary Target, the City of Kokura, a city of a quarter million inhabitants. Arriving at its destination, the B-29 opens its bomb bay doors and makes a bombing run on the center of the city. However, the weather being cloudy, there is poor visibility over the target, and the bombardier cannot release the bomb. Then the bomber makes a second bombing run, and again there are a few clouds obscuring the city center. Finally, the bomber—with its Plutonium bomb armed and ready to drop, and the bomb bay doors open (so that anyone on the ground might look up and observe the bomb still in the plane)—makes a third bombing run. Once again, however, there are intervening clouds, and the bombardier cannot release the bomb. Having made three bombing runs, and growing short of fuel, the bomber departs Kokura and flies to its Secondary Target, the City of Nagasaki. There, on the first run, there is a break in the clouds, and the bomb is dropped. Thus, in that city 40,000 lives are obliterated in an instant, but in Kokura, the moment passes without notice.

  This is the event which possesses for me the same poetic, spiritual power as a sacred natural formation. Three times the bomber passes over the City of Kokura. Three times the bombardier holds his finger over the bomb release. Three times he searches for a clear view of the target; but each time a great and unknowable will so stirs the atmosphere that there should be a few clouds dimming his sight. And because of that, the city of Nagasaki, old and beautiful as it was, awakens to annihilation and despair, while in Kokura, its inhabitants suffer no more than the gloom of a cloudy summer morning.

  Now, dear reader, if you think of this or that which you regret, or feel yourself a champion, first among men, remember this: That if it pleases Him to let so much turn upon so little, do not think He does not have a hand in every great event of your small fate.

CHAPTER 28
One True Thing

Now I will turn my attention to a subject which you may feel I have sadly neglected. This is the subject of organized (and, I suppose, un-organized) religion. Here I must tell you that I am a Christian—a Protestant—and was brought up in those beliefs. Now even if you were brought up in some other tradition, I hope you will, nevertheless, feel that up to this point in my meditation I have not expressed opinions which are outside the general scope of "acceptable" religious thought. Although I have, from time to time, made plain certain of my beliefs, taken from this or that Scripture or based upon one or another story from the Bible, still I trust that there is nothing so far contained in this meditation which—while it may not be part of the beliefs of another faith—would shock or appall a believer of another religion.

This is as we might expect. Perhaps, in ancient times, believers of differing religions would have had as one of their fundamental religious impulses a complete and violent rejection of the beliefs—the God or gods—of other then-existing faiths. No doubt this was a reflection of the fact that, long ago, peoples and nations lived a far more isolated existence, seldom coming into contact with those following other gods, and, thereby, not encouraged by circumstance to tolerate obvious differences.

Today, of course, we are not wholly free of these conflicts, and we have only to turn to a newspaper to see that there are believers alive today who are at least as fanatical and uncompromising in their fidelity to their (one true) faith and their (one true) God as when the founders of those religions first wrote and spoke.

Now, I want to learn: How you or I—or any other man or woman—having been led to this place in eternity by a loving guide, might ask (and be answered) the question: "What is the truth of my personal faith? My own religion? Of that great and most holy church (or mosque or synagogue, temple or shrine) to which I have joined myself in devotion?" How might it be that my guide, wishing to make clear to me the truth of the world, will answer or explain this mystery? (Which, while alive, I have resolved in favor of my personal faith, but which, in the afterlife, will no longer be a matter for belief or speculation, but rather, I expect, no more than some self-evident fact … but which fact?)

One observation immediately leaps to mind. If I ask my guide: "Which is the one true religion … from among all the religions of the world?" I might find he asks me in return, "Do you mean from among those which are practiced today? Or those which have ever existed?" So immediately I must lift myself up to a higher perspective, viewing not just those faiths which are commonly practiced today but also countless others—among them many which were founded long ago, endured for many generations, and now have passed away, leaving little from which we might reconstruct their wisdom and vitality.

I see that if I had lived (and passed away) in ancient Egypt, in the time of the Pharaohs, and if I had then asked, "Which is the one true religion?" no doubt I would have expected an answer reflective of the gods of the time: Perhaps Isis or Osiris of the Egyptians, Ashur of the Assyrians, Marduk of the Babylonians, or (once the existence of other lands was revealed to me) the gods of the Aztecs, the Hindus or the Bushmen.

But now my guide, having before him the universal tableau of human piety, shows me this, too: A time in the Ice Age, when glaciers still covered most of the world. A cave and the first small band of humans, clad in skins and furs, surrounded in their shelter by colorful murals depicting wild animals (plentiful, fat and bountiful) and hunts (by the gift of their god) always successful. Such people, I see, are primitive, indeed, having recourse only to the most limited vocabulary with which to call-upon and praise their "God of the Hunt." And my guide tells me: "Look. You see. When these men lived (there being only this one first religion), there would have been only one possible answer to your question (the one true faith). And so it was … from this ancient time forward, there were in the world many pious voices, many hearts and souls uplifted (each in its own way), and many faithful prayers to God, as many as the countless languages of men."

My reaction is what any person might experience. I feel exasperated, peeved … and I tell my guide: "Stop playing games. I'm serious. Which is the one true religion? They can't all be true." My guide, now with a look of amusement on his face, and motioning for my attention, points to a place not far off where, from among the universal catalogue of times and places, people and events (which were or might have been), he shows me these ... instructive lessons:

A street scene in New York City, present day, and a boisterous parade, well-peopled with groups, signs and costumes signifying all things "Irish" ... bands and floats, police and politicians. The revelers stop at Fifth Avenue and 51st Street before a large, imposing place of worship, all of stone, old and well-used. Now quieting themselves, they go in and make offering to ... Our Lady Isis. Giving fruits and cakes, bolts of cloth and coins, they celebrate the Feast of the Flood, on this same day when we know the Nile crests, and all are deeply moved and praise Her Holy Name.

And this ... our present day, the Spring equinox at dawn, and in Rome a great and imposing place of worship made of marble, granite and bronze, and on the ceiling, a painting by Michelangelo (in which a white bearded deity stretches forth his hand to spark life in the human form), and down below, a great assemblage offers prayers and devotion to their God. Among their number is one man first in honor among the priests, that single representative of His True Church on Earth, who over his shoulders wears a breastplate of iron and on his head a helmet of beaten bronze. This chief priest offers up a newly slaughtered ox to the Great God Odin. Then raising up the Hammer of Thor before him, he calls down judgment upon Loki—the Trickster—Lord of treachery, deception, cowardice and lies (of which this lesser god holds sway) now and forever more.

And finally this ... Still present day, a joyous morning throughout the Holy Land. There, crowds of worshipers, with humor, tolerance and calm forbearance, crowd the streets and lanes on their way to the center of Jerusalem, most Holy City. No rancor, conflict or opposition clouds this day—or their sure expectancy of worshiping the One True God. There, before them on the Holy Mount, they see the domes and spires that mark His chosen city. Now they come close, and some lucky few enter this most holy sanctuary. There they are surrounded by sacred images, huge and magnificent drawings on the walls of this, His Most Holy Encampment, where burns the Holy Fire. We see these drawings, done in charcoal, whitewash and ocher, images of stag and caribou, auroch and deer, bear and boar, prey of every ancient kind in this, the Sacred Temple of Him, Giver of All Bounty, God of the Hunt, the One True God, and His the One True Religion.

When we have seen these scenes, we pause a while, and I try to take them in. "How might I put these things into words?" I ask my guide. And he answers: "You need not fear, nor lose your faith. It has been said: 'Our Lord is a Great God and a Great King above all gods. The world is His, and He made it.' Do you think He made it a trap to deceive or injure you, His children, or to lead you any where astray? He knows that you seek answers and, not finding certitude, never pausing in your search, might offer this or that invention in its place."

My guide concludes the lesson: "You asked me, 'Which is the one true religion?' Listen carefully. Here is how you may obtain your answer. You must gather together a great multitude of believers, each one a devoted follower of one of the numberless religions of man, so that there is no faith which is not represented. Then, when all are quiet, and He is moved to act, our Heavenly Father will speak and call forth that one single worshiper of perfect faith— sole representative of the One True Religion—in this manner: Our Father will look out over that number of the faithful and ask, 'Which of you was present, when I laid the foundations of the world? Let him come forth now.'" And so I had my answer.

CHAPTER 29
All of Them Kings

As time went by and my experiences with the universal record of human history became more numerous, I noticed a recurring theme. I saw that, over and over in those times and places which I visited, and again in my meditations on those things, I found myself witnessing events put into motion by some one man who was a "king." After giving this observation much meditation, I decided I would ask my guide to help me see the truth of this all-powerful office.

Thus I went to my guide and asked, "Can you show me the origin of this common human experience—to name a man a king or give oneself in loyalty to serve another man (that man a king)? Was there some one man (in history) who might claim that he, alone, was first among that line of men whom other men called 'king'? I would like to go to the record of the universal pageant and see that time and place where first a man placed on his head a crown."

My guide gave this matter some brief consideration, then asked me, "No doubt I could do that, but first I would like to hear your thoughts about the role of 'king.' At any earlier time in history, I would have felt confident that I could predict what attitude anyone might have toward those who claim some sovereign majesty. But for you, coming to the afterlife at this time, I feel I need to hear a little more from you about your opinion of royalty.

"You see," he continued, "until fairly recently in human history, there was no other relationship binding those who had wealth and power in the world to those who daily labored to produce their bare and modest living. If we look over the thousands of years of human history, we see countless kings and queens and kingdoms, and everywhere we look we see the office of 'king' is uniformly and predictably designed. A king in one kingdom, at one time and place, might substitute for another king (on another continent, perhaps hundreds of years earlier or later in time) and, but for his kingly robes, his language and the gods he serves, no one would be aware of his imposture, or fail in any way to serve his royal will.

"Now, however, the world in which we live is a world where democracy holds sway. We see, still today, some few tyrants (a very different thing from 'king') and some few countries which still claim to have 'royalty' (but without any real power, being merely an ancient symbol of that people's honor, pride and culture). So, what, today, do you make of this period of human history—so many thousands of years—during which the world was all (as one) the domain of kings? Nobility, then, an emblem of authority which (like a magic talisman) might cast its spell of subservience and submission over all who fell within its sway, but which now we see no longer earns our loyalty nor compels our obedience? What do you think could have been the source of its universal and long-lived hold upon the hearts and minds of men?"

I was quiet for a while, trying to come to terms with the question my guide had asked me. Finally I said, "Now that you ask me that question, I have to say I have no idea what might have been the circumstances leading to the crowning of that first king. I can only surmise there must have been something about the world, back when this first occurred, that encouraged or nourished men to see in royalty a thing accommodated to their lives, and only later, after many, many kings and queens had come and gone, did society or nature or some such forces (subtle and ephemeral) change our world in such a way that men no longer needed kings.

"I do believe, however, that there is one unmistakable, common token which denotes a king. It is not riches, for I have seen many kings and queens who have had little wealth to command and who have had to exercise much diplomacy and tact (and use much skill in parsimony) to keep the crown upon their heads. (I could not go on without taking special notice of the first Queen Elizabeth, who managed to defend her realm against an overwhelming fleet of invading warships with little more than puddle-jumping barks and livestock scows.)

"That one, unmistakable sign of a king is likewise not his warlike skills or strength or arts in battle, as I have seen all too many kings who were as awkward and inept as any average young man might be—yet still they wore a crown. And finally, I saw that having a face and form of 'royal' aspect (as if the king a 'storybook prince' must play) is also not any indicator of who might wear a crown. I saw many kings (and all too many queens) who, taking off their crown and royal robes and jewels and changing with a humble stable boy or kitchen wench, might never more regain their crown or robe or jewels, if only by perfection in their form or face or figure they could reclaim it.

"It seems to me that the one, universal and infallible indicator of kingship is this: That in each place which does embrace a king, we see that knights and soldiers, artisans and priests, and every man and woman gentle, wise and honest, does freely and unreservedly give to that one man—the king—an oath of loyalty, trust and obedience. This they do in humble gratitude. Not out of fear (of his anger or his strength) nor out of need (that he has riches, and might purchase their devotion) nor yet out of ambition (as who can say if their servitude will bring them gain or woe?) but only this: That in this man they see a dim reflection of that greater King, and in his goodness (which they see and trust), a promise of that greater Good. Thus bending low before his kingly gaze, they trust that by this promise they might raise his goodness up above the common man and place his word and will above the rest, where all might see and follow him.

My guide stood up and, motioning a little way off, said, "Good. You are ready to see the first kings and queens, the first kingdom, and the source of that energy which for many generations has fed the flame of duty and loyalty throughout the world."

A Command Performance

My guide and I were immediately transported to a place which now we would say is in southeast France. The landscape is lush and green, with numerous river valleys and low mountaintops. At first we see no people. Then, after studying the scene for some time, I see a small gathering of what look like lodges made of animal skins stretched over tree limbs and animal bones. These lodges are located off to the side of a river valley, on a lower slope where they might keep watch over the comings and goings of great herds of animals using this river valley as a path connecting two larger, verdant plains at each end. This group of lodges is arranged around a central common space where, from time to time, a larger fire is built (larger than the small cooking fires burning in front of several of the lodges) and where all the residents might gather on special occasions. At length I ask my guide, "What year is this … by our calendar?" He pauses, thinking perhaps he will ask me to guess, but then relents and answers, "The year is thirty thousand years before your time."

Watching (unobserved) the residents of this small encampment, we see that these people survive by hunting. They have spears and traps and snares, and, by careful observation of their prey, they are able to anticipate their movements and place themselves in position to bring down some one animal or another. This they do often enough that they have meat to eat and skins and hides with which to fashion clothing and coverings for their lodges. They have devised crude methods for tanning the hides of animals, and they have learned how to prepare game in dry and smoked strips to sustain them on a hunt.

Seeing this small and primitive village—no more than thirty or forty souls in total—I could not imagine how this place could claim to have a "king." Nevertheless, I trusted my guide, so I pressed on with my observations. At this time in Europe, the climate was much cooler than what we know today, and I soon realized that this encampment was actually a temporary one, used only in the summer. When winter came on, I saw that these residents would gather up all their meager possessions and make their way down the river valley to the south, where better weather could be expected over the winter months. At the commencement of the following spring, they would then return to this same encampment for another summer's hunting. Thus I saw that, although these people lived a life more primitive in its technology (compared to ours), they were as clever and diligent, and as patient and observant, as we.

Watching the scene a little longer, I could see, walking along the river bank and then ascending the hillside to the encampment, a family—a man, his spouse and two children (a girl of 11 and a boy of eight). Each carries some burden on his back: Some articles of food and clothing, several rolled-up hides, a few spears and sacks of sharpened stones for cutting. They arrive in the little village and are greeted warmly by the people there. I ask "Who are these people? Is this man the king?"

"Watch and see," my guide says.

That evening, with all the hunters now returned to camp, there is a special gathering of all the village. There is a well-tended fire in the commons, and before it stands this visitor, surrounded by the children of the village, sitting cross-legged in the front. Then behind them are the adults and, on the fringes of the crowd, holding back from it (as if aloof, but not so far they can-

All of Them Kings

not hear), are those few we count as teenagers. When all are assembled, the eldest male, the longest-lived of all the hunters in that place, bestirs himself and, checking with his spouse to be sure she is ready, motions to the visitor, that he might commence some great and vital ceremony.

Then I see the visitor, all eyes upon him and all ears attentive. He begins to tell a story. He tells about a duck, a goose, a partridge and an owl, and how each came to make a friend—a fox—who played a trick (the same) upon each bird in turn. The ending of the story coming soon (the fox left hanging by his tail, to decorate a tall, tall tree) the children laugh (as so do all). Then the visitor has one more story to tell. This second one is more serious—about a little boy, a wolf, his parents, and a lesson that those children all might learn about integrity and trust (and unsupported cries of "Wolf!").

Seeing this performance (as professional in its way as any we might see upon the stage today), I perceive that this "visitor" indeed has his own calling, which is "storyteller." After these children's stories, the Storyteller calls a break. At once, all the young mothers take their cue to gather up their little ones and take them off to bed. Then, after the mothers have had ample time to tuck their children into bed (with grandma), allowing the mothers to sneak back to the fire, the Storyteller prepares to resume his performance. During the break, I see that the Storyteller and his spouse (now with much assistance from their children) have prepared a special dressing for this ice age "stage."

Off to the side of the fire, where the flames might easily illuminate it, and where it will be visible to the entire audience, the Storyteller and his spouse have assembled a kind of open framework on the ground. It is made of branches tied together at the joints—as tall as a man and three times as much in length. Hanging from the top, along its length, is a panoramic tapestry of hides, well sewn together and visible to all. Then at one end, along the top, a further length of hides (still rolled into a kind of scroll, and bounded to the frame as if might unroll at any time).

Then looking at this prop, I am amazed! I see it is a painting done with chalk (for white) and charcoal (black), red ocher and mineral oxides (which I do not know) for green and tan. I see displayed amazing life-like animals—there are caribou, rhinoceros, several aurock (a kind of primitive, over-sized wild bull) as well as reindeer, mammoth and—prominently—horses (wild of eye and mane). The artistry, I immediately perceive, displays exceptional talent and proficiency. The colors are vivid and lifelike. The proportions are all well-done; the body of each animal being shown in a kind of double (twisted) perspective, demonstrating a great sophistication of perception. What is more, each animal has been given some unique, personal expression on its face, as if each one were known to all who heard its story told.

Now standing before this display, the Storyteller begins to tell another story. This time he tells a tale of bravery—a young hunter facing a dangerous challenge on his first hunt. Pointing here and there at his great tapestry of ancient animals, the Storyteller captures all the fear this young hunter faced and how, with bravery and strength, and trusting in his Maker (and in the skills his elders taught him), he saved himself, brought down the prey, and lived to hunt another day.

The Storyteller pauses again to give his audience some time to recover from this exciting narrative, knowing that each of his listeners has been moved to relive this most frightening (and all too common) account of events which many here have shared. Now the Storyteller (again after receiving consent from the eldest living hunter) begins another story. This one, however, is only the first episode in what we today might call an "epic." A story of a man—a hero—and the challenges he faced: Of foreign lands and fierce predators, of loyal friends and clever hunting tricks, of bravery and unwavering determination, and of his Maker's periodic, timely intervention. This episode today is but one short link in this (the Storyteller's) lengthy tale, which week by week he parcels out to keep his listeners gathered round.

Here I must tell you about a wonderful bit of "showmanship" which this Storyteller has arranged. You recall I described the scroll (still rolled up) tied along the top of the Storyteller's frame. Well ... his spouse, in secret, sneaking round behind the tapestry (and taking hold of the leather cords that tied the scroll), at just that moment when the Storyteller reached the part about " ... that monster cave bear, with his glaring eyes and snarling jaws ... " let loose the cord, and so the scroll unrolled before the audience. And on the scroll! An image of a cave bear which they hope to see only in nightmares! His body huge and dark! His jaws' perspective twisted, as if he struggles to free himself from the surface of the scroll. His expression as fearsome as any hunter here has seen (and lived to tell).

You can imagine the reaction of the assembled audience. Much screaming (!) yelling (!) children awakened (!) dogs barking! Any prey they might have hunted within a day's full march completely "spooked" by all the noise and hollering. The eldest hunter (and his spouse)—it was the longest laugh they'd had in years! So then they bid the Storyteller to leave off for now and begin again in several days when all have had the chance to take it in and share it with the others.

As I continued to watch the activities of the Storyteller and his family, I learned much. He stayed with this one encampment for several weeks, later moving on, in turn, to several others, until, by summer's end, he had traveled a kind of "circuit" of his storyteller's trade. During those days when the encampment sent out a hunting party, he made himself useful in the village but did not tell any stories (well, not for the adults; he did tell stories for the children, to please the mothers and keep them all amused). I also saw that, as a very special favor and a (is it kingly?) courtesy, he went into the lodge of that eldest living hunter and his spouse and, there, using mixtures which he kept dried and rolled up in a hide, he painted on the wall – above the place where this great hunter lays his head in sleep—a painting of a bison (his greatest kill) and by its side a painting of its mate who loved him, mourns for him, yet feels her love complete (as someday will the spouse of him, this great and noble hunter).

All the while living in this encampment, the Storyteller and his family were supported by the other families. When there was meat and hides and bone, the Storyteller and his spouse were given what they needed, without reserve. The people knew he brought them humor, love, excitement and a passion for the hunt they all knew well. But stories were not the only illumination which the Storyteller brought.

The Storyteller's Secret
Never taking my attention from the Storyteller, I was privileged at last to see his greatest secret and the mystery which he so closely guarded (and which kept his family fed). One evening, when most were on their way to bed, the eldest living hunter (let me just call him the "Elder") called the Storyteller aside and, each of them sending away their wives, they (to all it seemed) went in to see the bison painted on the wall of the great hunter's lodge. Now I see, instead, that the Elder takes out from his bedroll a scroll of hides and rolls it out before them on the ground. I look and see that this scroll is another product of the Storyteller's art. It is a panoply of bulls, horses, caribou and bear. Another work of art, although in this case, looking at the images of the animals, I do not see expression in their eyes or true emotion in their stance or posture.

Let me pause, now, to explain one essential fact I have learned about this encampment. As I noted, these people reside here only in the summer when warmer weather permits. They are free to hunt throughout those warmer months, but when the seasons begin to change, it is essential that they break camp and start their journey to a more southern destination where fair weather is expected. What is critical to these people is that they do not choose the wrong day on which to break camp. If they wait too long, they may fall victim to snow and cold. But similarly, if they leave too soon, they will not have sufficient time to harvest all the meat they need to get them through the winter and following spring, when they can return to these summer hunting grounds. So these people—and especially their leader, the Elder—are dependent on their knowledge of the turning of the seasons to keep them from disaster. Delay too long … they will all freeze; depart too soon … they will all starve. And this is the key: To know the summer solstice. The day of summer's longest light. The day as far from winter's longest night as it can be. If only this one day they know, then they by longest years of counting out the seasons day by day, of watching flocks departing, foxes molting, bears beginning feasts for slumber, by all these things they count the days until that day when by the moon's presage, it tells them "Go!"

Now we look over the shoulders of the Elder and the Storyteller as they study this secret scroll unrolled before them. The scroll is perhaps three times as long (from left to right) as it is tall. Across the scroll I see painted a panoply of animals. There are four enormous (aurock) bulls and one great horse, and, along the bottom, numerous other animals are portrayed: some caribou, reindeer and bear, but these are (in some unspoken way, I feel) mere decoration. I see that the right half of the scroll shows two great, black bulls in side-view silhouette, both facing to the left. Then on the left half of the scroll, I see three equally large animals: a bull, a horse and then another bull, again in side view, and all facing to the right. I could not avoid the conclusion that some greater hand or will or art had placed these animals in these positions (giving to them all a common purpose) so that each might fix its gaze upon some vital sign or portent which (within that space provided in the center) we, too, expect to see.

I hear these men talking. First the Storyteller (telling), then the Elder (repeating, for emphasis, and to be sure he got it right) and then once more the Storyteller tells, so never will mistake be made. Here, now, is the secret teaching, which this scroll reveals: The bulls and horse are all constellations. In our time, we (seeing the stars differently, and grouping them in ways unknown before) call this first one, the bull upon the farthest right, "Taurus." Then the next bull, second from the right, we see includes those stars which we call "Orion" and "Gemini." Now looking to the left side of the scroll, we see the bull farthest to the left includes the stars we call "Scorpio" and "Libra." Next, the horse (as grand and tall as any bull) we call "Virgo." And last that final bull, third animal from the left, we in our day call "Leo." But as I say, these men have their own names for these celestial beings.

In order to keep things clear, I will give these animals the following titles: The two bulls which are standing "nose to nose" I will call the "Watchful Bulls" (the bull on the right, the "Right-side Watchful Bull" and that on the left, the "Left-side Watchful Bull"). Then the bulls located outermost, I will call the "Servant Bulls" (for in our story, this is their role and purpose). The bull on the far right is the "Right-side Servant Bull" and that on the far left the "Left-side Servant Bull." Of course, we do not forget the Great Horse, who holds his place and serves some purpose still unknown to them (and us).

So this again the Storyteller tells: The secret which alone he knows and which (before) he shared and painted out and gave the Elder to be safe. There will be a full moon which appears as if it stands upon the horns of him, the Left-side Watchful Bull. Then the next full moon to occur will stand within that space (which we have seen is set-aside for portents, prophesies and signs) between the nose of him, the Left-side Watchful Bull, and him, the Right-side Watchful Bull. If so, this moon (full moon) is that which comes within a day or two of that, the day they need to fix—the summer solstice.

But wait! This is not the secret! This much any man in the village might know and calculate, and, if he did, then by a deeper science (which the Storyteller tells) that in one year in ten, they all must die! Because one year in ten, the first full moon falling between the noses of the Watchful Bulls is not the only full moon which will this space bestride. One year in ten there is a *second* full moon that occurs within that space: And this—the fact which all must know (or die)—that only one of these full moons is that which shows the solstice.

Now, this much of the mystery is only half the secret which the Storyteller and the Elder are at such pains to rehearse. Here is the remaining part of that vital secret which the Storyteller must teach and the Elder must know: The true full moon (the solstice) will show this (the following) image in the stars:

The Left-side Servant Bull must stand upon the earth (horizon) as if his purpose is to wait and serve his master Watchful Bull (which now the proper moon he does behold).

The Right-side Servant Bull, as well, must stand upon that same horizon where his master Watchful Bull does fix his gaze upon the one-true Moon.

The other moon (imposter) shows this:

The Right-side Servant Bull, as if in excess of exuberance, and recklessly failing to keep himself ready to serve his master Watchful Bull, now flies up in the sky, his body as high above the horizon as he might jump.

The Left-side Servant Bull, as if he sleeps in heedless disregard, does not yet serve his master Watchful Bull, as he, forgetting his vow, has not yet fully arisen from his place of rest below the horizon.

If these two outermost bulls are not in their proper places, that moon is death (!) to all the people here.

So once more they, in private, do confer to read that secret scroll which tells those hidden mysteries by which they keep the calendar complete. When I have understood these things—and given these two men my honest admiration—my guide interrupts. "You see this is a story deeply linked to the stars, the moon, the seasons, and their regular, recurring cycles, which long years of observation have revealed. Now, let me show you one more (almost) endlessly repeating cycle."

Then he showed me this Elder, when he is a few years older, pass away. His place is taken by another hunter, equally brave and skilled and trusted.

In time, the Storyteller returning to the encampment, he grieves to see his old friend gone, then taking aside the new elder of the village, he unrolls a new scroll and explains the secret of the moons, the bulls, the horse, and how his word alone might keep his people safe. And so, in years to come, the Storyteller, too, his time on earth complete, his son continues on the path he knows so well. And, too, in time, the loving spouse of that young son (a little girl who once reviled that little boy who called out "Wolf!") is now the one who pulls the cord and sets that monster cave bear free to rage and snarl and live within a hundred dreams of bravery and fear.

The Four Horses
After witnessing all these things, I turned to my guide in exasperation. "You are determined to show me everything except the origin of kings! How much more are you going to delay before you finally show me what I want to know?" My guide found my outburst enormously amusing, and he spent a little time laughing before he replied.

"There were a few things you needed to see and know about these people. As I told you, these are the last people who knew nothing of kings— the last who knew no oath of loyalty or obedience. You need to see how pure and generous were their hearts and what a promise meant to men as brave as these."

My guide took me to the same encampment, but a year later. The Elder and the Storyteller were present, as were all the residents whom I had seen recoil in shock (and glee) at the fearsome image of the cave bear. The date was early summer, and the weather had been fair. Hunting was good, and the hero's epic journey had advanced but a little from the point it had reached the year before.

I heard a great hue and cry in the village, and I followed all the residents to see what had transpired. I saw some little distance from the village a gathering of hunters, they standing and conferring beside a sort of natural pit or deep depression in the hillside. I saw the hunters had devised a large trap or snare by which they sought to capture some prey. They had used branches to block off one end of a sort of small box canyon and, using additional branches, had obscured one end of the pit so that animals on the hoof might easily mistake their surroundings and become entrapped in this deep and inescapable enclosure.

Looking down, I saw that these hunters had been luckier than they could have dreamed. At the bottom of the pit (some many yards square) were four full-grown horses, uninjured and alive! Each one breathing deeply and looking 'round in fear, they saw no means by which they might escape. Unless the hunters chose to remove the imprisoning branches, none of them would ever run free again.

Now as you can imagine, the residents of the encampment are as excited about this good fortune as any group of hunters could be. Here are four large animals, each rich in meat and hide, which the hunters have entirely at their command. Indeed, I hear some of them already voicing their plan for these animals. They will for now keep all of the horses imprisoned. Then in a few weeks, they will kill one, butcher it, take its hide, and prepare its meat for use. Then after another few weeks, they will take down the second animal and use what it has to offer in the same way. Finally, the third and the fourth they will deal with as the others before, and, with careful use, they might still be consuming these fine, fat animals next winter when (unlike this day) the snow lies deep upon the pit.

Even you or I, as little as we might deserve the title "hunter," can well appreciate the wisdom of this plan. Did these people not live by hunting? Were these animals not the very prey which, daily, in many difficult and dangerous hunts, these men labored to bring down, so as to provide their families with food and clothing and shelter? At first, there was general assent given to this plan, as who among them could scorn the value of these animals to people as poor and rustic as these?

Nevertheless, I saw that, within the space of only one day, there was dissention and a kind of angry, violent revolution brewing! I saw there was a group of residents who had a strong objection to the plan. This group, I saw, included all those younger men and women (teenagers) who before I had seen stand off aloof (as not a child nor yet a full adult). This group loudly and angrily objected to the plan. They gathered at the side of the pit, as if to reassure the horses with their strident cries, and over and over bewailed the injustice of the plan.

Here was their objection: That these horses were made to run free. That their Maker, having given them long legs, powerful lungs and untiring muscles, it was His intention that these creatures should be permitted to run unfettered and unbound. That to ensnare these creatures in this, a base and unyielding pit within the ground, is to go against His will, as they, the heirs and offspring of hunters, know it to be. To show the sincerity and consistency of their argument, they even allowed (as a matter which none could contradict) that they would not have objected were their fathers (forgoing this trap) to have hunted down and killed with spear and rocks these very same animals (as they ran free upon the plain, then fled as prey before the hunters' arrowheads and blades). For that, they said, is also by His will: That horses must run free—until some hunter's lance does bring them down—but 'till then … free!

After this revolt had been under way for some hours, the arguments of the Youth were brought to the Elder, that he might consider these things in private before having to confront these rebellious voices beside the pit (and in the full audience of the entire encampment). The Elder had already examined the pit and seen the hunters' wondrous good fortune (four large and captive prey) which, until this moment, had been received as a gift unencumbered with any obligation to the giver. Here were four horses bequeathed to them by the forebearers of all wild horses (which was a bounteous gift), but now it seems they owe a favor to that same Maker who gives these horses (and the Youth) their spirits wild and fierce and free.

The Elder spent some time contemplating this objection to the plan, and in so doing he discussed all aspects of that plan (and the grievances of the Youth) with the Storyteller and their respective spouses. This encampment was too small a place to permit any such vocal and emotional grievance to persist. After several hours of discussion, the Elder emerged from his lodge and descended the hill to the side of the pit.

When he reached the place of captivity, the Elder saw all the Youth arranged on one side of the pit (all of them seething with anxiety and fear, lest one of the horses be killed at any moment). On the other side of the pit were the adult hunters, waiting quietly to hear how the Elder would dispose of these infantile and immature objections by these mere children. Nevertheless, having given the matter much thought, the Elder saw that there was a serious and divisive truth at stake in this dispute. What is it that sustains his people? And by what bounty and dispensation do they live? He hears one truth from one side of the pit, and yet another from the other side.

The Elder standing quietly by the pit, in a few moments all the others present became quite. He, looking down into the pit, soon caught the eye of first this one, and then another, of the captives. He saw the fear that burned within these horses' eyes. And shocked by what he saw, he realized, then, that in this pit was yet another truth that beating heart and racing breath might tell. Drawing himself up in an attitude of authority, and raising his voice so that both sides of the pit could hear, he instructed both groups of disputants to go back to the encampment. He said that he would spend the night there, beside the pit, and open up his heart to receive what judgment their Maker might reveal. Then, the next day, he would communicate to all the will of He who makes the seasons turn and lights the sun and brings the grass (which horses eat—as they eat horses).

That night I kept watch with the Elder, sitting quietly beside the pit; some hunters and a Youth or two some distance off (to watch and keep the Elder safe). I saw the sun go down and the stars arise. And watching further, soon the darkness gave its way to light: the moon came up and showed itself in shape most full. The Elder, seeing this, recalled the message of the secret scroll and thereby found within his heart the judgment which he sought. He noted well the place whereat this moon did stand, and recalling vividly the secret of the Celestial Bulls, he saw in this a verdict from on high. The Elder knew that in another month the next full moon would stand upon the nose of that Great Horse which pastures in the stars: Who strides beside those Watchful Bulls that keep his village safe. He knows this horse—Great Horse—runs free in that unbounded pasture which their Maker stretches overhead. And, meditating on this fact, the Elder learns his Maker has a place for horses (serving Him both in the stars and here), and so he knows what he must do, and what His judgment is.

The next morning all the people of the encampment gathered at the side of the pit to hear the words of their Elder. When all were assembled, the Elder gave this order: The horses were to remain in the pit—unharmed—until that day (one month hence) when the full moon stands upon the nose of the Great Horse in the sky. Until then, he charged three of the village's most skillful hunters and three of its most vocal Youth to be responsible for bringing the horses food and water and keeping the pit clean and safe for these animals.

Thus, the dispute dividing the village remained in a state of suspension for another month. Every day, the appointed caretakers brought the horses what they needed and kept them quiet and safe in their enclosure. It was not long (the Elder saw) before bonds began to form between the horses and their caretakers. Where before these animals had been no more than prey, now each revealed its own personality, which the caretakers could not fail to observe. Even the Youth, who by their strong conviction believed that these horses must remain free and un-entangled in any snare, soon saw that the horses, as if by some secret agreement accomplished among themselves, came to forge strong and living ties with their caretakers—and among them even the Youth.

All of Them Kings

At last the appointed day arrived. The full moon would (that night) stand upon the sign of the Great Horse. The people of the village, anxious to hear the final judgment of the Elder upon the lives and freedom of the horses, gathered around the perimeter of the pit. The Elder, choosing that moment most fitting to deliver his verdict, stood forth at sundown when all might see the daylight by degrees extinguished, the stars (ever in those places assigned to them of old), by increments revealed.

It was His judgment (the Elder stated) that, inasmuch as it pleased their Maker to place the Great Horse in the sky, where (they all believe) he serves his Maker in some secret way, they, too, seeing in the pit these helpless, captive horses, must, by His example, seek some other (hidden) purpose which these animals might serve.

The Elder then recounted to one and all the mystery of the strong bonds which had developed between the horses (heretofore only prey) and those men who gave them care. He said that he had been shown an answer which, were it not the self-evident culmination of events which they had all witnessed, he might have ascribed to some dream or prophesy of the Storyteller. But this was not the case.

"No," he said, "until today it was a deeply hidden secret (which their Maker meant for them to keep, but now released them of) that they—these horses—share a single, sacred oath which they have sworn to serve their Maker's will. And by that oath we see that hidden purpose which these animals must serve."

The Elder (in solemn show of this eternal mystery) did then look up, and, seeing (in its place) that Great Horse illuminated by the moon, commenced to read (from that one over-arching scroll which our Great Storyteller's hand did once paint out in stars across the dark) these sacred words of royalty; and by these words, this first coronation did decree:

Now hear my words! And witness this ...
That men and horses ... passing through this world but weakly ...briefly
   ... gaining all we have to show by hand and hoof,
Do gather here within the sight of this one moon, which shall this night
   denote eternal sire of these few brave and trusting steeds.
Though they be brutes, and may not speak nor count nor pray,
   we know do run and race and graze, in equal earthly imitation of
   that immortal (equine) form our Maker placed among the stars.

So let us, now, with speech (that we be men) mark out this sovereign
> *oath which (never spoken out in words) we do but witness when*
> *we see that even hooves might fall to bended knee.*
Now do we swear (our gentle hands be pressed against our purest heart)
> *that from this day, we shall embrace that sacred oath—*
> *which now revealed—*
We see these beasts have sworn to men, and which, thereby, to make
> *of men all kings.*

The Elder, his head bowed before him, and his eyes thereby cast down into the pit, paused for a few moments, allowing these words to find their place in the hearts of his people.

Then silently observing the faces of the four horses, the Elder, honestly and faithfully obedient to that one wish which he read there, gave voice to that patient and forbearing oath which these mute creatures shared, saying:

Now shall I speak! As if I did possess that form ... that going
> *forth by hoof and mane, and voiceless to defend our kind—*
Still do we swear this single vow, which looking up, we see
> *enacted in these stars.*
Where our Great Sire does ever keep that selfsame oath.
Hear, now, our pledge! This vow of ours be sounded out in
> *heartbeats strong and fierce and proud—*
As constant as those signs migrating ... passing through that starry
> *meadow nurtured in the vastness of His boundless sky.*
Once running free, we shared with men this common, earthly
> *pasture, trusting, all, that One Great Will:*
Now from this day (by oath revealed), He stays that bloody hand
> *of man that would have thrown the killing lance—*
> *and thereby made of us but prey.*
Behold these kings! Who practice His forbearing mercy:
> *a dim reflection of that greater King.*
And in our awe of their kindhearted goodness (our species does but
> *see and trust): an echo of that greater Good.*
That by our promise, we might raise that goodness up above this
> *worldly realm,*
And so enshrine that sacred vow within His pasture of eternal stars.

All of Them Kings

So let us, now, in wordless show of our devotion, mark out this sovereign oath which we do swear—
Where taking up this one eternal burden, it drives us to our knees in grateful prayer.

And this, he said, is what these horses pledged: That they shall ever after carry burdens on their backs, and trusting in the love and care that men provide, shall live a life ennobled—paragons of constancy and trust.

Thus I saw what I had asked my guide to show me: That first, great and royal oath of loyalty, service and obedience, sworn to and adopted not by men (fickle creatures, and lacking in the necessary noble impulses) but by these horses. Four noble and exalted horses, each made in the image of that Great Horse. Finding it their destiny written even in the stars that they should by their own oath, freely given, become ancestors to countless descendents who, by this same unwritten covenant, will live out the years which their Maker has allotted to their kind, evermore in trust to men.

The verdict of the Elder upon the fate of the horses having been given, all in the encampment were relieved to see the divisions within the village healed. The hunters, soon finding that a live horse is worth at least as much in its labor and strength as it might be in the form of meat and hides, they rapidly became as adept at caring for and tending to those horses as any Great Horse might wish. Of the effect upon the residents of the encampment of this great revolution in society, we must leave that to the true record of all the events of human history, where we might someday see the final chapter written. Is it any criticism of men to say that they, lacking in those noble sentiments which underlie the state of kings, at least did not let false pride deter them from adopting that great office as their own? Perhaps they could sense that this reservoir of so much nobility and grace must have its source in that heavenly pasture, where dwells the Great Horse, perfect pattern for the role of "King."

My guide turned to me and said "I will leave it to you, now, to tell me, in as few words as you can, what yet more simple truth might be etched upon the foundation of every earthy throne." I paused a while to compose my thoughts, then answered:

"If men did not keep horses, the world would not have kings."

ᛉ ᛉ ᛉ

Despite the rightness of the Elder's judgment, and notwithstanding the peace and calm which followed his decree, I saw that there were still some (among the Youth) who found themselves unable to accept this result. Seeing those horses delivered into what they believed to be no more than subjugation, they grieved to see these animals—made in His perfection to run free—now bent beneath a heavy burden and so encumbered with ropes and fetters as evermore to live a life of bondage.

These Youth continued to be despondent, and, although they accepted the verdict (as in its way just), nevertheless they were possessed of a sadness that could not be healed. The Storyteller, seeing that the hearts of these Youth remained innocent and naïve, he knew that, unless something could be done to relieve their anguish and despair, they would never be reconciled to the fate of the horses. Thus, he went to them and offered to make for them a record—a true and lasting memorial—capturing for all time the images and spirits of these four horses as they appeared when they yet lived unfettered and free. Finding higher on the hillside above the encampment an entrance to a deep cave, the Storyteller took these Youth far into the earth. There, finding a suitable wall and using his mixtures tied up in a hide, he painted out the faces of those horses (using all his artistry and skill), capturing that spirit which they had before they fell into the snare. At last finishing this commission, the Storyteller saw that the Youth were now satisfied that there would forever exist a record of that time: Before any horse had yet been tamed or sworn an oath of servitude to any man (and showing them in all proportions sure and true).

There in that cave you may see them still, the Four Horses of the Cave of Chauvet, their eyes and faces flashing fire, eternally free.

All of Them Kings

CHAPTER 30
I Question My Guide

Let me see where I have come with my guide. I have been shown that the events of history might have been different. I have asked my guide to show me, regarding some of the great tragic occurrences of history, how these events would have appeared if, because of some trivially changed circumstance, the tragedy in each case had been avoided. So, I will see JFK not shot, Abraham Lincoln attend the swearing-in of his successor, the Titanic make port in New York harbor. I can imagine there must be many such singular occurrences—tragedies or disasters or merely unfortunate outcomes (the Venus de Milo loses her arms)—to witness (or rather, to see not occurring) throughout history. I will ask my guide to search the universal catalogue for such instances and let me see them.

    Now I must explore a further complexity. Here is one instance of a potential turning point in history that I would like to experience. During World War II, there was a plot by some of Hitler's generals to assassinate him. A bomb was prepared, and on July 20, 1944, Hitler went into a large conference room in the city of Rastenberg, East Prussia, to review his army's battle plans. Numerous maps were spread out over a large conference table. One of the plotters brought the bomb (hidden in a briefcase) into the conference room, and he placed that briefcase under the conference table at a place near where Hitler would be standing. Unfortunately for the plotter, he placed the bomb (let us say) to the *right* of the table leg so that, when it exploded, the force of the bomb was largely absorbed by the table leg, and Hitler was only slightly injured. Now, I ask my guide, "Show me what would have occurred if the plotter had placed the bomb to the *left* of the table leg."

    So we see the bomb have its intended effect, and I am privileged to witness the events which might then have followed: Hitler dies. Power is seized by a highly placed German general, and this new leader rapidly seeks an end to the war, etc. Certainly this example fits with those others we have already considered. There is some trivial change of circumstances (the bomb goes to the left of the table leg rather than to the right), but the results of this small change are enormously far-reaching. And I expect my guide would not be surprised to review this turning point with me, and, had I not suggested it to him, I would have trusted him to have brought it to my attention as a moment of great potential interest. A "teachable moment" as they say.

But there is more, here, that I need to know from my guide. I note, first, that this incident occurred in July 1944, so World War II in Europe had already been under way for almost five years. Many, many lives had already been lost, and even if new German leadership had immediately sought to end the war (which we assume, but cannot be sure of) it is unclear if the situation would actually have been improved. (At that point, had Germany been occupied, it likely would have been the Soviet army doing the occupying. Who can say what that would have meant for the people of Germany, France, Belgium and the Netherlands? The whole European continent might have come under the control of Stalin—not necessarily an improvement over Hitler.)

No. I would like to see another, less problematic outcome. So I ask my guide, "Show me this: Show me a world in which Hitler is killed while still serving in the German Army during World War I. Or show me that he dies in childhood, or that a wealthy art collector 'discovers' him as a painter, and he decides to pursue a career as an artist rather than politics." These things might have been, and I want to see them.

(Did you know that, for a time, while Hitler was a young man, he lived in Vienna, Austria, and, visiting that same city also during those few months in 1913, was a young man from the City of Tiflis, the country of Georgia, who later would take the name "Stalin." It is even possible that these two young men might have crossed paths, perhaps even sitting side by side in a streetcar. So I ask my guide, show me what the world would have been like if that streetcar had been involved in some horrible accident, killing, let us say, just two passengers. I would like to see that world. Would we envy them? My guide will know.)

So, to be clear, my question is: When did Hitler come most near to some event that would have prevented his becoming Chancellor of Germany? Was there a moment when, but for some trivial occurrence, the world would have been spared so much destruction and misery? I don't know what answer my guide will give me. I do feel that my purpose in writing this meditation is to anticipate what sorts of questions I will ask and what sorts of answers my guide will have. Certainly, I must prepare for the possibility that there will be questions for which my guide does not have answers. What might such questions be?

My Guide Explains
You have, of course, seen that I have a fondness for mathematics, so perhaps you will not be surprised that I now turn to the science of mathematics for a question to which I believe my guide will *not* have the answer. Suppose I ask him, "Show me a world in which there are no prime numbers." Or, and I hope this is not too much math for you, "Show me a world in which there are all the usual multi-sided polygons (5-sided polygons, 4-sided polygons, etc.) but no 3-sided polygons." In other words, "Show me a world in which there are no triangles."

Thus, we come to a question that has challenged religious philosophers for ages. It is a debate in which one side will argue: "If God really is omnipotent, then there is nothing He cannot do. Therefore: He must be able to construct a world in which there are all the usual theorems of mathematics—except that there are no prime numbers, or no triangles." Then, on the other side of the argument are those who say: "No, even God could not create such a world. You simply cannot have all of the other principles and theorems of mathematics and then somehow leave out such an indivisible element." They argue that even He cannot create a world having a number system like ours but which, let us say, has no number "12" (skipping from 11 directly to 13).

I will not spend long on this question. The answer—for the purposes of this meditation—is clear. Our Heavenly Father in indeed omnipotent. This world is His, and He made it; and, had it been His intention, I have no doubt He might have given us a world in which we would not have the faculty of counting or any awareness of polygons or prime numbers. (Who knows what other senses or abilities He might have given us instead: Magic? Psychokenesis? Telepathy?) I do believe, however, that having given us the whole numbers ("1, 2, 3, 4 ..."), even He cannot withhold the prime numbers or triangles or the number 12.

How do I describe this? Well, to me it is a kind of Godly "integrity." Yes. He made the world. He made it to such-and-so plan and with such-and-so laws and dimensions and effective energies. We, living, always, ever-attentive to His plan, are daily reminded that this world has its own rules, leaving but scant room for capricious chance. We somehow know that, in this world (which we see might have been different) the dignity of His creation is not some casual happenstance that might have been sacrificed in favor of some other whimsical fortuity. What does this mean for my questions about, let us say, the assassination of JFK or Martin Luther King's death? If I ask, "Show me the events in Dealey Plaza, Dallas, in those fateful moments, but now, show me that the fatal bullets stop in the air before reaching their target." Or, I ask, "Show me the events in Memphis after the shots have been fired and have found their mark. Now show me that, nevertheless, he does not die but fully recovers."

What I understand is that there will be questions I might ask, alternative series of events from history that I might request to see, which, although I think my question has an answer, are in fact no different from seeking a world in which there are no triangles. These are questions for which the answer is, in a sense, "No" or "Nothing" or "This you cannot see." I ask to see the Titanic, after hitting the iceberg, not sink and not take so many to their deaths. The answer, I perceive, may be "It always sinks; the passengers always drown." Not out of some predetermined fate or irreversible judgment of God, but out of the integrity of His creation and the unshakable dignity of His word.

His Further Explanation

I ask my guide, then, how I should pose my questions so that I will receive meaningful answers—answers that serve the purpose of my lessons. If I want to learn from the events of the past, perhaps a more general approach might be more instructive. Let us try one example.

Suppose I say to my guide, "Show me the Titanic … without loss of life." No other pre-conditions or stipulations. Then, my guide shows me, first, the Titanic, half-way across the Atlantic, and the ship's telegraph operator (at the critical instant) pauses a few moments from his task of sending out-bound messages and so receives a message from the Carpathia warning of icebergs in the area. So the captain slows the ship to just a few knots, and the Titanic never comes near any iceberg, or if it does, we see it proceeds at so slow a rate of speed that there is no danger of collision. Or I am shown one of the ship's lookouts who, troubled that he has not been issued any binoculars to help him in his watch, breaks into a locked cabinet on the bridge and, finding what he sought, later catches sight of the iceberg at such a distance as to give a timely alarm, so there is no collision.

Then another possibility: I see the story beginning with the design of the vessel, and I see that now the designers add strong, water-tight tops to the water-tight compartments of the vessel, and then the ship is built to that design. Later, when the iceberg is struck, the compartments remain airtight, and sea water does not pour over from one compartment to the next. So the ship does not sink, and many lives are not lost.

This, then, is the common characteristic of my guide's answers. That every new outcome that I desire to see is not some simple result of one trivial contingency—one gentle push this way rather than that. No, there are multiple steps, sometimes manyfold in number and complexity, to reach whatever result I might desire. As we have seen, none of the steps can violate the integrity of His creation. This is not permitted. But also, no doubt, without contravening that limitation, we can employ a boundless creativity to reach whatever outcome we desire.

Let us go back to our two passengers in the streetcar in Vienna. Now, I had asked, "How might it have happened that these two young men suffered a common, fatal accident?" Well, when we look, we see that Austrian streetcars don't travel very fast, and even a derailment must seldom cause serious injury. There were, at the time, no other vehicles on the road that were so heavy or moved at so high a speed that a collision could result in the death of the streetcar passengers.

No, we would have to imagine some other circumstance, which is starting to look more far-fetched. We imagine ... a truck, carrying construction supplies, has a few lengths of iron pipe tied (poorly and loosely) lengthwise along the top of the truck. Then the truck, speeding, crashes into the side of the streetcar, and the pipes are catapulted forward so that they crash through the side window of the streetcar, striking each passenger in the back of his head, killing each of them instantly. But my guide points out, this result, while not contrary to the laws of space or time, nevertheless requires a great many steps to be realized.

Some worker has to have a truck, and he has to be carrying pipes of the right size, weight and number. He has to tie the pipes on his truck in just the right fashion. Next, he has to speed the truck to some minimum speed, and he has to lose control of his vehicle at just the right instant. Then the streetcar—with its passengers in the exact seats we have specified—has to be in just the right place (and at just the right time) to be hit by the truck.

This is the explanation that my guide provides. That, so long as my requested outcome is not prohibited (as against the integrity of His creation), it can be shown but sometimes only as the end point of some long series of otherwise commonplace events (nevertheless moving as if by some hidden and secret intention) to an outcome that appears improbable only because it was so specifically described in advance. We see the complexity of His creation: That every outcome stands finely balanced upon a multitude of simple common circumstances. The triumphs and tragedies of our lives are ... not running wild, but tethered securely to the fixed guideposts of our journey. They progress from one moment to the next, not by some magical power that He wills but by our own choices bounded in the moment.

What is the practical lesson of my guide's explanation? Looking at the two young men in the streetcar, suppose my guide tells me, "This was the moment when each of them came nearest to an untimely death." (Before the time when, we now know, each of them did die.) In such a case, we would have to conclude that, without their lives or the suffering and misery they caused ever having been predetermined, necessary, or by God's will, nevertheless, except for some other intervention in the events of history, the evil that they caused was in this sense an Inescapable Fate. If this were the complete and final instruction of my guide, I would be devastated, indeed, to foresee such a bleak horizon. But there is more that he must teach.

I Take Stock
The last few sections have been complicated and challenging. I feel a need to sum up where we have come. Recently I have seen that it was His plan that our world as we know it—and all of history leading up to today—might have been different. I saw that there are a few cases in which, but for some trivial cause, a great harm or tragedy might have been avoided.

So I see I might commence this part of my lessons by asking my guide to show me those great events—in this case, disasters or tragedies—that might have been avoided but for one single trivial cause. No doubt there will be many more than I suspect. Next, I will ask my guide to show me other similar "great events" that, but for two trivial causes, would not have come to pass. Now, I recognize this is a simplistic approach. I start with those events which turn upon the fulcrum of a single event, then go on to those that might have been altered by two, then three, then four (etc.) such trivial causes. Perhaps it is not correct to count them out in such a childishly simple way, but you see my approach.

First we see those events which were, as we hypothesize, "hanging by a single thread," then next, those events more deeply imbedded in the moment (where, seeking what we believe to be the originating cause of each, we soon lose our way among the ambiguities of life's general chaos and disorder). Finally, we come to events which would require, for their non-occurrence, some lengthy series of self-evidently implausible occurrences to have intervened. But my guide will understand all this. I trust him to present these alternative histories for my improvement. For here is the basis of this lesson: That a great harm might be avoided by one single choice made rightly. That the "good" that actually results from a kindly, compassionate choice may be wildly out of proportion to the results we expect. And finally, that failing such a timely choice—made rightly—the resulting harm may be (even when seen from the standpoint of His divine omnipotence) inescapable.

At this point in our journey we are not primarily observing the individual moral choices themselves. Instead, we want to recognize the fragility of the historical narrative. That it might have been unrecognizably shattered by a single or a few occurrences:

- An archer shoots his arrow differently. Alexander is killed in his first battle; he never conquers the world.
- Julius Caesar is not assassinated. He lives many more years, and shortly before his death, restores the republic. Rome endures as a republic for 1000 years.
- Archimedes is not killed by a Roman soldier at the siege of Syracuse. Instead, he is taken prisoner, transported to Rome, and spends years pursuing the development of science and mathematics. The Dark Ages never occur.
- Einstein does not write a letter to FDR urging development of the atomic bomb. There is no bomb to be dropped in August 1945. More than 2,000,000 Japanese die of starvation over the winter of 1945–46, and when the U.S. invades in April 1946, another 2,000,000 Japanese soldiers and civilians die. The U.S. suffers 50,000 killed, 200,000 wounded in the invasion.
- Pharaoh, tiring of the "disloyalty" of his Hebrew captives, sends them into exile in the swamps of the Upper Nile. There they are decimated by malaria. Pharaoh has the survivors killed.
- Jesus and his follows, returning to Judea from his years of study and teaching in India, are set upon by robbers, and He is killed.

Now, let me apologize to my devout Christian and Jewish friends for the two examples above. Believers may say such alternative histories are not possible—that it was His will that the Hebrews should be delivered from slavery and that His Son should spread His gospel and give His life for sinners on the cross. I only mean by these examples to observe that these events in the scriptures of these great religions do not, in our journey, show any signs of undeniable necessity. Here they seem as fragile as any other events. They might have happened otherwise—or not come to pass at all. Certainly, this only reinforces the conclusion that such occurrences are the gift of a loving God—not built into the fabric of the universe as if some natural law unchangeable even by His pleasure. Such events are truly the most joyful, uplifting and loving messages freely given and willed by His inexhaustible compassion.

CHAPTER 31
I Calculate Anew

It is time, again, to improve the way in which I keep my Total to This Point. You recall where I last left off: I had my old Bible with its thin, onionskin pages, and on each page I wrote (in as fine a hand as I could imagine) my total of 70 times 70 zeros per line and 80 times 80 lines per page.

Finding this method of counting the number of moments I will need in the afterlife inadequate, I considered what improvement I might make. Thinking back, I remembered that my previous practice (when I needed to add more zeros to my Total) was to add additional pages to the back of my little book. I thought perhaps I could use this same procedure to greatly increase the number of my now newly improved record, having so many more zeros written on each page. I hoped I would have to add only a few more pages. However, I soon saw my mistake: I would need to add many, many more pages, indeed. My little book of zeros was becoming unmanageably thick. Thus it became clear to me that I had to find a better way to expand the Total I was keeping.

Here is what I imagined: I took my little book and cut the pages into strips—actually one long, narrow, continuous strip of onionskin paper. So instead of many, many pages, I had just one strip of paper with zeros written along its length and—this is important—zeros written along its length on the back, as well. So, we might imagine, the start of my total, at one end of that long narrow strip, has some few actual digits. Let us say it starts with "678" and then goes on into the zeros ("678,000,000,000…"). We then follow that string of zeros all along that single narrow strip … as far as it continues … until we get to the end. Then, at the very end of the strip (" … 000,000,000"), the total goes over onto the back side of the paper, and it resumes the count, never stopping until it returns to the starting point, where it ends up ("…000,000,000.") on the back side of our starting numbers "678."

I Calculate Anew

All of this must seem to be a considerable amount of trouble for very little purpose, but here is the next step: I go to the end of that strip of paper (the opposite end of the "678") where the zeros stop and jump over onto the back side. There, taking careful hold at that point, I start wrapping the end of that narrow strip of paper around itself, as if I were starting a ball of string. I wrap and wrap, always keeping the paper flat, wrapping more and more length, but adding only very slowly to the diameter of the ball.

What benefit does this ball of zeros give me? Well, if I find I need to add to my total—some additional numbers, or even multiples of our current total—I can do so easily. I just find that point on the ball where the numbers began (the "678" point), and I attach at that point—as if I were attaching a length of string to the outside of an orange—the end of my new strip of onionskin paper. Having done so, I now proceed to wrap this new length of onionskin around and around my ball of zeros. Thus we see my newly produced record increases in size only slowly, but the total it records increases with great rapidity; accommodating even numbers of near immeasurable quantity. So once again, I manage the task before me.

CHAPTER 32
The Wisdom of Stan

A Mighty Fortress
One day, pausing to reminisce about my earlier experiences in the afterlife, it occurred to me that it might be instructive to go back and see, again, that individual who presided as "speaker" at that ceremonial Affirmation of Unfaithfulness which my guide and I attended during our visit to the Village. Some curiosity welled up in me, and so deciding to make a proper expedition of it, I set off by myself to go, once again, to the Village and meet that man who acted as spokesperson for the unGodly.

Thus availing myself of the freedom given to me in this place of rest, I returned to the square in the Village just at that moment when the ceremony I had earlier witnessed was concluding. I waited for the attendees to leave, and when the speaker likewise finally departed, I followed him at some distance to see where he might go. I expected him either to stop by one of the coffee houses in the Village (this being, after all, not late on a Sunday morning, when a cup of coffee is usually welcome) or perhaps to retire to one of the cozy houses I had previously seen when touring that modest town.

However, I was surprised to see that after crossing the square, he mysteriously ducked into a gap in one of the hedges which lined the stream passing through the square. I quickened my pace in order to keep up with him, and doing so I soon found myself following him down a path hidden from the view of anyone passing by on the road.

This path—which seemed to follow along the bank of the stream—was by no means a wide one; suitable, really, for no more than one person to pass at a time, and now and then requiring me to duck down to avoid some low-hanging branch that impeded my way. I walked as quietly as I could, not wishing to reveal my presence to the speaker until I had a chance to introduce myself properly. I hoped that—as before—I would be invisible and inaudible to this resident of the Village, but being still a newcomer to this world I could not be certain I would be able to watch him unobserved.

At last the path delivered me suddenly into a clearing, on the other side of which I saw a modest house set back into some forest of foliage. There was a pleasant front porch in view, and on the porch I saw the speaker already leaning back in a wicker recliner and making himself comfortable. I had thought to watch him a little while before deciding my next move, but instead I was shocked when he looked directly at me—immediately catching my eye in recognition of my presence—then motioned for me to join him on the porch.

Now, it mildly disturbed me to have been found-out in my attempt to do a little harmless spying, but there was nothing to be done about it. I walked up to the porch and, as invited, took a seat in another wicker chair near the speaker. My host, I observed, was a man of early middle age, not much younger than me, if at all, and of average height and build. His features were regular and his hair was combed back in a style altogether complimentary to those waves and curls which it naturally produced. Taken at a glance, I found his appearance unassuming, as if (imagining all things about him to be the product of his art, and his art likely to produce among his patrons some painful case of buyer's remorse) he desired by his visage to provide as little to be remembered about him as possible.

"You are surprised that I can see you!" he greeted me. "Well, there's nothing to be concerned about. I won't hurt you, and if anyone else should show up, I promise not to reveal your presence."

"I … I apologize for following you, and for seeming to sneak up on you," I stammered. "Really, I assumed you couldn't see me, so I guess I thought I can't really be spying if I'm invisible. But since you can see me, I have to say I'm sorry for sneaking up on you like this."

"No problem," he replied. "I am sure you meant no offense, and I will take none. Actually, it pleases me to have a visitor from outside the Village, something I haven't had in a long time."

Having made my apology, and feeling more comfortable with my host, I settled back in my chair and explained. "I am … not a resident of the Village—as you have recognized—nor am I a permanent resident of the afterlife. I am, in fact … a traveler—and have been for many months, now. Some time ago I committed myself to a deep, end-of-life meditation, from which I hope to gather valuable lessons to serve me when I am everlastingly arrived in the afterlife.

"I thought as much," he observed, "but where is your guide? You have one, naturally." "I came on by own," I replied. "Sometimes a little exploration is good for the soul."

"Well ... we'll see about that," he said, betraying some undercurrent of hostility in his voice. I could not help but notice that my host instantly assumed a manner and tone of voice all out of character with his mild and unobtrusive physical appearance. In fact, he seemed to have taken on a persona at once scornful, arrogant and overbearing. "I see I shall have to introduce myself, if we are to get anywhere with this interview," he announced.

"I am (!), he thundered (as if, drawing himself up with all possible dignity, he intended to read out some pronouncement of supreme importance), that singular and incomparable personage who has been known to one and all throughout history as Satan, himself! Yes, yes, he continued (as if he were weary of being disbelieved, or perhaps only fishing for some unearned adulation), it is, indeed, I whom you have no doubt heard about, spoken of and been repeatedly advised to keep behind you. My appearance, he said (addressing that all too obvious disconnect between his words and what I saw to be his utter lack of horns and tail and color red) is something which I have altered so that I might come and go freely in the Village.

"Nevertheless," he continued, "you may be sure that I am that one, clever, powerful and malevolent spirit which your species has on so many occasions bowed down before, and which, in all due time (as I aver), you will at last come to worship as your better in all things."

At that moment, I heard from behind me a derisive snort.

I quickly turned to see the source of that angry sound and was relieved to see my guide emerging from the path into the clearing. His face, I saw, expressed some confused and troubled excess of aggravation, as if he were exasperated not only with his wayward student (me) but also some equally wayward fellow-denizen of the afterlife. He walked purposely up to where we were sitting, and I instantly stood up, expecting to receive from him some teacherly discipline which my misbehavior merited. Satan (being Satan) remained seated, seeking thereby to show as much insolent discourtesy as his languid, dismissive posture might communicate.

"I wish you had told me you were coming here," my guide said, looking upon my guilty countenance in gentle admonition. "Not everything here is as harmless as it seems." "And you," he said, turning to the Devil, who lounged derisively, "what have you told him? You know the rules. Out with it."

The Wisdom of Stan

Satan, being, it seemed, deeply wounded in his unequaled self-regard by these preemptory and intemperate words spoken by my guide, sat unresponsive, staring out into the distance as if he had heard not one word that was said, and doing his best thereby to demonstrate his immeasurable scorn and contempt for my guide's authority.

"Oh, I see you are going to pout," my guide observed. "Well, you just sit here a few minutes and try to get as much pleasure as you can out of this outrage, and in the meantime, I will tell our traveler, here, about this place—and about the rules which you obey." Thus motioning to me, my guide walked off across the clearing and back into the woods where he picked up the path, again, as it continued along the bank of the stream. In a few minutes we reached another clearing where my guide stopped. I walked up and stood next to him, and together we surveyed the scene.

There, at the edge of the clearing nearest the bank, was one end of a now-decrepit bridge, constructed of timbers no doubt taken from this very forest, and still spanning the stream to the other side. There were, I could see, places here and there where rot and weather had broken through the boards forming the pavement of the bridge, and it was obvious that anyone, today, desiring to cross that bridge would very likely end up in the water.

On the other side of the stream, near where the far end of the bridge was visible, I could likewise see a grand and forbidding fortress gate, and on either side of it some short distance of fortress walls. (Gazing at that gate and walls, I could not help but feel that I had been transported back to some ancient time when great sovereigns raised tall and impregnable walls of stone and timber to guard their rich and populous realms.) That gate, I saw, was in an equally ruinous condition; its hinges long since parted, allowing the castle doors to fall haphazardly to the ground where they were now covered with vines and detritus. It was a scene of sad disuse, so much labor still evident in the crossbeams and foundation stones of the bridge abutment and fortress walls, but all of it showing that decay which tells of its complete abandonment.

We stood for a few moments so that I could inspect that scene of ongoing dissolution. Then my guide spoke, "This is a most famous and historic location. Look carefully," he said, pointing to the space above where the fortress doors once came together. Shading my eyes to better perceive what was hidden in the overgrowing gloom, gradually I began to make out letters. Indeed, I seemed to see remnants of some grand inscription equal to itself in pride of place and bearing down in overawing boastfulness upon those passing through (or been a beacon to any seeking shelter there). I tried to read aloud that one-word proclamation, beginning "H" then "E" and finding next a space where time and weather had conspired to rot away some letter, then next a "V," an "E" and ending up an "N." Thus I read out to myself (as much as to my guide) the letters "HE VEN" which at first blush presented some riddle which needed a bit more time to be unraveled. My guide, however, leaned over to me and in a voice of quiet revelation, whispered, "It only lacks the 'A' it had before."

"Let us go back to the first clearing," my guide suggested, "and I will let the Devil have his due."

A Great Transformation
We returned to the porch where we had left Satan steaming in some bitter, agitated stew of which, it seemed, he could not have his fill. We took our seats, and my guide at once commenced. "First," he said, looking at me, "this gentleman is not THE Devil but rather only one of his minions. What is your title, again?" he asked, addressing the heretofore silent demon. "I am," our host replied, with no little evident pride, "'Chief Malevolence Officer and Senior Executive Vice-Minion, Second Class.'" "Good for you," responded my guide. "Now," he continued, turning to speak directly to me, "it is important that you be aware that our 'Second Class' friend, here, as a condition of his being allowed to remain in this place, is required to observe one unbreakable rule, and that is … that he may not tell a lie. He can tell half-truths and painful truths and inconvenient truths, but he cannot tell a lie. Now, you would think such a rule is one that no devil or demon or minion (of whatever class) could possibly observe, but as I shall soon show you, this is not the case."

My guide now changed direction. "Before I go on, however, I feel that the rules of good manners and polite society (which are observed even here, in the company of our satanic host and mortgagor) require that I introduce you to our (malfeasant) companion *by name*. Accordingly, you should know that the name which he uses in the Village—and the name by which I and the other guides know him—is "Stan." You see, long ago he resided in a similar dwelling not far from that decrepit bridge and fortress gate I showed you, and now that that ancient wooden signpost has lost its 'A,' all of us who knew him in those days have agreed that (despite what we know of his character) he also should (in sympathy) give up an 'A.' Thus we call him 'Stan.'"

Stan shifted uncomfortably in his chair. We know it is not easy for any of us (even those of us eternally committed to doing evil, and looking gladly

The Wisdom of Stan

upon any who would do unprovoked harm upon our fellow creatures) to sit quietly by and be spoken of as if we were not present. At length, Stan (clearing his throat) signified his desire to participate actively in the conversation.

"Whatever else you my say about me," he declared, looking reprovingly at my guide, "you must admit that there must have been something I said or did at that Ceremony of Unfaithfulness that so touched our traveler, here, that he would take leave of your oversight and return here, to the place where I ply my trade. So, do not be too critical of me. You may be surprised at the value of what I have to teach.

"Very well," my guide replied. "As I promised earlier, I have brought my student back here to the very threshold of your dwelling where it is my intention—as I believe it must be yours, also—that you should tell him your story and (always obeying that one unbreakable law which I have explained) share with him what measure of wisdom your words contain.

Stan, looking, now, as if he felt his estate in life was now more honestly respected, and having convinced himself that my guide's words contained within themselves some weak and watery taste of 'sorry,' now commenced his lecture, which, despite its show of promised wisdom, I found in all ways overbalanced by its cunning.

"I presume," he began, "that your guide has taken you to see the other clearing where you saw an old, decrepit bridge and some equally old fortress gate. Now, I gather you have been here in the afterlife for some time, and therefore you must long ago have realized that the lives of we who reside here are extraordinarily long. Thus you will not be shocked when I tell you that it was I who attended to the design and construction of that bridge and fortress wall. And what is more, I tell you—truthfully, as I am bound to do—that I was continuously resident at that other clearing from the day those stones and timbers were brought together until the day I moved my hearth to this place where we now sit.

"Now, that bridge and walls and gate were, from the time of their construction through to the day of their abandonment, no more than 'props' designed and intended to serve my purposes. You see, it was at that place where, some man or woman coming to me as in a dream or fantasy or imagination, and facing, then, some test or trial that sought to balance out The Right against The Wrong (wherein the scales were yet in motion, and will and choice might tip the beam this way or that), I gave them what they came expecting. Employing all my arts of showmanship, I put before each undecided patron just such an allegorical work of stagecraft as their moral sense required. I gave each man some symbolic, emblematic quandary that, by acting out my drama where those paths diverged, I never failed to offer him that choice which evil knows.

"A man, for example, coming there (in his indecision) to the foot of that bridge which might safely convey him to the Gates of Heaven, I find he brings with him some choice which vexes him. Then, I, ever helpful, am there (conveniently) to offer him some answer not previously apparent. I say to him,

> 'Sure, you could do the 'right thing,' and such determination would not fail to take you over that bridge which stands before us, but really, have you considered all the alternatives? Why, a man as wise as you, having all those talents which I see you have, would he be so dull and ordinary as to take that common, obvious path which anyone might easily survey?'

"And, you know, often, despite the path lying unobstructed at his feet, and the Gates of Heaven prominent in his sight, such a man will sometimes choose what I have to offer, and so he passes by that bridge, leaving behind him that gate and walls, and striking out into the forest where in time he finds all possible solutions to his dilemma (except that one which would have carried him spotless over the flood).

"You see, it was my purpose to play upon the greed, vanity and other human weaknesses of those who appeared before me in their indecision. We know, after all, how universal are those errors and infirmities which infect the human heart. Thus, you will understand that I had readily at hand a great variety of inducements with which to tempt any man or woman to the path of wrongdoing.

"Now, I was resident at that place for a very long time, I can tell you. There were many who saw through my schemes and (in their imagination) took that narrow bridge over to that welcoming gate. However, there were also many (more than I believe you would willingly admit) who succumbed to my enticements and went off in search of their own personal ruin. But I remained content, continuing in my occupation for a very long time, believing, then, that the vanity and folly of the human heart are inexhaustible.

"However, there came a time when—to my shock and horror—those coming to my place of temptation more and more failed to heed my words or desire those allurements which I placed before them. Can you imagine my amazement? I asked myself, has human nature undergone some transformation of

The Wisdom of Stan

which I was unaware? Immediately I undertook an investigation, and this is what I found. Where, before, a man coming to the foot of that bridge would have been susceptible to flattery and appeals to his personal vanity, now such a man suffers so much from self-hatred, guilt and lack of self-esteem that all my words of unmerited praise have no effect on him. Where I, theretofore, might have pointed out to him some (non-existent) aspects of his character which all might envy, such a man now argues with me, telling me that such talents as I claim he has (even supposing them to actually exist) are in no way any credit to his name. Or, finally, such a man being offered some apparently infallible road to riches (if only he might turn aside from those who need his help or care or love), now I find he refuses to embark upon that journey unless he first plots out his every step by highways, off-ramps, bridges, exits, tolls and intersections!

"These men I offer riches, fame and earthly honor, and what do they reply? They dither! They argue! They question! Why … if I (meaning to tempt them to the path of unrighteousness) offer them the gift of a horse, they (ignoring any moral implications) decline and say they'd rather walk!

"So you see, this very great revolution in human nature did not constitute any elevation of their moral sensitivities (as if the choices that I offered them had suddenly become morally transparent) but rather the opposite! I saw that the 'youthfulness' and 'vitality' with which these men and women had previously approached their moral choices had been replaced by 'impoverishment' and 'enfeeblement.' Those souls coming before me every day I soon saw to be already on a path to Depression, Despondency and Despair. Well, you can imagine my joy at seeing this result!"

"Giving these astonishing new developments deeper consideration, it soon became apparent to me that I was—by my efforts there beside the bridge—only making things worse! Yes! There I was, by all my labors focusing on some moral dilemma faced by some confused and tortured soul, and by doing so I was unwittingly reinforcing the value and importance of the decision which that person had to make—and concurrently, of that immortal soul, itself. Why, I was doing the work of religion! (An involuntary shudder coursed through Stan's features as he said this.) You see, religions are full of *Thou shalts* and *Thou shalt nots* and every one of them reinforces the idea that the choices which a believer makes are important—from some moral, religious and eternal point-of-view. In whole, those precepts and prohibitions unambiguously communicate the message that 'Your choices matter … and your soul matters, also, to Him.'

"So, you see, I knew instantly what I had to do. I gave up my station at the foot of the bridge and began construction of the Village."

The Devil's Arts
Now, at this place in his story Stan felt the need to pause and receive some words or signs from his audience which, if not necessarily rising to the level of unqualified approbation, might at least provide him some encouragement to press on. However, no doubt to his discomfort, my guide seized upon this moment to correct the record.

"In fact, Stan," my guide interposed, "the Village was already here before you arrived, and it was only due to the temperance and charity of our Maker that you were permitted to take up residence here and insinuate yourself into the life and culture of this town. You may be sure that if your activities here did not, in some way, serve His greater Purpose, you would not be here."

These words being spoken, I saw that they must have had some profoundly painful effect upon the demon, as his face fell and his voice went silent. My guide, evidently not feeling any sympathy for our companion, went on with his criticism. "One more thing I should point out, Stan, is that once again, you have come perilously close to breaking that one law which you obey. First, earlier you claimed to be THE Devil, when in fact you are no more than Demon, Second Class, and now, you have claimed to be the founder and architect of the Village, which, again, you are not."

Stan had his reply instantly to his lips (as if, being accused of some ugly and malicious falsehood, he might have been willing to shoulder such an accusation manfully and with some self-satisfying pride, but being accused of some harmless and inconsequential fib, he could not bear it).

"My understanding of the rules," he angrily replied, "is that while I may not lie, I am in no way prohibited from the usual arts of exaggeration, embellishment and puffery which are allowed to any who come to this place. It seems to me I should be judged no more harshly than those politicians and elected representatives who annually stand for office, hoodwink the voters and ever after claim they did the public good. And let me remind you, as well, that any practice, support or encouragement of religion being forbidden in the Village, if I am found to discourage the practice of the virtues, support the vices, and encourage all forms of backsliding, then that is not to be considered any form of 'lie' but only some essential subterfuge. Do you disagree?"

The Wisdom of Stan

My guide, seeming to have at last realized that he had been too hard on Stan, merely shrugged his shoulders, as if to indicate his disinclination to pursue the matter, and motioned for Stan to resume his story.

However, Stan, at that instant looked down at his watch and gave a start. "Oh, damn me to hell!" he expostulated. I thought his words extremely odd (that he would invest so much emotion in such an obvious redundancy), but he quickly resumed, "I am late! I have to go back and lead a service in just a few minutes. Look, I am sorry that we will not be able to continue this interview, but if you will come along to the service, your remaining questions may yet be answered."

With that Stan stood up and set off across the clearing to where the path to the Village was to be found. My guide looked at me questioningly, as if soliciting my willingness to undertake such an expedition, and I nodded my assent. Accordingly, we, too, followed the path back to the Village where in a few moments we had entered that great assembly hall on the square and were soon sitting side-by-side on one of the benches (which, although it was hard and uncomfortable, was of a design in no way comparable to a pew).

I saw, surrounding my guide and me in the other benches, a goodly number of residents of the Village waiting quietly for the service to begin. This service, I was soon given to understand (checking the Order of Service handed out at the door), would be different from the one my guide and I had visited earlier that morning. This one would not contain any of the usual activities calling for the participation of the attendees (such as hymns or responsive readings), but would be limited only to some eloquent speech or lecture (by Stan) affirming (in the presence of all) their shared and unshakable commitment to their common unbelief.

Now, looking around, my guide and I saw Stan enter the rear of the hall and saunter loftily, indolently up to the front. There on the left side of the stage (seen from our perspective) was a raised platform (as high above the stage as a man is tall) having a sort of projecting balcony at the front (the forepart of which served as a lectern) and an attractive (though merely decorative) bit of roof over it. Upon his arriving at the front of the hall, we were surprised to see Stan reach over to the wall beneath the platform and unloosen the end of a rope ladder. He then proceeded to climb that ladder, entering onto the platform (and its attendant balcony) as if lifting himself by this life-saving device to some comfortable place of safety. Next, we saw Stan turn and pull up the ladder. His intention: (at once evident to us all) that my guide and I (and the assembled multitude) being collectively present in some low and inescapable pit, and now (very democratically) all equally vulnerable to wild animals and rising floods, we were thereby advised to look to our own fate.

Upon reaching that elevated lectern, Stan paused briefly to allow those in the hall to finish their conversations and fall silent. He then commenced his speech (which, in recognition of its logical consistency, I shall set forth below in full, uninterrupted).

ཞ ཞ ཞ

The Wisdom of Stan
"As I look out over your upturned, inquisitive faces, they seem to ask but one question: 'How is it he gets to be up there, where he can look down on us with that smug and superior expression on his face—and we have to be down here, where we are prey to every visitation of predatory animals and raging floodwaters?' Well, it's a long story, but I can share it with you if you will follow along what I have to say. I shall begin at the beginning by telling you what it was that brought me here, to this Village, from the place I was before.

"You see, long ago the world was a simpler, more elemental place. It was a place of Right and Wrong and Good and Evil, and having few gradations separating the two. Then, in time, mankind discovered the value of science, logic and rationality. Where before men sought to explain the world by reference to disembodied spirits, magical spells and divine intervention, gradually they abandoned those superstitions and began to rely upon science and reason. Many were the treasures of technology which were thereby bestowed upon mankind as the gift of science.

"But this is not all that science and reason had to tell us about the human species. No, imagine the following: A large rock stands upon the top of a mountain. A strong wind blows, or perhaps some few pebbles under the rock shift, and the rock begins to roll down the mountainside. Now, as the rock bounces from place to place on the way down, we would all agree that, using the laws of physics and the tools of higher mathematics, and being given the weight of the rock, its shape, density, temperature, etc., we would, in principle, be able to calculate its entire journey down the mountainside. First hitting here and bouncing off at such-and-so angle and velocity, then hitting the next location there, and so on from place to place down the mountain until we might accurately and confidently predict the exact location where it will come to rest at the bottom.

"So, looking at this journey of the rock to its predicted destination, we would never say that the rock 'chose' to bounce this way or that; or that it made any 'decision' to strike the earth at this location (where it did) rather than another (where the laws of physics would not have permitted). We look at this chain of occurrences and we do not see—do not perceive any scope for—'choice' of any kind. Once the rock is set in motion with whatever mass, velocity, density, temperature, etc. it may have, its final resting place is preordained by the fundamental laws of space and time.

"Now going one step further, and applying other (but analogous) scientific laws, we might conduct the following similar experiment (and reach the identical conclusion): Taking as our experimental 'subject' some young man who is facing some critical, life-altering decision, we might picture him as if standing at some imaginary fork in the road, one path taking him over a narrow bridge to a place of safety on the other side, the other path leading off into a forest where uncertainty (and yet, perhaps, glory and riches) awaits. Now, as in our example involving the rock, if we are given this young man's age, upbringing, education, ambitions and beliefs (and those hidden circumstances which constitute his habits, desires, fears, faults, wishes, and more besides), and if we carefully and conscientiously apply the laws of science, we will have no difficulty in predicting the choice he is likely to make (and, if we have the opportunity, perhaps we will encourage him to choose that forest path which, in time, may lead to wealth and notoriety.)

"Thus science teaches us that this young man's decisions are as predictable as any other events occurring in the natural world, and if we wish to explain or describe his choices, we have no need to refer to any transcendental, intangible talent which he might claim for himself (what some might call 'free will') residing in some equally implausible and imaginary organ of his body (what others call the 'soul'). No, if we think this young man exercised something we call 'free will,' we observe that this is merely a 'perceptual illusion' (similar to an optical illusion, but of a more subtle and powerful kind). 'Choice' becomes a kind of universal, ever-present attribute of human behavior which, when looked for, retreats more and more deeply into the crevices of reality until, finally, we admit that we could explain the world perfectly well—and with no resort to supernatural forces—without it.

"We, in our scientific age, no longer say of disease that it is the 'judgment of God,' or if some great natural disaster occurs, that 'God was displeased.' We see that these things are fully explained by our greater scientific knowledge; thus we do not think as humans did long ago. Why, then, do we still attribute the choices which people make to some self-actuated, unmeasurable but ever-active power to direct human capabilities this way or that?

Every time we think we have finally located this ephemeral thing called a 'soul' we see, instead, that we have merely discovered some previously unsuspected predisposition resulting from biochemical or psychological factors readily measurable by science.

"Accordingly, if you are one of those who still believes that you possess an imperishable, immortal soul endowed with the power of choice, I say to you: 'You are only clinging to some superstitious delusion. Of that intangible, immortal soul you claim to have, our science finds no evidence.'

"Now those of you who have been following attentively my rustic and naturalistic imagery will be prepared to accompany me to the next and final stop on my journey to this, our Respite of Reason, our own Village. Thinking back to that precariously placed rock which we observed a few moments ago resting at the top of some hypothetical mountain; there may be a few of you who object:

> "Why is it that that rock—no doubt having been placed there by the actions of some (now melted) ancient glacier, or by the uplifting force of two tectonic plates—should have chosen just that moment to start its trip down the side of the mountain? Was there not, perhaps, some 'spiritual' if not 'Divine' hand at work, reaching out at just that instant to unleash those scientifically predictable results?"

"Such a question, my fellow unbelievers, merely demonstrates the illimitable power and subtlety of science. For it is an intrinsic characteristic of science—and equally, of our world explained and described by science—that when we seek the 'why' of things, we do often find remaining at the bottom of our experimental test tube (after we have boiled away all the rest and residue of our speculations) just this one irreducible fact: Sometimes the only explanation is 'random chance.'

"Let us go back, in our imagination, long ago, to see that first scientist, keeping some careful and comprehensive tally of some natural event (let us say, the date of the first snowfall, or the date on which some herd of wild animals commences its migration to the south). We see that after many years of observation and recordkeeping, this first scientist at last reaches a point where he feels confident to predict the date of the first snowfall and the date migration begins. But he soon learns something else, as well. That no matter how detailed and precise are his calculations, the actual dates for such events will often vary from his predictions—sometimes by rather large amounts. He learns that the final answers provided by science are not 'certainties' at all, but only 'probabilities.' If his science is trustworthy, the probabilities he calculates will be dependable, but if not, there will be some (perhaps considerable) element of uncertainty in his predictions.

"Now once again, there may be some of you who object:

> "Going back to that young man standing at the threshold of some life-altering decision (where you claimed that the tools of science will unfailingly predict his every choice), why should we not believe, instead, that his choices are dictated by that transcendental and spiritual power which we call his 'soul' (a thing no less unmeasurable and unpredictable than 'random chance,' itself)? Why, have you not just this moment admitted to us that even when attempting to predict such mundane events as the date of the first snowfall or the date migration begins, science can provide no more than 'probabilities?'"

"Oh, you have found me out! You have caught me in a lie—well, a half-truth, anyway. Indeed, I was not completely honest with you when I told you that story about the rock or the story of that young man facing some challenging decision. What I should have said is that even taking into account the power of our science, we might easily be mistaken about that rock's final resting place; and in the case of that young man, we are equally likely to be proven wrong when we predict what path he will choose. And the reason in every such case is the same: Science does not provide us with 'certainties' but only 'probabilities.'

"But if you think I am going to apologize for the 'probabilities' of science, or for any of those countless benefits which science provides us, you are sadly mistaken. No! Look around you and see this grand and imposing edifice which science has built for us! You see a rich and capable society surrounded on all sides by the fruits of our technology, great advances in medicine, transportation and communications, and a mountainous piling-up of knowledge about the world, its laws, and our place in it. This is an achievement of which our species may take the greatest (undivided) pride!

"Thus I say to you … you who object to this mighty Edifice of Science (designed and constructed using no more than the tools of 'reason, logic and mathematics'), is it now your wish that we should make room in it for spirits, spooks and apparitions? For preachers, pontiffs and sermonizers? Shall we, perhaps, as if in former times, open up one suite of rooms for those anthropomorphic gods of ancient Egypt—for Isis and Osiris, for Horus and Anubis? Or perhaps you would have us make a place for those quarrelsome and combative gods of the ancient Greeks—for Zeus and Hera, for Apollo, Athena and Aphrodite? Or, if you like, we might move all of them in together (!) and let them set up housekeeping alongside Bigfoot, the Lock Ness Monster and some heavenly convocation of departed Catholic saints?

"We will do no such thing! Our species has not raised up this glorious storehouse of unquestioned scientific truth merely to open its doors to every 'spiritual' or allegedly 'Divine' power which might from time-to-time take up residence in the human heart. No! This edifice—this Radiant Repository of Factual Exactitude—has but one occupant who might properly call this structure 'home.' That occupant, we know, is 'Random Chance.'

"So I say, open up every door and window and cast out those weeping spirits! This is not a place for tears, repentance or words of His forgiveness. Here we know only silence! Wander, if you will, from room to room, and you will encounter nothing but some vaulted, voiceless emptiness having but one occupant: that one unmoved mover, that one Ascendant Master who has for us no prayers, no commandments, no words you might believe could heal, forgive or mollify. Never! In this … our one palatial 'Edifice of Science' there dwells in sovereign glory only that one inanimate presence who (by his unvaryingly varying variability) proclaims the Uncaring Indifference of the universe—Our Lord and Master, Random Chance.

"Somewhere, in one of those infinite number of universes which science and mathematics tell us may exist, there may be found what we would all agree to be … immortal souls, living eternal lives in ceaseless gratitude of some Forgiving God. But not here! Here, we recognize but one Arbitrary and Omnipotent Monarch, one Capricious and All-Powerful Progenitor, one Apathetic Apostle of the Careless Inattention of the universe, and that, we say, is 'Random Chance.'

"In conclusion, standing, as I am, at this lofty vantage point, I feel an obligation to sum up those logical and rational conclusions which I have shared with you this day. Thus if anyone were to ask: 'What have we learned?' I would answer: 'First, that no one here has any need to speak about 'immortal souls.' There's nothing here would 'stir your soul' assuming that you had one, and (it is universally agreed) no one can enjoy 'immortality' who does not cheat death, and here it's rather the opposite. We know, as well, that the entrance to our Village being unprotected by any Pearly Gates, we do not need to give thanks for our presence here to any elderly, white-bearded gentleman wearing a long white robe and wielding pen and record book. Indeed, it seems that our existence, here, owes more to our own, shared, militant disregard for Right and Wrong than it does to any Final and Eternal Judgment in our favor.

"Now I shall share with you the following two Psalms of Indifferent Fate which, being shared aloud in words which I give voice, you may hear in them that pace and gait of cold, unyielding logic.

> *"If loving once some child or spouse who, being gone, you feel some pang of loneliness or loss, give up that sense, at once, that any thing of value might be missed; that soul you knew it never was, and now that body being likewise gone, there's nothing left, and of that smile ... you'll find that even memory does finally fail."*

> *"If we might find our sleep in any way be troubled by our shame, remorse or self-regret, we must not think that such emotions have their source in any error that we did, but see in them, instead, some common natural processes impelled to their predicted end by random chance."*

"Accordingly, in final summation ... If you think it might be pleasant to dream upon that other universe of which I spoke, wherein 'immortal souls do live eternal lives in ceaseless gratitude ...' I say to you: 'You shall not witness such a world, no matter how you search the roads and paths of this, our modest land, nor shall you find here any Merciful and Loving God—who I do promise you, no more exists than ... fairies.'

ઢા ઢા ઢા

Having concluded his remarks, Stan looked expectantly out over the hall (as if seeking from his audience that excess of adulation which he felt his performance deserved). However, there being no instantaneous and impassioned standing ovation to be heard, Stan's features took on a downcast air and, the silence becoming more and more prolonged, the atmosphere in the hall began to radiate some tragic and oppressive energy. Seeing the Order of Service before him on his lectern, Stan seized upon it as if providing him a door by which he might escape this humiliating silence.

"I see here," he said, "that our service today is to be concluded by the reading of a passage taken from our Book of Truth. Usually I would do the reading, but since I have been doing a lot of talking, I would like to ask if anyone in the audience would be willing to read this entry?" At this, Stan stopped speaking and looked around the hall.

Of course, as soon as Stan began looking around the room, so did everyone else. As I did so, I could not help but notice that the other members of the audience had upon their faces an expression which might only be approximated by combining—in one emotion—first, that feeling which came over me during that mathematics class when my teacher explained to us the theory of logarithms, next, that moment when I learned (in fact) there is no Santa Claus, and finally, the day my dog died.

Seeing that unconcealable despondency on the faces of my fellow audience members, and finding in my heart some unexpected pity for the speaker, I raised my hand and called out, "I'll read it." Stan, as much surprised to see that I had volunteered as he was relieved that anyone had done so, motioned for me to come up to the front of the hall where I could read to the entire gathering. This I did, taking with me the Order of Service where, on the back page, I found that brief passage from the Book of Truth which I proceeded to read aloud, as follows:

> *All things occur randomly; I shall have no expectations.*
> *Haphazardly I come upon green pastures; fortuitously I find still*
>   *waters.*
> *I restoreth my system software; my reason leadeth me down paths*
>   *logically consistent in all things.*
> *Yea, though I walk through the valley of the shadow of His spirit,*
>   *I will learn no wisdom: for I have an advanced degree.*
> *My science and my math they comfort me.*
> *Evolution preparest for me an advantage in the presence of mine*
>   *enemies; servers downloadeth my data; my storage devices*
>   *runneth over.*
> *Possibly goodness and mercy shall follow me some of the days*
>   *of my life: and I will dwell in the edifice of science*
>   *for some indeterminately long time (but not "eternally").*

After I had finished reading I returned to my seat, by which time Stan had declared the service over and the hall had begun to empty out. Stan, I could see, was in his spirits much relieved that his lecture had been ended upon some poetic, supportive note. As I came up to my guide, I could not help but notice how crestfallen were his features. There was no hiding the disappointment and hurt which he obviously felt. Immediately I saw what troubled him, and looking at him with sympathetic affection, I tried to reassure him, "Remember what you told me," I said, "Stan is not permitted to tell any untruth … but I have no such limitation."

CHAPTER 33
That Great Sovereign

When I had progressed deeply into my meditation, I was surprised to see how prominent a place I found to be occupied by lives and events involving kings and queens. Living, as I do, in a self-governing democracy, and having seen many nations and peoples of the world throw off their archaic bonds of servitude in favor of democracy (even if, in some aberrant instances, these turned out to be "people's democracies"), I would have expected to hear little, indeed, of "kingdoms" or "realms" or "sovereignties." Nevertheless, as you will soon see, there was much I had to learn.

I went to my guide and asked, "Will there come a time when the world again witnesses kings and queens possessing power? Not merely symbolic, but actual power and authority over their fellow countrymen? Or has the time of kings finally come to an end, never to be revived?"

Hearing this question, my guide seems overtaken by some familiar, pleasurable emotion, as if meeting a friend he knew well but who he had not expected to encounter at just that moment. His wit, as ever, was light on his toes (as if, taking advantage of this dream-like state, he had dispensed with all the substance of his now incorporeal body and thereby—free of all inertia—might jump immediately to his conclusion). He has these words ready for reply.

"No doubt we shall find the answer to your question," my guide begins, "if we but look in His eternal playbill under the proper heading. And no doubt we shall be able to sort those plays and players revealed to us there according to events which we are certain to see—and then others less and less likely—until we come to those scenes which we are not likely to find in any drama produced by Him. Still, however, as I have put to you before (now doing my duty as both your guide and your teacher), I ask you to tell me what you would expect the answer to your question to be?

Having been placed in this position several times previously, I am ready to expound my own thoughts on the question presented. "Well," I begin, "here is how it appears to me. We have seen that the office of 'king' arose at a time when, society being then less complicated and the king's subjects not so numerous, a kingdom could be successfully established and perpetuated on a 'command' basis. That is, all those things needing to done, especially those things difficult, dangerous or onerous, could be accomplished solely at the will and command of the sovereign, with nothing more required or expected.

"However, as society progressed and became many magnitudes more complex, we saw the natural development of a market economy (incorporating the creation and use of currency) which, in time, grew to be so powerful as to be outside the control or command of any king. Nevertheless, still possessing, if not a monopoly, then at least some pre-eminent and unchallengeable primacy of military power, the king might still rule his kingdom by force of arms. We saw that the sovereign's royal court then served as a sort of 'clearing house' and 'court of justice' where any of the king's subjects might bring his grievances, supplications and ambitions to have these things weighed, judged and disposed of at the pleasure of the king.

We know, of course, that as the centuries elapsed, the limitations of this kingly office became more and more apparent. Science, technology and commerce continued their relentless development, and great wealth was thereby created (but very little of that was created in the hands of the king). Likewise, where in ancient times a man or woman of ordinary skill and ability might ably serve as 'king' or 'queen,' in more recent times the burdens of the office grew to overtax the capabilities of even those few men and women (elevated to that office) who possessed extraordinary and uncommon genius.

Thus, in time, this office of divinely ordained sovereign more and more failed to meet the challenges which it faced. Then the world, casting about for some more suitable arrangement by which wood might come to be chopped, and fields to be plowed, and metal to be fashioned into pots and coins and harnesses, a more serviceable example was at last found in what the Greeks called 'democracy.'

Where before a man residing in some kingdom might have humbly and respectfully supplicated (not to say 'bribed") some servant of the king to grant him entry to the king's court, there to present his request or grievance for the king's judgment, now that citizen has the 'right' to bring his request or grievance onto the floor of some 'congress' or 'parliament' where, being honestly advocated by himself before his fellow citizens, it may be that he will obtain his request or satisfy his grievance by joint and collective 'vote' of all such citizens so assembled.

Thus, in a democracy, all requests and grievances are brought forward in the light of day (not secretly to the king in private, where lies, flattery or misrepresentation might go unobserved, and so uncorrected). And, the officers and officials of this democracy being selected by vote of the citizenry, we can expect that (these positions being competed for) a more talented and capable number shall come to fill those positions (more so than counting upon some ill-defined improvements owing to heredity).

"It seems to me," I say, nearing my conclusion, "that, in recent years, we have seen several developments which have greatly improved the operation of the wheels and levers of the engine of democracy so that now it runs ever more smoothly. We know that the world comes ever closer to universal education, whereby every citizen has learned to read and write and has received a broad and liberal education, making each person well-capable of exercising a thoughtful, rational and informed judgment on the issues of the day. Likewise, the world enjoys a (some would say 'surfeit') of media by which every person might be informed (sometimes much against his inclination) concerning people and events of the world. Thus, citizens today are well-placed and well-prepared to exercise their rights of self-government, a reality which our ancestors would have been glad to have experienced.

"Accordingly," I conclude, "unless the people of the world are made less-educated, less-informed and less-numerous (or, indeed, unless they are rendered altogether unfree), then I see no circumstance which would induce this world to re-establish any 'kingdom' or place above them any king to rule or give command that any would obey.

Her Namesake
I wait patiently for my guide to comment upon the answer I have proposed. He stands, gazing off to one side out into the distance, as if he needs some few moments of inner reflection to collect his thoughts. At last he speaks. "That is ... a good summary of the case. In the most general terms, that sums up where the world has come as of this present day. Now, as you asked, let me take you to that time and place where you might see acted out in lives and tears and treasure the answer to your question. If the world is ever again to witness a king kindly, wise and powerful, let us see that kingdom and measure out how lightly (or how heavy) does that crown repose upon that sovereign brow.

That Great Sovereign

My guide motions a little way off, and instantly we find ourselves standing on a street corner in some city which I do not immediately recognize. There is a sign hanging over our heads attached to the building before which we are standing. On that sign I read the words "Blue Boar" and see some sort of crest of heraldry featuring a boar, a lion and what seems to be a unicorn. Glancing in the door of this building (standing open before us), I see it is a pub, and instantly I know I am in London! Eagerly, I look up and down the street, hoping to see something distinctly "British." Initially I see vehicles (having shapes and purposes unknown to me) which drive silently (and, I notice, odorlessly) past our corner. Likewise I see pedestrians out on some domestic errand, or on their way to work or leaving work, several of whom head in our direction and then duck in the door under the sign of the Boar, paying us no heed.

"I see we are in London," I say to my guide, "and I see that whatever year—or century—this may be, the residents here still retain that most characteristic habit of theirs formed of old—a love of sports, especially hunting and pursuing wild beasts, even into their lairs!" My guide smiles, and nodding his head in the direction of the open door, we are soon leaning on the bar, two pints of ale standing within our reach. After we have sampled the taste of these revivifying drafts, and after we have allowed our eyes to become accustomed to the pleasantly subdued light favored by the Boar, my guide resumes his explanation.

"We are, indeed, in London, as you have correctly concluded, but the year I shall not specify. Only this: that it is a time some dozen or so centuries after your time. Also I will tell you that this London you see remains the capital of what the people here still call 'England,' and that England has its 'King'—although, in point of fact, this sovereign being female, it has its 'Queen.'

"Now, you must not suppose that this England lacks democracy. No, there is also in this city a parliament, gathering representatives of the people from throughout the land, all such representatives being elected in regular, periodic and honestly conducted elections. The usual organs of government are staffed by public servants selected or retained by the representatives of parliament, and there likewise exists a system of courts and judges where justice is impartially and objectively administered.

"Nevertheless," he continues (first ordering another round, as so much explanation is a dry and desiccating thing), "I tell you this England has its Queen, who exercises not a little power, as you will soon observe. And, this England (in its present form a 'domestic partnership' marrying the ever-renewing vitality of democracy with the primordial gift of divinely inspired sovereignty) is by no means a new thing. Indeed, the present Queen, humbly respectful of her long-ago and well-regarded ancestor, is known as Elizabeth VIII (as if, now taking her place in some anointed sequence, she does with this even more ancient numerical appellation give honor to that Nobel Sire who gave the world that first Elizabeth).

My guide lifts his pint to his lips (showing, thereby, that it constitutes some prudent virtue even in this dreamlike, spectral world, to not waste ale), and, finishing his glass, he says, "I will take you, now, somewhere special where you might learn much about the state of kings—on this occasion (if you will pardon the disrespectful pun)—directly from the horse's mouth." Once again motioning with his hand, we are immediately transported to a sleeping chamber in the Palace of the Queen. The room is dark, and we, in all ways silent and invisible, observe the Queen in her sleep. I see that she is of tender years (no more than in her early twenties) and unmarried (as yet the equal of her First-Named ancestor).

My guide begins, "You see the Queen now sleeps, and (the same as any mortal) you may suppose she dreams. Now, as we have once before witnessed, it often happens that, some uncertainty or conflict or unacknowledged truth coming to us in our dreams, we might be heard to speak honestly of it from our hearts, setting aside for the moment any diplomacy or tact, fear or reticence, that might disguise or hide away the truth. Soon this Queen will join us (in her dream), and then, by speaking briefly and with measured words, you may hear that truth which only purest heart may tell.

In moments, as my guide had promised, we are joined in our dream-like state by the apparition of this Queen. Her earthly, sleeping form lying motionless in her bed, there now appears standing before us her twin, in all ways equal in beauty and grace to her somnolent majesty (who we can hear does softly snore). The Queen is, of stature, on the shorter side, though her hair, soft and lovely as it plainly shows, is worn the longer, resting lightly on her shoulders. Her face is gentle—features being finely drawn, her eyes expressive, hinting at some kindly favor. Involuntarily (for I have never had an earthly Queen), I bow my head.

The Queen looks about her as if taking in the room (which would be right, since she's asleep), but seeing us, as well (and who are you?), we see her stop and ponder. My guide, knowing that those who dream are prone to wakefulness, if the sleeper be too much disturbed, speaks to her in a soothing voice. "My Queen, forgive us for this unscheduled and unasked-for intrusion upon you serene repose. You may consider us your devoted servants who ever treasure your undoubted goodness. We trouble you only to hear from your all-knowing lips such truths as we would not hear of any other."

The Queen, now seeming to have accommodated herself to our presence, smiles at my guide as if to encourage him to go on with his speech. He, first bowing to her in deepest supplication, then drawing himself up in all his humble dignity, this most difficult of questions now propounds: "Good Queen, what are your works? What power do you claim, in this your earthly kingdom?"

The Queen, seeming in no way troubled by this question (which, touching as it does upon the very essence of her earthly state, I thought must sure give some offense), provides her answer straightaway, as if she has considered this question many times before.

"It is this," she replies. "This is my sovereign oath: That in this place and ever and again before my people, I do read out that judgment which our Maker shows; and doing this, I keep my people safe and serve His greater Will." She then falls silent, observing my reaction and no doubt sensing that I do not yet grasp the wisdom of her reply. Accordingly, patient of my slow and plodding understanding, she (having some more swift and nimble gait) motions for us to be seated there on the floor—my guide and I sitting in a place where the moonlight falls upon the tapestry behind us, she standing on the other side before the fire still burning in the hearth.

"You see," she begins, "long ago there was a time when England gave up its kings. There was then no sovereign, and no other will than the one will of the people, reflected in its parliament assembled. There was … only that one place (in no way set aside to honor Him or keep His name or Words or Will above our own) where any man or woman might seek compensation or justice, charity or deliverance. For, as you have seen, it is the function of democracy that every man might bring into this one congress every greedy and avaricious impulse, every unforgiving and undying grievance, every unexpressed and insatiable desire for wealth and power, influence and fame, and there see all and every such impulse meet with those of every other such man or woman, and thereby see all these things (each in its own way irresistible) so counterbalanced, one with the others, that there remains only the one single will which this assembly might declare.

"It is," she continued, "as if we might say … "

> *If all the greed were one greed, what a great greed it would be,*
> *And if all the envy were one envy, what a great envy it would be,*

And if all the resentment were one resentment, what a great resentment it would be,
And if all the men were one man, what a great man he would be,
And if all the swords were one sword, what a great sword it would be,
And if that great man took that great sword and cut down every object of that great greed, that great envy and that great resentment,
What a great and everlasting retribution it would be.

She continues her explanation. "Just as we see that every human emotion being contained in the one heart, and that heart ever and again falling into anger and excess, error and ingratitude, we should not expect any collective representation of those imperfect hearts (however comprehensive and well-imagined it may be) to be free of the same imperfections, or escape the same defects or limitations.

"It is my sovereign oath which I have sworn," she concludes, "that when we see that Great Man striding forth across the land, holding in his hands that Great Sword by which he would do the One Will of men, I, ever obedient to that One Great Will whose judgment is written in the stars, shall stay his hand, where mercy does require.

Thereupon falling silent, the Queen watches for my reaction, as if she knows what confused emotions contend silently in my heart. Then, walking over to the window, she beckons us to look out.

"Tomorrow," she relates, "I will take part in a very important ceremony, which, if you will attend, you will see more clearly what I have tried to explain."

"You see," she gestures, pointing with her finger to the sky, "tomorrow night the full moon will stand upon the constellation Virgo ... and, you remember, my namesake was known as the 'Virgin Queen.'"

In Parliament
My guide and I take leave of the Queen, permitting her to rest undisturbed in preparation for some great labor which she must perform the next day. My guide, then, transports us directly to a busy public plaza located immediately in front of some large and imposing public building. This building I do not at once recognize, as it has been much altered from its form of which I was familiar from my high school history class.

"This," my guide explains, "is Parliament—not the same style or construction as you remember but built upon the same ground and having (equally with these stones and mortar) much the same foundation as that original once erected at this place. Let us go in."

Passing in the large and ornate doorway, we find ourselves in a space dark and cool to human senses. Our eyes gradually becoming adjusted to the dark, we see small groups of people standing here and there in this large reception room. Some of those groups are obviously tour groups who have traveled (in some cases great distances) merely to examine the ancient, commemorative statuary lining the walls. Here, I think, is some fondest dream of every voter of all history—a Parliament wherein every politician must stand entirely mute, forever listening silently and attentively to the words and opinions of the common people.

Alas, we pass from this reception room into an even larger room behind it, where we are greeted by the sight of politicians still in full voice and vigor. My guide explains, "This, you see, is the floor of Parliament, where the laws of the nation are debated and adopted. Now, England, like most democracies, has but two competing parties. For our purposes, we shall call them the party of the Right and the party of the Left. Each party seeks supremacy, gathering unto itself as many lesser groups and interests and advocacies as it can, thereby hoping to obtain power for its members. Of course, the other party pursing the same strategy, we see the balance shift back and forth from the Right to the Left and back to the Right as events in the world (whether due to His devices, or based upon some words or deeds or thoughts of men) might momentarily tip the scales this way or that.

"Today, this moment ... ," my guide is about to say, when he is stopped by the pounding of a gavel and a loud cheer arising from the floor. We look up and see that the Member presiding over this session (standing on some elevated platform opposite the main doors) is pounding his gavel, signifying to all that the bill before this congress has been adopted. That cheer (seeming to have arisen from but one side of the room—the Left or the Right, I could not say which) dies rapidly away, as we know the human heart cannot long deceive itself when it has committed some deed of which it is certain to repent.

"That," my guide resumes, "was the adoption of the budget by Parliament. You have just seen these representatives agree upon a fiscal plan which will guide this nation for the next year. Now, there are two important points which I must make clear to you.

"First, you must know that this budget is divided into two independent and self-contained parts. There is, first, that portion of the budget which represents 'expenditures' (called the 'Public Purse'), setting forth in unequalled detail all those purchases, disbursements, costs and expenses which this Parliament proposes to spend. The other portion of the budget sets forth (in no lesser comprehensive sums) all those items of 'revenue' (comprising every known synonym for the word 'taxes') which Parliament proposes will fund that first-noted portion of the whole. This second, unavoidable portion of this nation's annual fiscal plan is called the 'Public Revenue.'

"That long explanation is, as I noted," he repeats, "the first essential fact that you must know. The other is this: that today—this day on which I have brought you to see Parliament at work—is *not* the day following the night during which you and I visited the Queen in her dream. No, this day is that day one month *before* the night of the Queen's dream. Presently, you will see why I have presented these things to you as I have."

My guide once again motioning in the usual way, we soon find ourselves back at the Palace of the Queen, but this time standing in the Palace's large, ornate and private Audience Hall. Here we see the Queen seated on her throne and looking with attentive interest at two members of Parliament (and their respective Deputies) standing respectfully before her.

"What ceremony is this?" I ask. "What Members are these? And what do they wish of their Queen?" My guide leans his head over to mine and whispers, "Just watch a few moments, and whatever is not clear to you, I will explain later."

We watch in silence, and presently one of the Members approaches the throne, first bowing, then raising his head, then speaking, "If it please Your Majesty, I am the most senior Member of my party, the party of the Left, and I hold the office of Minister of the Purse. It is my duty, and also my honor, to serve you in whatever way I can." He then turns and motions for his Deputy to bring forward a weighty and disorganized stack of papers (tied up with ribbon and surmounted with a bow). "It is my pleasure to present to you Parliament's newly adopted portion of the budget constituting the Public Purse."

This first Member now falling silent, the second Member approaches the throne. He also bows, first, as deeply as his brother, and then speaks, "If it please Your Majesty, I am the most senior Member of my party, the party of the Right, and I am privileged to hold the office of Minister of the Revenue. I, likewise, have a duty which I am honored to perform." He then turns and motions for his Deputy to bring forward yet another enormous stack of paper (tied up with some bailing twine and fastened with some showy, elaborate knot, that one stack might not be mistaken for the other). He says, "I am pleased to present to you Parliament's freshly adopted portion of the budget comprising the Public Revenue."

The Queen, for her part (as if in accordance with some secret ceremony, which I can not divine), only looks on in silence as several of her servants rush forward to take possession of these two enormous stacks of papers. The two Members, their Deputies, and all other "outsiders" (who are not servants of the Queen) then taking their leave (and the doors of the Palace being closed behind them), we watch to see what commandment the Queen will issue—some no doubt ceremonial and heavily symbolic acknowledgement of the wisdom of the people's representatives, thereby bespeaking the honor, dignity and majesty of her iconic role as Head of State.

"Oh, bollocks!" the Queen exclaims. "What idiots these people are! Do they always have to wait until the last possible moment to adopt these budgets?! And then, they have the nerve to show up here with their ' ... please Your Majesty ... ' but they can't even put these pages in a proper binder! Look at this *used* ribbon! This ... cheap string! Honestly, you'd think if they knew they were going to present something to the *Queen* they could have at least gotten a sturdy box and some wrapping paper. If it were up to me, I'd put them all in the Tower! If I still had a Tower."

Watching this outburst, I could not help but recall that she (the *Queen* ... the *only* Queen ... the one who answers when you call out "Queen!" in some congested, noisy coffee house, and you've a Double Mochachino Latte to give out beneath that name) is a direct and lineal descendant of that decisive King who, when his wife displeased him, divided her head from her heart; the thought thereby pressing itself upon me that these Members came closer than they knew to that bipartisan Heaven where they have their hearts present on the Left and their heads present on the Right (or visa versa).

I continue to observe the Queen to see what disposition she will make of these two towering and disorganized stacks of documents. Turning to her chief advisors, the Queen first divides them into two groups. Then assigning to each group one of the stacks of documents, she instructs each group to make a thorough, honest and educated evaluation of the contents thereof, most especially taking note of that final, summarizing "bottom line" which each contains.

Thus one group commences to study, index and compare all of those objects on which money is to be spent, while the other group investigates, calculates and cross-references every thing-of-value to be separated from its private possessor in favor of the Revenue. And, always of primary interest, each group checks and double checks those final "bottom lines"—first measuring one against the other to find the one "too much," then turning both around to hold them up and see the other one "too little."

Now, it is not only the Queen's servants who I see are busy studying these documents. I see the Queen, also, busy herself investigating matters pertinent to Parliament's proposed budget. At her "command" (where, in fact, her popularity is such that her "request" suffices), men and women from across the land come before her (in the Palace, in private) to tell their stories and answer such questions as the Queen might ask. Whatever ceremony it is that the Queen must perform (which I hope to witness), it is clear that all participants take this process very seriously, indeed.

Thus I watch for one month's time. During these weeks the Queen and her servants make a wide-ranging and fearless study of the Public Purse and the Public Revenue. Day after day the Queen meets with many of her subjects, both the rich and powerful and those destitute and afflicted, and during this period I see strong bonds between the Queen and her subjects grow even stronger.

Her Judgment
At last the appointed day for the Queen's ceremony arrives. My guide and I (silent and invisible to all) are present in the Audience Hall of the Palace. The time of day is sundown; when the Queen might speak to all her Kingdom as if at one feast where all might share the bounty of this land—its food and drink and fire. We see that the Audience Hall is filled; the seats on one side occupied by Members of Parliament, judges, and members of the military, diplomats and priests; all the seats on the other side occupied by common citizens, in no way distinguished.

This great assemblage now falls silent, and from the back of the room, progressing in single file down the central aisle toward the throne and chairs at the front, we observe the Queen and some small group of men. We hear majestic and uplifting music accompanying this small number to their seats, and the smell of incense (ancient emblem of nobility) is apparent to all.

In the front of the Hall, I see that several chairs have been arranged side by side, facing the audience, on the floor before the throne (which is on a higher, raised platform at the back). There are, I perceive, five chairs spaced equally in the sight of the audience, but there is no one chair which we might suppose is provided especially for the Queen.

In a few moments the Queen and her party reach the front of the Hall. This small number (made up of these persons whom we know) are seated in the following places: The Minister of the Purse sits second from the right, and at his left (the furthest on the right) is his Deputy. Then on the left side, there is the Minister of the Revenue sitting third from left, and at the furthest left of all, his Deputy. Of course, there is the Queen, who takes her seat second from the left, where her purpose in this ceremony remains hidden from us.

I see that, as the Queen and her officials take their seats, they are guided not by any confused or haphazard fortuity, but take their places solemnly and confidently, as if they know what ancient and essential stage direction they must take. This small group being at last seated in their proper places, I soon become aware that they—and in loyal imitation, all the Hall—now pause in voiceless anticipation of some moment which to me does seem but counted out in heartbeats strong and fierce and free. Thus, when it seems her own heart moves her, the Queen (yet voiceless) stands ... then walks around her chair (taking care to keep herself between the Minister and his Deputy) and ascends the steps to the raised platform immediately before her throne.

The Queen, now standing at the edge of the platform (and thereby looking down upon all those assembled within the enclosing walls surrounding us), begins her speech (which setting forth below—I will not interrupt):

"This is my oath ... which I have sworn to Him, that by my words, my deeds, and in my person, I carry on my back the burden of the people, and loving them and keeping them forever safe, I do His work, and serve His greater Will.

"In long-ago and ancient times, we in this land feared, in nature, two recurrent and ineradicable dangers. The one: That being inattentive to His signs (or seeing them, that we do not give them their due regard) and thereby sleep or nap or doze when (having in our minds that picture of His bounty which He keeps for us) we ought to wake, tie up our tents, and travel to some other place where meat and drink and warmth are waiting there.

"That other danger which we know is this: That being surrounded on all sides by examples of His inexhaustible bounty, we are thereby borne aloft in joyful celebration, and, our reason being intoxicated with wealth and pride and self-regard, we (mistakenly) conclude that no more labor will be required of us—that we are free to start upon some pleasant change of scene.

"These being, as I say, dangers known to us of old, we do not often suffer them in this, our modern times. Nevertheless, this being a world wherein He has set aside a burden for every back, and stones loose and easily stumbled upon by any number of shoes, we find even in our time that there are signs (denoting danger) which even those of us favored by His grace must walk around.

"Thus I have before me, this day, two not easily calculable quantities (these being the Public Purse and the Public Revenue; each but the work of human hands) of which it is now my purpose to sum up, write down and parcel out in humble supplication of His eternal, faultless Wisdom.

"What is it that we fear (and sometimes see) when reading out that Public Purse? That where, in ancient times, we saw brave and skillful hunters pursuing fat and bountiful prey across the plains, now we see many such men find their paths lead only to Parliament, where they hunt only favor. Or, we see men who might have planted crops or tended herds or gathered grapes ... now cultivate only Public preference (as if the floor of Parliament were some never-fallow, ever-fruitful soil). Finally, we see young people bright, earnest and inquisitive who, in the past, would have studied science, medicine or mathematics (and thereby acquired knowledge worthy to be written down), now, instead, devote endless hours to study of the laws of Parliament, where (such legislation having in it no compass in reason, logic or fact) they do in time lose themselves in some inescapable jungle of Sections, Sub-Sections and Parts.

"And going on, I find that Parliament—in some Quixotic quest for Public Betterment—will sometimes open wide the Purse to pay for plans (concerning, for example, agriculture) by which our Public servants hope to usher in a New Millennium Favorable to Eggplants; whereby all the people of the kingdom are to be provided with all their 'needs' for eggplants (and, if that quantity be insufficient to employ all the idle farmers who have ever seen an eggplant, all their 'desires' for eggplants, as well); it being necessary, however, for us to set aside the fact (an inconvenient observation) that such a quantity of eggplants might be produced in this kingdom by no other means than discontinuing entirely the cultivation of all other crops and grains and forage, solely in favor of 'eggplants.'

"What, finally, might we also often read, when flipping through those pages of the Public Purse? Indeed, we often see this: That Parliament, considering the need (this year) to replace certain bridges which (all agree) have fallen into disrepair, does then decide (in some excess of enthusiasm—or total failure of restraint) that 'The Kingdom always needing bridges' they will provide, as well, for next year's bridges. Then, no doubt wandering off the floor of Parliament into the reception room before, and seeing several groups of school children gathered there, the Parliament next concludes that 'These children must have bridges!' (as who would dare to venture that, when all these youngsters do grow up, this land will lack for rivers?). Then, giving the matter as much additional deep thought as Parliament is able, the members at last conclude, 'Our children's children needing bridges, we must not deny the children!' Thus, we see (this year) that Parliament will build *bridges*—so many that, the trees necessary for their construction we find growing not merely in every woodland, copse and forest of all the land, but the majority thereof existing as but a twinkle in a woodsman's eye.

"Now next, I ask, what it is that we fear to see when reading out the Public Revenue? That where, in nature, we know that drought might come no more than once in every seventh year, and plagues of locusts come no more than once in any twenty years, and even great storms and floods no more than once in every fifty or one hundred years, still do we see 'collector' (of the Revenue) does never yet his yearly visit fail, nor does he once delay, forestall or by a single day put off that moment of his dire demand.

"That where, in justice, we who labor to produce some increase in our crops, our stores or our devices, do often see those crops which we expect to harvest, nevertheless (by some hidden disposition) wither away; our stores, which all our science tells us should come on to us in a flood, nevertheless ebb away; and those of our devices (which we have never seen to fail of their essential purposes) are by some unforeseen events now serving purposes which no one wants. Then, in spite of all these things, we see that the collector (that one judge who will hear no evidence of inequity, oppression or injustice) grants neither reprieve nor pardon: He, standing solitary and pitiless, unmoved by any empathy.

"And finally, there is this: That where, in the ancient past, we might have suffered the visit of the collector no more often than annually, in our more modern times we see his visage (first) as regularly as the moon. Then, that being (to his purposes) insufficient, next he comes as regularly as the dawn, and finally (seeing that so much going-away and coming-back is in its way tiresome and inefficient) he concludes that his duties require him to stand ready at the shoulder of every man and woman from dawn to dusk, that of every dozen eggs collected, he will be there to take the Public's predominating share, of every batch of cookies, bread or biscuits baked, he will be there to take the Public's ever-rising share, and of every draught poured and placed before the lips of every man who has labored the whole day to earn it, he will be there to drink the Public's first and thirsty share.

"For the profession of the collector is the one profession that recognizes no natural, periodic season, nor yet any inherent, essential limitation (unlike the farmer, who feeds himself and his family upon the increase of his fields, but never upon those seeds which he knows are necessary for next year's crops); nor does the collector know of any pity, forbearance or moderation, if the same be not provided for in that Public Appetite which (we have all observed) is never satisfied.

"Now I come to the end of my judgment. I have reminded us of those two great errors into which our great Public assembly does repeatedly fall; these being ... not secret or in any way hidden from us (as if more hours of deliberation by Parliament might make such mysteries clear) but rather written in our stars, each being but a part of that most ancient world wherein those first, most-noble kings did dwell.

"It is my judgment ... that of all those expenditures which I have seen written out in the Public Purse—and of the sum thereof—subscribed to by all those representatives of the people (no longer giving utterance to any disputation; and speaking as if with one voice telling their One Wish), I find that such amounts are over-valued by three-parts-in-fourteen. Let them be so reduced.

"And of all those items for collection which I have read in Public Revenue (which I perceive it is the Wish of our generous and open-handed Parliament unfailingly to exact from my productive subjects), I judge that such amounts are likewise over-valued: These by the proportion of seven-parts-in-forty. Let them be so reduced."

ಶ ಶ ಶ

The Queen, now having delivered her judgment upon the lives and fortunes of her people, did bow her head (as if, her burden for the moment being lifted, she could, at last, give thanks). My guide and I remained standing where we were, watching in silence as the Queen, and then the members of the audience, departed. Though we were now alone in the great Audience Hall of the Palace, I found myself unwilling to take my leave, feeling that I could not do so until I had written (in my heart) some appropriate summation of all that I had seen.

At last I said, "It seems to me ... where once I heard a man of humble, caring heart cry out (in bitter irony),

> *'Am I not the greatest of all kings? You see, no man might milk a cow or mend a pot or plant a melon except at my royal sufferance and command.'*

That Great Sovereign

I hear, too, as if by Echo, this great Queen declare,

> 'Am I not the greatest of all sovereigns? You see, no man might keep his oath, nor bear his burden, nor serve his Maker's Will except—as I do show—he first reads out His judgment in the stars.'

CHAPTER 34
I Travel Far

My journey has brought me to a place in my lessons where, with the assistance of my guide, I will make great progress. I recognize that I have a soul which is richly endowed with talents, inclinations, habits and desires. These, unmeasurable and in many cases invisible to me, are known to my guide in exhaustive detail. Next, all of the common, everyday circumstances of my life that are measurable and knowable by science are likewise known to him. He sees both and knows in each case, for each moment, where the line is drawn between the deterministic facts of the world, that overthrew my will and pushed me this way or that in response to materialistic forces, and those other events which are properly ascribable to the choices of my soul, acting freely.

And it is not just that my guide can draw that line for each moment of my life. No, it is also the case that he can survey that line from moment to moment, across the months and years of my life, until he finally connects the moment of my birth to the moment of my death, thereby marking off two separate domains: This the sum of my choices, freely made, the other, the sum of all of the natural forces of this world, before which I traveled unsheltered and adrift.

My guide knows, too, wherein each domain might be different, and where not. So, I ask my guide to show me, first, those pivotal events of my life where, similar to what we have seen before, a very great outcome turned upon a trivial choice. Perhaps it was my choice, or perhaps the choice of someone close to me—a parent, spouse, teacher or friend. Or some stranger, whose seemingly random choice steered my life in a new direction.

You may think: "We have come this way before." You recall that earlier in our journey, I was permitted to review and re-experience the many events of my life, including being witness to the thoughts, intentions and inner monologue of myself and those around me. Indeed, this is true, and there was a benefit to seeing those events (both open and visible, and secret and invisible) unroll as if in the form of a theatrical film of which I and my guide were the sole audience—one event after the other, occurring in their true and original order, mixing willy-nilly the mundane with the profound and pivotal, but always keeping faith with the true and honest narrative of my life.

Now, however, my guide gives to me a new platform from which to sum the choices of my life. I am shown, first, a particular, selected event from the narrative of my life (taken from such-and-so time and place and having its own self-evident lesson to teach); then, next, from some other time and place, no doubt far removed in years from the first, another event, its lesson adding to the first, expressing something more complex, profound and personal. Who can say how many such pivotal events I have experienced, or avoided, in my lifetime? How will my guide present this lesson to me? Perhaps he will show me, first, those instances where, due to some (apparently trivial) intervening cause, I was able to avoid death or injury. Next, instances where I was lucky to avoid the loss of a parent or sibling, or choices (seemingly inconsequential) that allowed me to meet my future wife, to have my career and profession, or to avoid losing any of those things in some unforeseen way.

Here is how my guide measures it out for me: This I might have lost or suffered, but did not; this other what I had or gained and by what fragile thread it all came hanging down upon. From the beginning of my life through its final hour, he shows me these moments—sparkling, fragile, reflective of so much that turns upon them, as pearls upon the thread of my lifespan, precious evidence of the precarious joys of our existence, and unknowable by any but Him.

But I know there is more. There are also, as we saw, those other outcomes that depend upon two trivial causes … and three, and four, and so on. We saw that there are those occurrences which are more or less embedded in the fabric of the past. More so than those we saw earlier that turned upon one single choice or event, but less so than those others that would have been near unchangeable certainties. How many such further "turning" events might there be in my life? My guide will know … will show me.

How unrecognizable might my life be by the end of this lesson? Was there much that I created by my own will? Or was the general plan laid out by others in a way that bypassed all my choices? Show me. Show me those great events of my life that turn upon a choice or efforts by others. What is it that I have truly accomplished? And for which I, in this final accounting, can place by my name and to my credit? My sense of honor? No, place that to the credit of my father, who showed me that one day, as my guide reveals, how strong is honor and how it shelters. My love for my family? No, place that to the credit of my mother, who, when I thought I had done some unforgivable folly, only took me in her arms and comforted me and wiped away the tears as though they never were.

I Look Out a Great Distance
My guide has much to show me. He starts in my childhood and comes to some pivotal point. Then he shows me the "road not traveled." His is the power of knowing the secret inclinations of my soul. Also the limitless possibilities of the materialistic, deterministic world. He sees them both, and he takes me, in my lesson, first one way and then another. Here (let us say), I am a child, climbing the plum tree in my backyard, and my foot slips, but I catch myself. Now, he also shows me … it slips, but I am too slow to catch the limb. I land one way, and only my dignity is injured … or, I land another way, and my leg is broken.

How many lifetimes might my guide and I devote to this experience? Many, no doubt. So many choices in a lifetime, and so many fortuitous circumstances that, taken together, paint the rich and complex picture of our lives. How much more so if we might go back and change this or that upon which all succeeding events depend. If I change a key event when I was, let us say, just 12, how many more lifetimes of possibilities might I want to see? And each of those lifetimes has its own turning points, trivial and otherwise, that would show me much about our world and about myself.

And neither I nor my guide will stop at just my one life. We will see my parents, grandparents and others; their pivotal choices and events, and how they might have fared in this or that aspect of their lives. No doubt I'll see my parents not meet each other and not marry (a sad story for me, their son!). I'll see my grandparents and learn how narrow the paths that brought them together to be married and have families.

But we won't stop with this small group. No, we go on to the whole number of the human species. My guide shows me the universal and unedited story of the human race, true and complete in all its variety and common folly, but then he shows me more. He shows me all the choices that might have been made (but weren't), the accidents that might have occurred (but didn't), the worlds that might have been (but weren't) and more, because he stands astride the line between the free choices of our souls and those inescapable destinies written into the laws of space and time. He shows me where lies the authentic judgment of a just God: Here there is guilt, as there is so-much measure of free choice; there no guilt at all, but only sadness that so much misery could be the result of a clock-work fate.

This is the vantage point on which I and my guide stand. We are at so lofty a place that we can see not just all the actual persons and events of history but also all the events that might have occurred, all the lives that might have turned out better, or longer, or happier. All the tragedies of history avoided. And those avoided, now to be seen and estimated, weighed against the authentic tragedies of life to see which is the greater. All that might have been different with the natural world and how our human narrative would have been changed. The books, music, art and philosophy that we never enjoyed because some chance event intervened and the author or artist died before its creation.

What a limitless and inexhaustible outpouring of people, events and experiences. Pleasures never, in truth, imagined, and it is my destiny to experience every sensation they have to offer. Beautiful women who never attained adulthood, now they are mature, and I am gratified with the pleasure they give. Empires that were proud and optimistic, now I see not fade or weaken but live on. The greatest kings and conquerors, their names famous in our history books, I do not see in these other worlds that might have been, but other names, unknown to us, and in these other worlds the emblems and icons of the endless ages, symbols of the greatness they achieved. Crimes that were committed, I see no longer occur. Victims' suffering, I see no longer suffered. Can my guide show me? Yes, my guide shows me all.

Indeed, I shall see this: Two young men, passengers in a streetcar. There is a fatal accident, but only one of them is killed. The other in time attains his position of power in Germany. The first, not having survived, is not there to assume the position of General Secretary of the Communist Party. As a result, Bukharin, not so decisive a leader, assembles a loose confederation of theoreticians to rule the Politburo up to 1941, when invading German armies threaten the Soviet Union. But now Bukharin, unable to maintain his power, is deposed in a coup. The new Soviet Government seeks an end to hostilities, but Hitler, perceiving weakness, presses on with his attack. In December 1941 Moscow falls to the German armies, and the Soviet Government flees to the east. Soviet forces are no longer a factor in the War. Hitler moves his armies to the west, where they are in place when the Allies attempt an amphibious landing at Normandy beaches. German armies, heavily outnumbering the Allied invaders, repulse the attack. Secure in Fortress Europe, Hitler embarks on development of the atomic bomb.

Is this the inevitable outcome of an event that occurred with a slightly different result on that earlier day in the streetcar? Well, no. It is one outcome, but there are many others. My guide shows me multiple possible outcomes of ever-more uncountable choices, chance occurrences and fortuitous events. He calls upon the universal catalogue of human history. The true record of this world and all the choices that might have been made differently, and all the altered events that would have thereby resulted, and then all of the further events that—not absolutely required by the laws of space and time—were themselves subject to alteration, and including their variations, and so on. Can I find a path out of this wilderness?

All the Numbers
I am at a point where I must add considerably to my Total to This Point. I had, from before, not only the world—the universe—as it was in all its uncountable variety, but now I see I must find some way to accommodate every other event in the history of the world "that might have happened differently." How can I count up such numbers?

Indeed, I need to strike out into new territory, never before exploited, to add many more zeros to my moments in the afterlife. Here is the new land to be explored.

You recall that I have my ball of onionskin paper—so many recorded zeros, each representing so many additional multiples of ten, written out in the language of the universal catalogue—wound round and round, and as rich with zeros as it can be. Now, imagine this ball is reduced in size. No longer written on onionskin, I find even that paper too dense for my purpose. Instead, I use now a kind of "fairy paper." Still a long, narrow strip with zeros written down one side and back the other, this new paper is so thin that the same number of layers of paper—the same number of times wound 'round the starting point—is only in size the same diameter as an electron, that tiny particle orbiting the protons of a single atom. Now this new-sized ball of fairy paper starts as the size of this foundational particle. But it does not stop there. I go further and fill up all the space of the atom with many newly added layers of fairy paper, wound 'round and 'round until the whole volume of the atom is full. Packed tight with fairy-pages.

This is just one atom of the previous ball of onionskin. Now a microscopic pattern endlessly repeated, atom by atom, for the entirety of what had been that aggregation of paper strips, filling up even the particles of the atoms (the electrons, the nucleus, the space between), one atom to the next, the zeros continuing in an endless chain of counting: All the moments that I need in this, the afterlife, where I might see (and seeing, know) all those events that ever were, that might have been, or by His wisdom may yet be, and all this to be written out … and counted, too.

What size do I have now, my collection of zeros? I think a good-sized pebble. Maybe as big as a small marble. Not large in weight or dimensions, but very, very great in duration. So many layers of fairy paper, wound 'round and written upon, densely counted. Time enough here for my lessons in the afterlife. I trust my guide to know the count and keep it for me.

CHAPTER 35
The Queen's Bower

A New Friend
Any of us who has heard the phrase "quiet as the grave" would no doubt forever cease to use such words, if ever being induced to read this far in this meditation. Looking back, we must be amazed to see such a wealth of activity, stories and surprising outcomes. Who could have imagined that the afterlife could be such a busy place? Indeed, speaking, now of my "eternal rest," I see that I will have what must be an infinitude of distractions to occupy my eternity of time, but I have not yet found any place in His one afterlife where I might find "rest."

Now, it was not merely my sense of order (seeking what pieces must be missing from that one perplexing puzzle of my eventual reward), nor was it the rigor of my intellect (which, solving some all-inclusive formula, had need of some one factor representing "lassitude"), but rather, that I found I had been overtaken by some inescapable weariness: A fatigue that had, I saw, no readily identifiable cause, bordering upon some pouting sadness (that does not fail to make its presence known, but will not speak or tell its just complaint).

At last my guide came to me and said, "I cannot help but observe that recently, you seem to lack your usual curiosity and high spirits. Questions I would have expected you to ask, now you let them pass you by in silence, not seeking what they would have had to teach. Mysteries which, being revealed to you, I would have expected them to give you pleasure, instead you display only irritation and annoyance that such answers should have been so long hidden from you. I cannot help but conclude that you are in need of rest and renewal.

"I will not disagree with you," I said. "For some while now I haven't felt quite right, and now that you point it out, I admit I have become fatigued and over-tired. So, what sort of leisure do you recommend?

The Queen's Bower

"Well ... " my guide began, but still pondering. At last he brightened, having come upon some idea which appealed to him. "I know! I remember you saying that you used to enjoy mountain climbing, and I know just the mountain we could climb. Now, this is only going to be an exercise in climbing—there is no special moral I am trying to teach. Just a refreshing day spent climbing the same sort of mountain you used to climb when you lived in Japan. How does that sound?

"Great!" I replied instantly. "Nothing so clears the mind and refreshes the spirit as a day getting tired and sweaty on the way to the top of a mountain!" Our adventure being agreed, my guide waved his hand and we were immediately transported to a location which, after some brief moments of initial confusion, I recognized to be a place I had seen before.

My guide and I were standing at the edge of a dense and overgrown forest, in the shadow of that decayed and abandoned structure which (even in that leafy gloom) I saw spelled out its message "HE VEN" overhead. This time my guide and I stood on the "hevenly" side of that small river we had seen before, and each of us now being attired in jacket, pants and boots, we were as ready to climb to the top of that decrepit fortress gate (where we might, perhaps, correct some gross misspelling) as we were to climb a mountain.

Nevertheless, I could not help but take a few moments to observe and contemplate that aged fortress, musing as I did that these great gates, never having barred a man from choosing "Right," they must have served our Maker's purpose well, being but that over-arching promise of His firmament which ... floating over torrents, floods and cataracts, a man in search of rescue must spy out.

"If you are ready," my guide began, "we will take the path that follows along this bank of this river. On the far side of the river, as you have heard, the path doubles around upon itself and goes off in this direction and that, never returning to the clearing by the bridge. However, on this side of the river, the path follows the river valley up the slopes of the mountain to the very source of the river, itself. Our final destination is not the top of the mountain, but it is enough of a climb to refresh your spirits, and the source of this river is something you will want to see. Shall we begin?

Thus my guide and I started our climb. Taking leave of that rotting fortress gate, we soon found the path we were seeking, and so began our climb. The weather was pleasant, crisp and stratospheric (this being, after all, that lofty elevation which many coming here before believed to be Heaven, itself). The path—though by no means easy to climb—was well marked and lying plainly in our sight. Stopping from time-to-time along the way, we paused here and there to contemplate some oddly growing tree or fractured rock or waterfall (that whispered subtle, sibilant secrets which we could not grasp). We climbed in silence, taking in the beauty of the quiet forest through which we walked, and, having no longer any choices to make along the way (having already made that one, first and fateful decision to begin our climb on this side of the river) we allowed our minds to wander in restful aimlessness.

We had been climbing for several hours, making good progress and reaching a considerable elevation—in comparison to the river bank where we had started—when we came upon yet another familiar place. It was a clearing in the forest, and surrounding us was that over-arching bower and stones gently emerging from the earth which was the place of my earlier humiliation. It was the same clearing where I met those fair and luminescent fairies, and where I had my audience with the Fairy Queen. Coming upon this spot, I could not avoid recalling those unexpected words which … my heart being then under the spell of Her Fairy Majesty, I could not help but speak.

My guide and I paused in the clearing, not yet deciding to sit and talk awhile, but as yet unwilling to press on and leave this lovely, quiet hideaway behind. Finally my guide spoke, "It has been some little while since you and I visited this place. Now, some time after we were here (when you learned that lesson of the Fairy Queen), I received a request that you meet with a certain member of that fairy race; one who has some further words to share with you in quiet conversation. Since we have the time, and since resting here might help to cure your weariness, I suggest that I send for this particular fairy, and we hear what he has to say." I readily agreed.

Accordingly, my guide and I took up those seats where we had once reclined when we met the Fairy Queen. In short order we made ourselves comfortable, and almost immediately we saw coming toward us out of the forest a man in his early 20's, not tall but rather shorter, and in silhouette roundish (not heavy, but giving in to flesh as if his humor, too, gave in to warmth and joy and friendship). His apparel performed some melodic chorus of green— his trousers of a sprightly, youthful green that warbled sunny fields of grass, his shirt and coat a darker green that sang of musty bowers, and on his head a cap of green (the like of which I cannot match) that trilled of leaves and buds that nestle vivid flowers.

This fairy strode boldly up to us where we sprawled upon the ground and, no doubt wishing to put us at our ease (that we do not find in him so much dignity that we feel the need to stand), he threw himself to the ground beside

The Queen's Bower

us with the words, "Hallow!! I'm Puck!" Thus saying, he looked at us with an altogether open and guileless expression (as if, having thereby written the first sentence of some lengthy, modern novel, he was perfectly content to let us fill in all the rest).

I was ... thunderstruck. In order to gain some time (and presence of mind) before replying, I swung my legs around to face him where he sat, then looked over to my guide. (I thought, "You claim to be my guide! So now, for once, some guidance, please!") But, like any teacher determined to be the equal of Socrates, he would not venture any hint of what I ought to reply. Thus once again thrown back upon my own dull dialogue and threadbare devices, I had no choice but to think back to that drama in which I had once played a part upon this woodland stage.

I began (tentatively), "Perhaps ... recently, well, since that incident when I had the opportunity to meet your queen ... uh, word, perhaps, got back to you in some way (which I hope was not in any way exaggerated) as to my grievance or (let us say) ill-feeling about ... well, certain comments (actually, just the one comment) which you may have made ... and I'm not saying you weren't fully justified to have said what you did; so, yes, I guess what it comes down to is ... How do you do, I'm pleased to meet you."

Having made this speech, scraping and bumping fitfully to the end, where my train of thought went entirely off its tracks finally in a heap at my feet, Puck continued to gaze at me transfixed in wondrous awe (as if, Abe Lincoln descending from his speaker's box at Gettysburg, he turned to Puck and asked him, 'How was that?') "And I am pleased to meet you, too." Puck replied, smiling slyly and giving me a look which seemed to say "We'll just pretend—between us—that all you said was, 'Pleased to meet you.'"

"The story which I heard," Puck began, "and you seeing it now from my point of view (which is not yours) is this: That there you were, a person only recently come to the afterlife (and only a visitor here, after all), and you having some problem (which was not particularly serious, from a "previously deceased" point of view), but, still, you claimed it was a problem, so alright, we'll pretend it was a problem. Then, in some way—and I'm not blaming anybody (he said, looking directly at my guide, as if, staring directly at him and speaking slowly, distinctly and loudly in the direction of my guide when he said this, there was any possibility of my guide not being aware who Puck was referring to)—your problem (such as it was—or is) somehow made its way directly to my Queen where, naturally, it took the efforts of three of my sisters and the Queen, herself, to solve this problem of yours ... which (I am not finished!), had it come directly to me, as it should have (my guide at this instant attempting to withdraw his head below the level of his shoulders, as if executing some deeply apologetic bow of which only his ears on either side of his head prevented him from bowing even lower in even greater self-abasement) I could have solved your problem quickly and with no effort or involvement of my Queen. You see, I hope, how embarrassing it was to me not to have been permitted to speak for myself from the first.

What an odd place this forest clearing was. Here we had been speaking only a few minutes (my guide not having broken his silence at all) and, to any observer, the words spoken by Puck could not be described as anything other than honeyed, sweet and liberal, and yet my guide and I both cringed upon the ground as if having been brought shackled in chains before some merciless and bloodthirsty tyrant attired in lime-green knickers. I looked sheepishly at my guide (who looked back crestfallen at me from out of the same flock), and then bravely trusting that initial goodness which we saw in him, we threw ourselves upon the mercy of this woodland Ozymandias.

Once again a kind and welcoming smile came over Puck's features, and my guide and I relaxed, prepared at last to give him all our sympathetic attention. "There are," he began, "several different ways that a person might approach the problem which you had (or have). That problem being: that you are guilty of some error, fault or misbehavior of which the consequences thereof are hurtful and cannot be condoned. This act of which you grieve, regret and would repent, you cannot find the words which being spoken out aloud in judgment might declare your crime to be discharged or pardoned.

"Now, I am sure you have given this problem much prayerful meditation," Puck said, looking at me. "What I would like to ask is that you now tell us what you have concluded—based upon your experiences thus far in the afterlife. Putting aside the lessons of my sisters and queen, how would you propose to solve your problem, today?" I was, surprisingly, animated and energetic enough to attempt to answer.

"I have, indeed, devoted considerable thought to this subject, having given it many long and sleepless nights in restless speculation. You know, I am sure, that in my meditation, I have traveled widely throughout all those times and places available to me in this afterlife, and doing so I have piled up a great summation of all the wisdom, knowledge and reasoning comprehensible by the human mind. Always I have before me this one, insoluble puzzle: How could it be that an error, once being made, might entirely and finally be erased? How could it be that some injury, sadness or disappointment, once being inscribed

The Queen's Bower

in that book entitled 'Shall Ever Be,' might be (instead) rubbed out and copied over in that other book we seek (but never find) entitled 'Never Was'?

"Here is what I suppose," I said. "I have seen that men and women, coming to the end of their allotted years, do gradually (and, it seems, naturally) give up what strength they have in body, mind and memory. Then passing away, they forfeit any further claim on life and likewise sever every passion, appetite and urge which bound them to this earth. Thereby it seems the road map of our lives does illustrate (our final destination being reached), that it is no more than the common expectation of all that we store away (as empty luggage—no longer useful to our corpse) those dreams and aspirations which nourished us along the way.

"Likewise, now standing upon that loftiest pedestal provided by the afterlife, if we but look back over those events of politics, commerce and religion which occupied our passions during life, we do also see that such eternally-disputed controversies—concerning, for example, Justice, Freedom, Equality and Religious Truth—do similarly escape us at the end. It seems to be a universal observation that, no matter which side of these earthly human conflicts we espouse while we are young and vital, when we do finally reach our body's end, these fade away to nothing.

"Now, finally, speaking of those most personal and intimate details of human life, it seems to me that if I were to describe some error of which I would be healed, there are those who would show me a ledger book (from that unbounded archive of the world) where I might see my error there inscribed, and with it written out all other such errors, so that anyone (turning to that page) might see how common, universal and predictable my error is. Indeed, it was once suggested to me that, my error being like any other (predictable as the first snowfall, or the date migration begins), I would not be unjustified to see in it some unavoidable necessity, as if it owed itself to nothing more than random chance. After all, is this not the inescapable destiny of all men? That they, heirs to what is 'common' and 'universal' in this world, come, in time (randomly, but predictably), to the one, same graveyard? I ask you, who of us being born into this world might be laid to rest anywhere else? And you, who are yet alive, is there any other property which is bequeathed to you unfailingly than this expectation of your own, private plot selected by the hand of random chance from among all of those open and empty in this one, great common Potter's field?

Finishing my answer, I fell silent, hoping by my speech to have painted for my fairy companion pictures of unfading reassurance. However, he glanced,

I thought, darkly at my guide, then spoke, "Yes, I see. Well, that was … interesting. Indeed, I see that my work, and the work of my fairy brethren, is not yet done." Whereupon he stood up, and my guide and I stood up with him, awaiting his instruction.

Her Bower

Puck hesitated an instant, as if he pondered which direction we should take in search of that solution to my problem which would satisfy him. Presently he spoke, "Now, if you had come to me in the beginning, I might have shown you an answer in some other way, but now that my sisters and our Queen have shown you much, it seems only proper that I should build upon that foundation which they have already laid. This I can do, if you will patiently attend what I will show.

Next changing the scene with a wave of his hand, Puck transported us to a different time but the same place. (Once again, all of us—Puck, my guide and I—were invisible to those we witnessed.) Our small group stood, as before, in the same clearing, standing beside the same stones and seeing the same trees and woods that I knew. But, kneeling on the ground before us I saw … myself! That image which I showed that day I stood before the Fairy Queen.

This "me" (this image of myself, my "counterpart") I saw had yet upon his cheeks those tears of his and hers (of Molly's) which I knew yet burned. My counterpart, I saw, remained upon the ground in sadness, grief and shame of his unkindest error. The Fairy Queen, herself, was no more there. Her time which she did grant to me was all used up, but there remained (still in the presence of my counterpart) that fairy which I knew before.

It seemed that this fairy (Fairy of Those Tears that Signify a Broken Heart) waited out some inner process which we could not know; then, while my counterpart remained kneeling in silent meditation, she once again reached out her gentle hand and gathered up those many tears which still remained upon his cheeks. I could not miss that as she did; she reached out with her other hand and placed it gently on his head, bestowing upon my counterpart some caring, healing, heart's caress.

Seeing that this fairy-servant had now taken up her watery burden, we waited for her as she straightened up and turned to go (and, I thought, did seem to glance at us—as if her eyes could see through any sham, including things invisible). Puck inclined his head forward in our direction and whispered, "Look sharp, now, we must follow her!" At this, almost before he had got the words out, the fairy started back into the forest, finding there a narrow, winding

The Queen's Bower

path which led off deeper into the woods. She walked briskly, but having her luminescent glow always before us as a beacon, we had no difficulty in following her through the gloomy shade.

In only a few minutes, it seemed, we emerged behind her into yet another forest clearing. We saw, at once, a lovely, over-arching bower of vines and stalks and flowers, having at its forefront an opening large enough to admit but one person (or fairy) at a time (and providing the human is willing to duck). In this clearing, however, our small expeditionary party was no longer alone with our phosphorescent quarry. Here we saw a group of fairies—each as gentle and fair as she who preceded us here—standing patiently in line. After a few moments of observation, we realized that the front of the line stood at the threshold of that leafy shelter and, now standing at the end of the line, was that fairy who clasped within her gentle grip those tears which I (and Molly) shed.

As we waited, and before we could react to what was before us, we saw a fairy (Fairy of Those Tears of Shame) emerge from the darkness of the bower. She paused to allow her eyes to acclimate themselves to the brighter day, then turned and left the clearing altogether; entering a path that led deeper into the forest on the far side of the clearing from where we stood. This fairy having departed the arbor, the fairy next in line (Fairy of Those Tears that Some Unkindness Knows) stepped up to the door of the shelter and, we noted, bowed deeply before entering fully into that leafy enclosure.

Puck turned to us and once again whispered. [Despite his words being already inaudible to this assembled grace of fairies, such evidence of his deference and respect was, for him, nevertheless not proof enough of his devotion to their goodness; accordingly, Puck, determined as he was in his own heart that his speech must not be permitted to echo or grate (and thereby shame himself silently in his own voice), did naught but whisper.] "We are going to go into this bower, but I caution you, you will not be invisible or inaudible to those inside." Then leading the way, Puck commenced to walk composedly in the direction of the arbor (my guide and I following) and presently we ducked down and stepped inside.

The interior of the bower was not large; leaving little space, indeed, even after we three pressed ourselves flat against the back wall on one side. There was no illumination—or rather, I should say, no other illumination than that supernatural incandescence emanating from the two fairies I saw before me. The one, standing in that place of supplication before the other, was the same fairy whom we had just seen enter the bower. She stood motionless, as if she paused in deference to that other, (seated) fairy who now looked in our direction.

I cannot imagine what spell of confusion must have been worked upon me that I had not, before this instant, recognized the fairy seated before me in the bower. This was—as if just now revealed—the Fairy Queen, herself! She looked at us in mild and benevolent curiosity, as if our visit were a daily thing, but she (forgetting this) did pause to wonder why it was that she had asked for us. Seeing her once again in all her sparking radiance, I could not doubt that in the world of fairies (where she reigned), buds blossomed only to shade her sight, vines traveled only to cushion her step, and stars burned in the heavens for no more reason than to ornament the dark (and so to please her fancy). Who could this be but that one, Unequaled Queen of all the solipsists of the world, whereby only in her all things that are (or wish to be) must measure themselves against the one standard of her perfection?

Noticing some movement at my side, I turned and saw Puck first close his eyes, then bow his head and pause his breath, in show of his obedience to his Queen. (He, not wishing to disturb her eminence, did not make such a grand and horizontal prostration as he was wont to do—there being no room for it, and his Queen being otherwise engaged paying audience to some other performance.) Looking back to where the Queen was seated, I could not help but notice that the stool on which she sat was only wood (not gold or pearl or ivory) and, on its bench, provided no more than some common velvet cushion (which even then, I saw, was threadbare from so many years of constant use).

The Queen, now returning her complete and undivided attention to her fairy-servant standing before her, nodded her head, and the fairy thereupon commenced some grave and momentous ceremony, as if placing some ancient and insoluble grievance before the one, all-knowing sovereign who might satisfy it. This fairy held up her hand (that hand in which she held those tears which she had collected) and, turning her fingers this way and that, presently we saw those tears collected into one, and that one now hanging down from her fingertip as if it were a sparkling teardrop pendant held out where all might see.

Then, taking out her fairy mirror, she held the face of that mirror up before her so that her other hand (holding the tear) was close beside it. Now, taking care to face her Queen directly, the fairy moved the mirror so that—taking into account where the Fairy Queen was seated—the mirror conveniently reflected (to the sight of the Queen) the image of the tear. Thus, the Queen could readily and effortlessly observe in that fairy mirror (which all too well, I knew, showed all) that tear which told of loss and lack, of pain and woe, of error, falsehood and deception.

The Queen's Bower

We three visitors had been silent during this ceremony but, at once, we all (as one) drew in a single breath and startled, marveling at her reveal'd, resplendent power. The Queen, seeing the image of that tear now centered in the mirror, she reached out gently with her hand and, instantly, the shelter was bathed in brightest light! It seemed that modest mirror now burned with all bedazzling brilliance (and cleansing power) of the surface of the sun! And, as we stood transfixed by this pulsing, mesmerizing blaze of light, we saw that from within the oval of the mirror's frame, now there showed forth images, motion, sounds and voices.

Our party being in no way prepared for this explosive show of radiance (some secret door having been opened unexpectedly into some violent, turbulent universe of perpetual sound and light), we could do no more than cower against the wall. The Queen, for her part seeming to take no notice of the power and illumination which she had unleashed, only focused her gaze attentively upon that mirror, taking in those scenes it showed and well-remarking all that was said and done, and wished and regretted, within that oval frame. When she had at last satisfied herself that she had seen all that this tear had to teach, the Queen allowed the mirror to go dark; the servant-fairy, still holding that looking-glass—and tear—before her (unmoved), she bowed her head in tribute to her Queen.

The fairy-servant now put away her mirror and, taking up that tear, again, into her hand for safekeeping, she prepared to depart. The Queen, however, motioned for her to come closer and, when she did so, the Queen whispered some few words into her ear. Having imparted these additional words of instruction to her servant, the Queen now turned to us to speak (the fairy-servant at once leaving the shelter).

"How nice to see you again," the Queen observed, looking pointedly in my direction. "I see that if I am going to get anything accomplished in this fairy realm, even I (its Queen) am going to have to go through 'channels' and not jump in and try to do the work of those (she glanced at Puck) who do it better. Even so, I require no fairy mirror to show me how things stand with you, my friend, who once professed yourself 'no fool' then later changed your plea.

Leaning back more comfortably in her seat, the Queen went on at length. "Considering what you have just witnessed, you may perhaps guess the nature and purpose of this exercise, but even so, there is much that is not yet revealed to you. No doubt Puck has brought you here so that you might understand these things which you have already been privileged to witness, but his purpose cannot finally be served until the rest is fully made clear.

"You know, of course, that it is the unceasing duty of my fairy-servants that they travel (unimpeded) throughout this universe of time and space, where it is their purpose to seek out every man and women who suffers and in whose eyes we will find that tangible evidence of their grief—which we call a 'tear.' You will not find in heaven or earth any place where, a tear being shed in sadness, pain or misery, there is not also to be found there one of my servants, watching, waiting and bearing witness. Thus, it is my sacred, loyal duty, that I and my servants keep that promise which our Maker pledged: that there is not any tear shed in solitude, nor any pain nor want, nor loss nor lack, that goes unacknowledged in the world; that any such thing should ever be unknown to Him.

"You have been told, I understand, about the uncaring, heedless indifference of the world, which some claim to be the foundation of all that is. Let me tell you, now, that if you were to plumb the deepest depths of that one stagnant well of apathetic, inattentive disregard, you would find those waters to be only as deep as my fairy-servants desire them to be; they having fed the springs of that watery randomness with their own fairy buckets.

"Now, concerning those powers of my fairy mirror which you have only just now observed, the explanation is plain. My fairy-servants collect those tears which represent tangible evidence of the sorrow, misery and loss which those human hearts endured. Then holding up those tears before some fairy mirror, I see before me every circumstance which they reveal: The nature of those tears; that they be due to grief or loss, loneliness or abandonment, or any other of a thousand similar causes; and of those tears, the 'fault' thereof, that they might show the error of some person (self or others), deceit, misfortune or necessity. And, finally, I am shown—of the heart which shed that tear—what words or deeds or only time which might repair that hurt.

"Here is a great truth better known in the fairy world than in yours; that there is nothing sure, true or eternal which does not have its own earthly exemplar (of which, being weighed and measured out in your world of dust and clay, you place upon it some 'price' in common, earthly currency, when, in fact, its true worth is to be found only in that one heavenly storehouse which accumulates all things of eternal value).

"You who would put your faith in science, logic and fact, what tangible proof would you adduce of that 'random chance' which you place at the foundation of your world? Would you, going out among all the men and women of this world—living lives unpredictable and unplanned—seek 'randomly' from among their number, and no more than 'fortuitously' from among all of those days and hours which are given to them, to find any tangible evidence of an intangible despair?

"So, you see, the 'truth' of every such tear is unfailingly seen, told and recorded; there is no heart which suffers alone; no voice whose just complaint is not heard; no one soul who, having endured some deceit, dishonor or betrayal, does not thereafter place such facts in evidence in this one fairy court where such injustice might be verified and sworn before my eternally unforgetting eyes.

"Now, finally, there is one further truth which you must learn, and it is this: That ... these tangible emblems of the loneliness, loss and misery of the world being here collected, and each of them being measured and appraised, and the stories which they tell written out in the hearts of me and my fairy-servants, these tokens are at last put away and no more regarded ... until that day when all is revealed and His eternal judgment totaled up in some just and final summation.

Some Ever-Verdant Pasture
This final lesson of the Fairy Queen being now at an end, Puck, first, and then my guide and I, in honest imitation, bowed to the Queen and silently exited the shelter. Coming into the bright sunlight outside the bower, we, like that fairy I observed earlier, had to pause to allow our eyes to adjust themselves to its radiance. As we waited, not yet having ventured any comment upon all that we had experienced, one of the Queen's fairy-servants came up to us.

I looked at her, and I was at once struck by the thought that I knew her; that I had seen her face before. Naturally, having seen but few actual fairies during my stay in the afterlife (and none at all during my time on earth, not that they were ever in any way absent), but wishing to match her face to one I had seen before, there were only a few faces from among those I had to choose. Quickly it came to me who she was. It was she who waited during that dream of the Groom (my own self, betrothed) and who could not help but witness those three vows which I placed before his (then) unseeing eyes.

This fairy smiled at me, seeming to have waited for me to recall her face and form, and no doubt intending that I revisit in my heart that moment when I dared the Groom to swear those oaths (and thereby risk his 'all' upon some modest home and fields and pledge of heart's fidelity to rule his fate).

"I am happy to see you again, she said, keeping her smile. It was rude of me, I am sure, to have been in your company, once, and to have had business there, yet to have failed to properly introduce myself. My name, she explained, is 'Fairy of Those Tears That Youthful Folly Knows.' It was my Queen who sent for me to come this moment, that I might attend to you, again, and show you more.

"You know, of course, what duty it was that I discharged that night of the Groom's dream. Thus, you have by your life's unkindest error—and by your attempt to undo that error—provided both me and one of my sisters with that sad duty of bringing to our Queen evidence of your heart's anguish and despair. You have, just now, by the thoughtful actions of my brother, Puck, been privileged to see what use my Queen makes of those tangible tokens of your heart's wrongdoing.

"Thus, my duty, next, is this: I have been charged by Her Majesty to show you that final resting place of those tears which you so heedlessly brought into the world." Then turning to her brother, Puck, and to my guide, she spoke, "Our Gentle Queen has asked that I take him alone to those places he has yet to see. Perhaps, in the meantime, you could catch up with some of your old friends who will be arriving here shortly?" They being agreeable to the Queen's request, Puck and my guide headed off to the edge of the forest to find some shade.

The fairy next held out her hand, pointing in the direction across the clearing where that path (earlier taken by others) entered the forest. With her in the lead, I followed her onto that path and deeper into the woods. We walked for some little while, in time passing out of the forest and into a wide and fragrant orchard where I saw blossoms of dogwood and plum, cherry and mulberry. When we had passed through all of these rows and columns of flowering branches, we came to another landscape where, looking in all directions, we saw fields (of flowers) growing densely with lilies and irises, blue bells and marigolds. These fields and orchards were as redolent with their promise of fertility as I remembered, having visited them already when I showed the Groom that second vow which 'he must make.'

After we had walked for what must have been an hour's hike, we came, at last, to the edge of a meadow. It was unfenced, large and growing green in succulent abandon. (I could see it had never been mowed.) Looking out over its gentle slopes and flats and hollows, I could not help but notice that the morning dew seemed yet upon the grass: the sunlight glistening and sparkling here and there across its profuse and proliferant surface, as if I saw some night's reflection of undying stars, scattered here and there by the hand of He who makes the grass to grow.

I was transfixed by the sight of that lush and ever-luxuriant landscape. I felt ... as if stricken; overcome by some profound and inescapable silence,

The Queen's Bower

wherein voices did not venture to intrude. "Allow me to explain," the fairy began. "You see before you a large and unbounded meadow—a pasture, in fact—which adjoins that mountain which you were climbing. You see before you an unbroken expanse of grass which, I will tell you, is interrupted only by a small river which drains its valleys and contours. Now, you have seen that stream before, I understand. It is that river which passes within reach of that ancient fortress gate which you observed, and from there, you know, it passes through the center of the Village where its residents—when they give it any thought—do so only to measure its depth and calculate its salinity.

I stood in silence; no more than taking in and ruminating upon what this fairy had just explained. Looking out over that expansive pasture—of virgin growth, unmarked by any road or ditch or furrow—I wondered, "Is there ever any snow? If I (disobeying my guide, and heedless of my footsteps leaving tracks) were to run out into that wilderness, to some unlooked-for, likely spot (my impulsive whimsy abandoning me there), and if I were to stop and call out, "Here's the Center!" would I find myself (again) bestride the axis of that Wheel of Fun? Could this be home to any 'Evil Fox' or 'Clever Goose?' Or mock-regret of 'corners cut?' Now see my footprints in that snow! Where—spoke to rim and rim to spoke—I seek that Innocence which 'spins the wheel' of childish fun. And never-giving-up the chase … I find, again, that joy I knew, and so I close that final gap and feel I win the game, at last.

While I continued to ponder these questions in my heart, my fairy companion gestured with her hand, and instantly there was revealed to me what until this moment had been withheld from my sight. Now no longer concealed; I saw appearing in the pasture here and there, as if materializing out of the ether, numberless fairies. Each, upon arriving in the field, looked around her, appearing to seek some tuft or blade of grass where as yet there was no drop of dew to be found. And each such fairy, I saw, held up before her at her fingertips a tear (or tears) doubtless collected in the same way as were my own tears.

It was at once evident to me that these fairies had but moments before departed that forest bower wherein the Fairy Queen held court. The words of that Queen were thus made transparent to my understanding: each such tear having once been held up before some fairy mirror, and having told its truth before that one fairy magistrate who will hear no falsehood, all of them were at last brought to this place by their attendant fairies; there being no more use for them in this afterlife than to serve that purpose which our Maker has for them here.

Now, watching one such fairy, I observed this common scene: she, having found some appropriate blade of grass, reached out her fingertips and placed those tears she bore upon that slender reed; then, having thereby delivered her burden to this eternal repository of all the world's misery and loss, she did but fade away, recalled to her place of service at the instance of her Queen.

"You see," my fairy-guide continued, "this great pasture is watered only by those tears collected by my fairy-sisters. And, those watery drops never ceasing in their abundant precipitation upon this celestial watershed, it is no more than some unavoidable hydrological necessity that the small river which you once crossed is (sadly) all too often given over to saturations, floods and inundations.

As I continued to look out over the pasture, I noticed that the area near where we were standing began gradually receiving fewer and fewer fairies until it reached the point where there were—temporarily, no doubt—no fairies coming there at all. Before I had the chance to ask my fairy guide about this odd occurrence, the answer galloped into view. Coming over one of the hills near us I saw first one, than another, then finally four (in total) wild and strong, fast-running horses! Each bore upon its coat no mark or scar of harness, and in its lips no space where any bit did ever bite or pull. Running at the limit of their illimitable energy, I saw they ran as much, today, unbounded, free and ignorant of fence and gate as ever in those days they knew before they fell into that snare (of limbs) which was the work of kings.

"There are," the fairy explained, "four horses which have their home in this boundless pasture. This was, I believe, some promise which our Maker made to them, that they might once more serve their kindred King, who is that Great Horse which grazes in the stars. You see, these horses run unceasingly throughout these fields and meadows, and by the actions of their powerful legs and hooves and flanks, they cause that dew of tears (yet adhering to the grass) to be thrown off in one final, fated disregard where (all such tokens of our earthly bereavements having been gathered together in trust of His eternal goodness) they pass finally into the soil and—as is their nature—do swell the banks of that small river and seek some outlet to the sea.

We watched those four horses gallop joyfully past where we stood, each one energetically traversing those hills and valleys which occupied the landscape between us and the slopes of the mountain on the other side. We could not help but marvel at the images of those horses—born wild and free—whose colors, we saw, did burn in iridescent hues of brown and tan, and black and red ... which all, we saw, were painted on their hides by fairy hands.

The Queen's Bower

After the four horses disappeared over one of the distant hills, the fairy spoke, "There is one more place which you must see." She thereupon turned and walked off, choosing another path which skirted the pasture to one side. We walked for only a short time before the path re-entered the forest and commenced once more to ascend the side of the mountain. We climbed, I would guess, no more than another hour before we came to our destination.

My fairy guide preceded me out of the woods and into another forest clearing, this one larger than the one which held the Queen's bower. This forest glade, I saw, was exceedingly calm and picturesque. On its far side was some rocky, overgrown shoulder of the mountain over which, at its lowest point, emerged a stream, thereby forming a lovely, gently-descending waterfall. That waterfall let itself into an otherwise waveless and serene pool of sparkling clear water; the pool making up most of the clearing. The air, I soon became aware, was as refreshing as anything I had ever experienced, and the sounds of the waterfall fell with an equally refreshing effect upon my hearing.

I watched this scene in silence, not wishing by my dull and cheerless voice to break any spell to which (it must be) I owe this scene of peace, healing and renewal. "Now, I was told," the fairy ventured, "that recently you have become … overtired, confused and fatigued. Thus my Queen instructed me to bring you here, that you might be refreshed and find some tonic for your weariness." Finishing this invitation, the fairy once more gestured with her hand before her, again revealing to me what (until this instant) she had withheld from my sight.

Now, I saw coming out of the forest (and making their way to the edge of the pool), numerous fairy-servants who, by their halting steps, did visibly show some aftereffects of the grief and affliction with which they were previously burdened. These were, I saw at once, those very same fairies whom I had recently observed put down their teary-burdens in that unfenced and gateless pasture.

Each of them, I saw, did suffer the effects of that most wearisome of all ascents, first starting out at that lowest low (where was found some human soul who suffered), next climbing up (encumbered) to that more lofty elevation of the Queen's bower, then finally ascending to that one, highest pinnacle of earthly attainment (beyond which there is no greater glory to be achieved): that common graveyard of His ever-verdant pasture where, having brought with them that unbearable, tangible evidence of the heartbreak of the world, it did seem that even fairy-souls must stumble under such a burden.

Each fairy, I saw, walked directly to the edge of that refreshing pool. There, finding on a rock or log an old and well-worn cup of tin, she dipped a cup of water from that pool and tasting it, she found herself renewed. Then returning the cup to the place where she had found it, each fairy turned and ascended the banks of the pool where (for some brief while) she gathered with her sisters in the shade.

My fairy-guide turned to me and spoke, "You may drink, if you like." Feeling at the same time both honored and obligated by this invitation (knowing that my own heart would not bear up as virtuous as these fairies in His sight), I steeled myself against my own guilty conscience and walked gingerly up to the edge of the pool. There I quickly found an old, corroded cup and dipped it in the water. Then, I brought it up to my lips and prepared to drink.

However, by what aversion I cannot say, I could not touch my lips to the rim of that cup. Perhaps ... already breathing in the scent or vapors of those waters, it was the mist from that waterfall which put into my mouth some taste of bitter scorn. Whatever cause it was, I found I could not drink.

I returned the water to the pool and the cup to the place where I had found it. Then returning to my fairy guide, I expected from her some words of admonition; however, she only asked, "I see you do not find these waters to your liking. Can you explain?"

"I cannot tell," I replied. "It seems to me as if ... that cup of healing is not mine to drink. Indeed, I know, now, that there is one other who, until she has first brought her own innocent lips to that same rough cup, drinking deeply of those sweet and all-renewing waters, I shall not find my heart replenished, nor find in any waters any freedom from my thirst."

The fairy smiled, "Do not concern yourself. There will be another opportunity to drink from these waters. You see that stream which forms the waterfall, coming down from a place higher on the mountain? The source of that stream is another, though smaller, pasture nearer to the top.

"Some day, when the time is right, you will come to that more lofty pasture, and you will see that it is as abundant with grass and vines and flowers as that pasture which you have already surveyed. I cannot promise you, however, that that higher pasture will be as grand and majestic as the one you have just seen (home to that noble herd of horses). That other, higher pasture, you will find, is home to no more than common rabbits: of all His creatures, the one, most sympathetic, mild and humble symbol of His forgiving spirit.

"You see, that higher pasture, too, is watered only by tears ... but in that place—they are but tears of joy, my friend, of joy ... and forgiveness."

CHAPTER 36
My Journey Ends

I Challenge My Guide

Many are the hours that I have given over in quiet meditation to the lesson taught to me by that Fairy Queen. Yes, I have been a fool, which when you hear that word, you think it was some (minor) falling-short of which I, in all due time, will pay the price. But this is not the case. No, is this not one of the most grievous of life's injustices? That, seeing my error, and feeling that painful sting of guilt of which, knowing full-well my sole responsibility, I do not resist nor seek to justify.

That, notwithstanding all the pain I feel at what I did and who I hurt and how so little I can do to make amends at this late date, here is the worst of it: That I, having done that thoughtless, hurtful error, it is she who suffers most for it. Thus, to my guilt and shame for my behavior I must now add injustice to those burdens which I bear.

In life, my error was like any other: Having once been written out by that all-seeing hand who keeps eternal record, I could not (in any way I know … nor did that poet) have any way to "lure it back to cancel half a line." But yet, am I not here in the afterlife, where much is shown to me? And is there not any lesson which my guide might teach me which, if I but asked, could take away this burning shame I feel? Meditating on this possibility, at last I conceive a plan, and (with hopeful apprehension) I go to my guide to ask if there is any help which he can give me in this way.

Here is the plan which I formulated and which I now propose to my guide: A simple question. Nothing out of line with our earlier lessons. I ask him "Show me my life … without this mistake, but otherwise the same outcomes, all the same, if there is such a thing." For, as we have seen, there are laws of space and time to which even our Heavenly Father owes obedience. And it may be that, for all I know, this mistake is one of those pivotal events upon which my whole later life—or that of others—might revolve. But here I assume not: that there is a world, easily possible, and within the bounds of probability, not against necessity, that omits this one mistake of which I am ashamed.

I ask him, "Take me to the place where there is recorded in the universal archive of human history … my mistake. The one place where it resides. Written not as a possibility among the numberless occurrences that fall within His sight, but the one, true record. And when you have found that place, I want you to write this—in substitution—the record of my life without this mistake but all the other outcomes just the same." I know my guide can go to such a place. And it is within his power to make this alteration, for the events of this world are, as we have repeatedly seen, fragile, and resting lightly upon the world.

Now I know this is my speculation, and it could be otherwise, for I cannot overcome the limitations of this meditation, of which I am keenly aware, but here is what I imagine: That my guide indulges me this far. He takes me to the universal archive, to the place where my mistake is written, and he shows it to me, and he tells me "Yes, this is the place, you see." And I read it, and so it is. There I am at the times and places, and her (the other person) and what I do, and how I feel about it at first. Then how it runs its course, and tears, and more events, all too trite … and then, in a way, it's over, and we don't talk about it any more, and we go on. But it happened, nonetheless.

So I say to my guide, "I want to change this. Take it out." And my guide pauses, considers, then finally says, "I will show you. And make the change you ask." And he does.

First, he writes—in the same hand as the universal archive of human history—the events of my life, complete and in detail, and all the same as I know. Except, in the one place, he writes not my mistake but, instead, some common daily routines, some characteristic activities of mine, and of her, some other choices. So, as he promised, my guide has made this merciful change, and I feel relief that this shame is taken away.

Then continuing, my guide, as he must, goes on to write the true record of all of my family, friends and co-workers. Expanding outward in succeeding waves of humanity, my guide records the totality of all the events of this world that we have so exhaustively considered.

And he, sympathetic to my efforts, adds up the numbers in the same familiar style that I have labored to produce. First, the list of zeros on a long strip of onionskin wrapped in a ball and added to again and again. He writes the events of the natural world and the inner monologue of all persons throughout history. He writes the transcript of all speech of all time and the music, books and science now known and ever to be known. He adds more to my little tangible record, more layers of onionskin, and presently he changes over to fairy paper so he can fill up the space of each of the atoms with writing—pages and pages of writing—counting the time of this world with my wish already recorded. But there is more.

I wait patiently. My guide presses on. He writes continuously for a time then stops, having come to the end. He opens his hand, and in his palm, a small, pinkish stone—the size of a robin's egg—and he tells me, "Yes. This, then, is the record. All the world as you knew it, and all the people, and everything that was and might have been. All there—and your change here, too. No longer is there any mistake … as you were guilty. Is this what you wanted?"

I am excited! I reach out greedily for the stone! To snatch it from him … but I am too hasty. I knock the stone from his hand, and it falls to the ground.

His Boundless Pasture
I quickly look down to find the precious stone that I have dropped. Oh, I must have it! Evidence that I am innocent! That I am not the person who did that thoughtless, selfish error.

But I look down and see … that I am standing on a wide, stony beach. By some body of water having no farther shore, but only the receding horizon. And I see that my one, small, pinkish stone has fallen on a limitless expanse of small stones, not dissimilar to my precious stone. All the same size. Smooth and rounded. I reach down and pick up a handful … can I pick the one by sight? By color? Is it still warm from my guide's hand? I look and study. What can I do? I look up again, and I see in every direction … small stones.

I hear the voice of my guide, "If you want to have your desire, you must find that one true record of the world wherein is written all that you wish. You must search for it. He has given you a very great time to find it. Shall we begin?" I follow him. We look from stone to stone. Each one a record of the universal archive, with this or that alteration, a record of this world, or that, that might have been, or was, or will be.

And I see the numbers of each stone are not separate from the others. But one continues to the next, and so on, throughout the whole of this vast expanse of beach and out under the sea. To the center of the earth whereon I stand. And there are only stones … and then the sea, too, is gone, and in its place yet more stones, and then there is nothing left but stones, and every one a record—written out in fairy-ink on fairy-pages—'round and 'round wrapped until there is

When Once I Lived

no space that is not the number of a moment—the smallest memory that I recall—here the taste of a popsicle on a July day when I was eight, next the memory of my sweetheart's smile when I first told her that I cared, and more besides.

All these numbers my guide and I pursue. We look and look, one stone to the next. Who can count these moments? But there is more. I look up and see the stars. Faint points of light. And here and there a sort of smudge that shows a further congregation of stars at even greater distance. And my guide looks and smiles and indicates these are—with his expression I now understand—not stars, but luminous collections of small stones, the tangible record of the time that I must devote to this, my search. These shining collections of stones, of unimaginable size and number, outpacing my plodding wit. Shall I count them all? Shall I experience all that they record? Every moment? As real and vivid as my first taste of sweet, or my first kiss?

My guide leads the way. We rise up weightless into some dimension where we look out upon our earth from a great height. I see that every substance—the soil, the stars and every other thing—has been made a fairy paper tablet upon which is written that endless catalogue of numbers. And then, in a twinkling, he shows me this record added to, expanded, made more complete ... and all the space between the stars extinguished. Wrapped 'round and 'round in fairy paper. Countless light years of distance consumed in numbers, one following close upon another. All the moments ... but not yet an eternity. I feel breathless. Dizzy. How can I take this in? Would my guide lead me to disaster? To some barren place where my mind fails?

My guide shows me this: It is all the universe filled up with fairy-numbers (each one reposing motionless in its sequential place, the whole as if rehearsing some procession of the dead). So it is that I might read these numbers. It is, let us say, a "1" followed by this many zeros, in the given order, starting in this place, the very stone I hold in my hand, and written out in order, continuing from one stone to the next, traversing the whole universe then coming back to the same stone in my hand. All one number ... of very great extent.

Now, my guide shows me, we have come to the end of one form of our numbers. We no longer have, in all the limitless universe, any place where we might write—even in a fairy-hand upon fairy paper—any further numbers. I look down at my small stone—the beginning point of this, the "Universal Number," and I see ... something is changing. I see that every space, having been filled with zeros, and there being no more place to add to them, that very number, that "1" followed by this universe of zeros, becomes symbolized by a small image. I see that symbol, a tiny image of a dogwood blossom, like

My Journey Ends

this ❀ written in place of the "1"

    ❀,000,000,000,000 …

And then, another ❀ in place of the first "0"

    ❀,❀00,000,000,000…

and then the second…

    ❀,❀❀0,000,000,000

and the third…

    ❀,❀❀❀,000,000,000 … and so on.

This fairy number, which until this instant I had thought to be very large, indeed, now leaps in size. No longer but a barren progression of empty zeros, this chain of fragrant, scattered ❀ now promises some more abundant, copious profusion, showing by this seamless, snowy blanket how much greater is the time which yet remains.

 Then, with added shock, I see my total suffers yet another transformation (even greater than the last). I see … that, where before I had recorded my total using "positional notation" [where, for example, "678" means $(6 \times 100) + (7 \times 10) + (8 \times 1)$, which, even for a number written out in only three digits, is not small], now my total changes over to "exponential notation" (which was, you may recall, that rare device which gave to us the chance to place those all-compelling Moments of our lives into some new relation "having in it power"). We discovered, at that time, how we might invoke such relation (which we observed "does cast its spell") by placing all such Moments (and now our Total) into that form which we would write as follows:

$$6^{7^{8}}$$

And thereby do we demonstrate (inferentially) that this unbounded sum does raise itself (exponentially) to some more lofty, elevated place; and so we read—

When Once I Lived

and calculate—this number (as we did before) as "6 to the 7th to the 8th" (and which, by climbing up these steps, we see horizons many worlds away).

Thus next I see is expressed (adopting this potent and effectual device), and in the same fairy-hand as before,

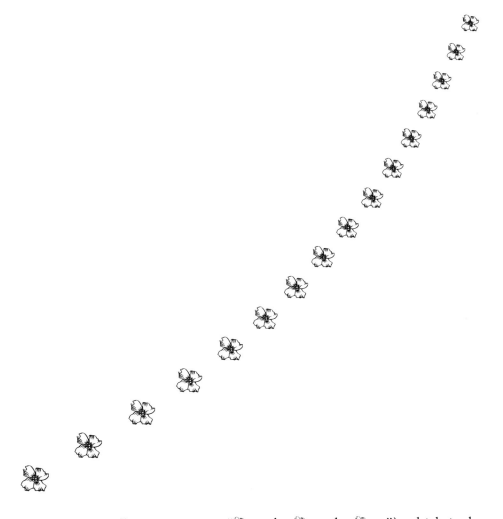

(which you recall, we pronounce "❀ to the ❀ to the ❀ ..."), which is the Universal Number raised to it own "power" first once, and then again, and again, and so on, until I see, looking down at the small stone in my palm, that this procession of ❀, replacing this one "0" and then the next, and then the next, goes out across all the universe, never pausing until (in time), its every (exponential) transformation made, it arrives back in my hand.

My Journey Ends

Now, here at this moment I feel a dread that I cannot express. Is this more than my soul, my spirit can tolerate? Am I being lead step by step into insanity? Suddenly I feel alone. I look around, but I do not see my guide. Have I come too far? Did I go off the path? Am I in some mysterious wilderness where my guide dares not follow?

I look down at my hand. I see the final "0" change over to a ❀. Then I see this, too, is changed. This new number—this endless strand of ❀ is newly symbolized. This time, I see a lily (✾) symbolizing … well, you know. And so it continues.

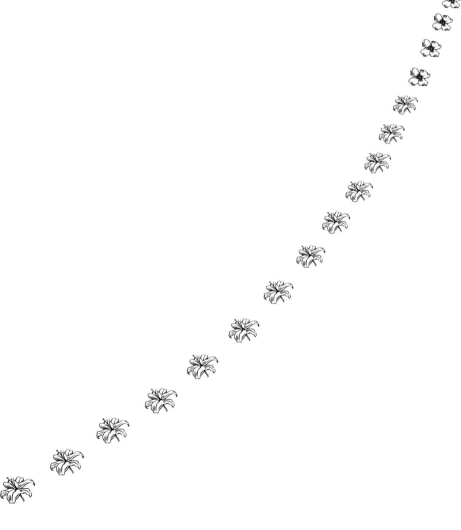

When Once I Lived

The endless sequence of 🌸 is changed, one by one, to an endless garland of ❋, the numbers undiminishing in the rapidity with which one follows on another, changing over, one symbol substituting for the next, going out to the furthest limit of the universe and then back again, until it arrives once more in my hand, and I see the final 🌸 wink out and a ❋ in its place.

Now I am dreadfully afraid. I shall not survive this. I have done something wrong, come somewhere I should not be. I know, now, that I shall never find that one, small, pinkish stone where is written my life without my shameful act. I see that now. The stain of my guilt is indelible. I have failed. I hurt her, and I cannot take it back. It is … it will always be. And now, seeking this impossible result, I have lost everything.

My guide has not returned, and I am powerless to look away from the stone I hold in my hand. I look closer, and my darkest fears are realized. Quickly, now, I see one symbol replaced by another. The Lily is replaced by the Marigold; the Marigold is replaced by the Blue Bell; the Blue Bell is replaced by the Larkspur. There is flower after flower; then the flowers are exhausted and (as symbols) there come all the varieties of trees and crops and grasses. Then the numberless species of fish, birds, insects, and more. Symbols only, but coming on ever more quickly, one after the other, until my eyes can barely focus or keep up.

My fear is great. All about me seems to be getting darker. Is it that, or are my eyes failing? Is there any place for me in this universal vortex of numbers? Have I transgressed some inviolable law, to seek as I did to change this one choice that I had made in life? I look at the stone in my hand, but I can no longer focus on the symbols changing over. They come too quickly. I cannot keep up.

I see this mad, convulsive transformation, symbol to symbol, each one explosively greater than the one before, each one going out in endless number to the outermost limit of the universe, then rushing back again to the small, reddish stone I hold in my hand. I see the newest symbol. Progressing as it has into the animals, this latest offers now, not merely beauty (as the Dogwood Blossom, the Lily or the Marigold) but now this … a spotted rabbit

its ears erect, and in its eyes a glint that says "Yes! We shall run! Quickly! To the farthest limit of all that is! We shall not weaken! We shall not rest!" But I cannot go on.

My Journey Ends

My hand drops, and the stone falls. I am no longer standing on the beach or anywhere I recognize. I see, instead, that I am running down a woodland path. Wait ... now I recall. I remember this from the time Molly and I had been married only a few years. The path behind our summer cottage. Through the woods to the fields beyond. But now I notice all around me—the trees, the flowers, and all—they are all the symbols. The living symbols of the numbers, ever changing, ever growing, and I am rushing past them. Past the Hickory, the Oak and the Maples. Past the Baby's Breath, Hibiscus and Mulberry. Beneath my feet an endless carpet of Lily and Marigold, Blue Bell and Larkspur. Out to the horizon, an endless flowering forest of Dogwood, Apple, Magnolia and Plum.

No longer dizzy, I feel invigorated—full of unaccounted energy. I look far down the path and feel—and know—that far ahead of me, which I pursue, is that one symbol which all the others serve. I know that now. My journey has brought me here. What symbol is it? Somehow I know it is a mystery, luminous and calm, where all and every number tends. But I do not see it. I only know. I know that I am here this moment, on this path, surrounded on every side by living symbols of the journey itself, ever growing, ever progressing.

Then I realize I am no longer alone. My heart leaps! The loneliness is over! I have failed in my desire to change the past, and I must bear out my guilt to the furthest extent of these numbers. But I am no longer alone! I turn, expecting to see my guide, but when I look, it is not my guide I see. There, running beside me, I see instead ... a spotted rabbit! And I know, without looking, that if could see my own body, I would see that I, too, have this same appearance. This universal symbol of the fleet of foot, ever running, never at rest, living by reckless, matchless speed, n'er overtaken, gentle, meek and fragile, well suited to live in this, His boundless pasture.

I look at the spotted rabbit, expecting to see my guide, but I do not. I see—I feel—the spirit that I know so well. The same eyes. The same gentle, loving expression. It is Molly, my wife! I see her and, in an instant, I understand. For in her eyes, I see that she forgives. That she, too, has had her guide, and she, too, has held that one small stone in her hand. That stone that promised no more hurt, no mistake, no choices wrongly made. But she tells me, with her look, that forgiveness is greater. That if we follow all the numbers ... all the moments ... out to the very end ... we will learn this one lesson: That love and forgiveness are greater than error.

When Once I Lived

So, we two, content in our love, forgiving, regretting nothing, in spirit fresh and new … we see the path before us. We feel His presence far ahead. We know that we have time enough to seek Him out. He has promised us an eternity.

I Cross Over
How long it was that my sweetheart and I pursued our common journey, I cannot say. Were we not in that one place where time—seeking its limit and

My Journey Ends

finding none—no longer held any power over us? That boundless pasture (wherein our souls, our spirits, striving ever onward ...) in time exhausting every effort that we made to mark its boundaries, became our home. And not only we, but our guides, as well, and those others who, in life, we knew as "father," "mother," "child" and "friend." These, the same living souls (each as pure and imperishable as we) who once we witnessed, experienced, measured out and enumerated in that one record of the world we came to know so well ... wound 'round and 'round and copied out in fairy-hand. And not just those few we knew who touched our lives, but the whole number of the human species: Those who traveled with us ... and those who went before.

And in this pleasant place, to pass the time, we ... each of us, in turn, a Storyteller plays. We share the story of our lives with others. No longer a solitary observer (perhaps in company with our guide) now we share our dramas, tragedies and travails with those (parents, children, friends and others) who might hear. Not as a lesson instructive of this or that moral, but the very same impulse we feel in this, our earthly existence, which is: That we never tire to tell and hear the story of our journey through this world (every personal journey like no other) and of His mercy and forgiveness (which triumphs over all).

I hear these stories—sharing many times as speaker or as witness—and that one ancient story (underlying all) to which we humans long ago subscribed: The hero and his journey, his road both long and dimly seen. His many trials and tests and fierce opponents, and then he chooses rightly (to be brave and trust his Maker's plan), and so he is not defeated but comes safely home. How many times I hear this story—how many times my heart, uplifted, responds in grateful praise—I cannot say.

Do you recall what I learned when I first embarked on this, my journey in the afterlife? I saw that long ago we each gave up, as our admission to this heavenly place, our physical bodies and all that necessarily accompanies our living flesh. We saw, at the time, that having done so, we likewise left behind many powerful human appetites and emotions. As who would not? These things, the common and universal exemplars of our existence on this earth, we do not list among the virtues or accomplishments of which we might boast, nor would we number them among those priceless, eternal gifts of our divine Maker.

Now I have been led to this place where, far from being compelled to leave anything behind, I find myself heir not only to what (in life) I lost or lacked or never knew, but also all the world—its sights, its secrets, its sensual pleasures, the sum total of all knowledge, and all possible inventions of human imagination. There is nothing of the universal pageant denied to me. And nothing lacking in the time available to me to see and touch and sample all that I desire. Is this anything less than His heavenly storehouse, to which, with generosity and open-handed love, He bids me enter and take whatever I will?

Many years have come and gone since my coming to this place. In recent years, the stories, which before I followed eagerly, racing to the finish before the teller could get it all out, now I find have little hold on me. Instead I seek solitude, serenity and calm. I often visit, now, alone, that selfsame beach where once I sought deliverance.

I stand upon that pebbled shore beside that wide ocean. Unhurried by any personal or selfish impulse, I reach down and pick up a handful of small stones. What might I see? I look closely, and I see this stone or that, inscribed with some singular narrative of the universal pageant: Perhaps a story of injustice from some ancient time, or sacrifice, or brave endurance; some story of a loving mother and of her child who died in infancy; or some other, of slavery, poverty, and loss; or a story of wrongdoing, crime and error, uncolored by any tint of redemption. So many stories.

I throw down these stones and, reaching for another handful, I see that these, too, have yet more stories to tell—of piety, solitude and lack, of gaiety, humor and shared pleasure. All these things I witness, now, not with the passion, gloom or wonder that was their birth mate, or which I might have felt when, first coming to this place, I experienced them for the first time. Instead, I see and know these stories—deeply familiar to me now (now that I, omniscient, have witnessed them so many times)—with the calm and loving wisdom of an angel's heart.

As I stand on this pebbled shore, I am joined by my guide (who long before no further lessons set me, but, still, we have witnessed much together). We look out wordlessly over the great ocean, its unceasing motion evidence of inexhaustible energy, its opaque surface signifying a mysterious, inescapable destiny.

He tells me: "This will be our final meeting. You will no longer have any guide. Do you know what now awaits you?"

Until this moment, it had not occurred to me that there was any other destiny than what I knew in this, His boundless pasture. Seeing around me all the universe of souls who ever lived, and having access to His perfect record of the world, it did not occur to me (before this moment) that there was anything here that might be lacking, or incomplete.

My Journey Ends

But my guide asking me this question was like a door opening upon an unknown land. All those things of all the world that I had witnessed, all the knowledge, all the stories, were like a landscape spread before me, but now my guide, speaking as he did, I felt as if I saw the setting sun, its radiance now falling behind a hillside, no longer color this scene with its vivid, vital energy, and so these things were dispossessed of any meaning.

I pause to meditate upon this revelation, and presently a greater truth reveals itself to me: That if we have laid down our physical body and all that is attendant upon it, shall we not also, in our eternity, come to a place where we do similarly lay aside our very selves—the life we led, the world, and all our memories of it, and all that these things mean to us?

My guide reaches down and, finding some one stone that he observed, picks it up and puts it in my hand. I bring it closer that I might better perceive what he wishes me to see. Very soon I understand.

I hold (in this one stone) that one true record of my life, collected and written out, without omission, honest, fair and true (including all my private prayers and dreams and aspirations, which then were mine ... when once I lived), and with it written out, His eternal judgment upon my life and all my choices—compassionate, just and fair, a judgment perfect in every way.

This the one, authentic memorial of my life, which I—my hopes and loves, my faults and errors—might see forever engrave'd here; and presently, turning it over in my hand, I understand that it is no more than this: The story of a journey ... written out in fairy-hand, wrapped 'round and 'round and lying here, beside this ocean, where ceaseless waves and tides might wear it down, until—even here, in this one place where eternal memory resides—you or I or some other might find this stone again ... and see all trace of me erased.

This, then, will end my journey. When all the world that is or was or might have been is in this place recorded, and I and others, having walked this shore in our eternal rest, and seeing all these things where once I was uplifted, this is for me at last ... my Moment Never Looking Back.

I ... now ... sensing that this eternal archive, this universal record of the world, no longer holds for me any fresh connection, nor any lesson yet unlearned, I travel on. My soul no longer bound to any certain past, I am transform'd. I cross over that unending ocean, leaving behind me this world and all we know and every memory of it, and seeing before me only the farther shore, I lay down all my burdens. I am uplifted.

Notes

Page 1—"Our God is a great God; and a great King … " Psalm 95.

Page 5—"a clever sort of answer to a puzzle which he knew." In 1877, the German mathematician Georg Cantor discovered a proof for the proposition that that the points of a plane have the same "cardinality" as the points of a line. That is, the points of a plane can be placed in 1-to-1 correspondence with the points on a line. Later, he proved that the points of three-dimensional space likewise have the same cardinality as the points on a line.

Page 12—"underdone potato." (*A Christmas Carol* by Charles Dickens. 1995 Modern Library Edition, page 21.)

Page 44—"I fear this most of all." (*A Christmas Carol* by Charles Dickens. Crown Publishers, 1977 page 113.)

Page 44—"Who can tell how of he offendeth … " Psalm 19.

Page 48—"wearing out of the world … " ("That wear this world out to the ending doom.") Sonnet 55.

Page 68—"The least of them." ("Inasmuch as ye have done it unto one of the least of these my brethren, ye have done it unto me.") Matthew 25:40.

Page 73—"Our secret faults." ("O cleanse thou me from my secret faults.") Psalm 19.

Page 81—"This copper…visible in rocks … " (*Michigan Prehistory Mysteries*, by Betty Sodders, Avery Color Studios, Au Train, Michigan 1990.)

Page 86—"the funerary god Anubis … " (*The Sphinx Mystery*, by Robert Temple with Olivia Temple, Inner Traditions, Rochester, Vermont, 2009.)

Page 87—"some certain Pharaoh … " (Pharaoh Amenemhet II, Twelfth Dynasty, 1876 to 1842 BCE. Temple, Op. Cit. page 195.)

Page 87—" … that prophetic dream … " Edgar Cayce. *Records of Association of Research and Enlightenment.*

Page 87—"each giving place in sequence to the next … " ("In sequent toil all forward do contend.") Sonnet 60.

Page 108—'is His, and He made it … " ("The sea is His, and He made it.") Psalm 95.

Page 114—"What fools these mortals be." *A Midsummer Night's Dream*, Act 3, Scene 2.

Page 116—" … that one soundest sleep … " ("We are such stuff as dreams are made on; and our little life is rounded with a sleep.") *The Tempest*, Act 4, scene 1.

Page 151—"that King of Kings, that Great King above all gods … " ("For the Lord is a great God: and a great King above all gods.") Psalm 95.

Page 151—"Vengeance is mine." ("Vengeance is mine: I will repay, saith the Lord.") Romans 12:19. "Overcome evil with good." ("Be not overcome of evil, but overcome evil with good.") Romans 12:21.

Page 154—"If you don't work, you die." ("The Gods of the Copybook Headings" 1919 Poem by Rudyard Kipling.

Page 166—"Great God, Great King above all gods" Psalm 95.

Page 166—"Which of you was present, when I laid the foundations of the world?" Job 38:4.

Page 174—"a panoply of animals ... " (The Hall of the Bulls, Cave of Lascaux, Spain.) (See "Aurochs in the Sky; Dancing with the Summer Moon—A celestial interpretation of the Hall of Bulls from the cave of Lascaux" 1995 Frank Edge)

Page 175—"by a deeper science ... " (op. cid. Frank Edge)

Page 263—"That boundless pasture ... " (" ... we are the people of his pasture, and the sheep of his hand.") Psalm 95: 7.

Page 264—"this pebbled shore ... " ("Like as the waves make towards the pebbled shore.") Sonnet 60.